Lucia

In the series

Voices of Latin American Life

edited by Arthur Schmidt

Lucia

Testimonies of a Brazilian Drug Dealer's Woman

Robert Gay

Foreword by Arthur Schmidt

TEMPLE UNIVERSITY PRESS PHILADELPHIA

Temple University Press
1601 North Broad Street
Philadelphia PA 19122
www.temple.edu/tempress

Photo Credits:
Introduction: *Guerra de traficantes na Rocinha,* taken April 13, 2004. Photograph by
Domingos Peixoto, Agência O Globo.
Chapter 3: Photo courtesy *Journal do Brasil.*
Chapter 6: *Toroteio na Rocinha,* taken April 12, 2004. Photograph by
Domingos Peixoto, Agência O Globo.
All other photos courtesy of the author.

All attempts were made to locate the people in the photographs published in this book. If you
believe you may be in one of them, please contact the publisher at Temple University Press,
1601 N. Broad Street, Philadelphia, PA 19122. The publisher will be sure to include
appropriate acknowledgment in subsequent editions of the book.

Text design by Kate Nichols

⊗ The paper used in this publication meets the requirements of the
American National Standard for Information sciences—Permanence
of Paper for Printed Library Materials, ANSI Z39.48-1992

Library of Congress Cataloging-in-Publication Data

Gay, Robert, 1958–
Lucia : testimonies of a Brazilian drug dealer's woman / Robert Gay ;
foreword by Arthur Schmidt.
p.   cm.
Includes bibliographical references (p.   ) and index.
ISBN 1-59213-338-X (alk. paper)—ISBN 1-59213-339-8 (pbk. : alk. paper)
1. Lucia, b. 1975 or 1976.   2. Drug traffic—Brazil—Rio de Janeiro.
3. Gangs—Brazil—Rio de Janeiro.   4. Marginality, Social—Brazil—Rio de Janeiro.
5. Police corruption—Brazil—Rio de Janeiro.   6. Rio de Janeiro (Brazil)—Social conditions.
7. Jakeira (Rio de Janeiro, Brazil)—Social conditions.   I. Title.

HV5840.B72R564 2005
363.45′092—dc22   2004062085
[B]

ISBN 13: 978-1-59213-339-0 (paper : alk. paper)

110807P

For Lucia

Contents

Foreword

Arthur Schmidt

Lucia's Testimony

LUCIA IS A RESIDENT of Jakeira, one of the many *favelas* or shantytowns of Rio de Janeiro, the second largest city in Brazil, the fifth most populous country in the world. Robert Gay, a sociologist from Connecticut College and experienced researcher on Brazil, pieced together this account of her life in a series of interviews conducted between 1999 and 2002. A woman of color now in her early thirties, Lucia is a survivor, her story a harrowing one. Her testimony offers, as Gay affirms, the "detailed and intensely personal perspective" of a woman struggling each day in a "male-centered and male-dominated world" of violence, fear, and economic hardship. In human terms, it brings to the reader one version of the precarious circumstances facing millions of poor people in the world's most rapidly growing large cities, the urban centers of the Third World.

Lucia's childhood was a short one. Her father failed to provide for the members of the family, and her mother could not lift them above poverty, despite her constant labors as a domestic for wealthy people. During her early to mid-teens, Lucia lost interest in school. By then, she had already entered the world of men, gangs, and narcotics that increasingly dominated existence in the favela as she grew up. Determined not to be a woman confined to housekeeping, she dreamed of a comfortable future through marriage to a rich man. In the world of the favela, however, drugs were the only route to quick and substantial money, and her life as a "drug dealer's woman" would prove anything but comfortable.

Rogério, a *dono* or drug lord, took the youthful Lucia as one of his women, eventually fathering her daughter Amanda in 1994. This liaison commences Lucia's narrative of several sexual alliances with *bandidos* or drug dealers that she maintained over succeeding years as her principal means of survival. "I hate being alone," she would confide to Gay in one of their interviews. Being alone meant total vulnerability—no income, no physical protection against the violence of the favela, no means of helping either her mother or her young daughter, no recognized place within the environment of drug-gang society. A successful bandido—and especially a successful dono—could provide in a day what it would have taken her a month or more to earn. Over the years of her life that she recounts to Gay, Lucia did find a series of short-term, low-wage jobs working for a neighborhood association, a supermarket, a Laundromat, a beauty salon, and stores that sold plastic items or clothing. Exploitation, ill treatment, boredom, and meager pay characterized every one of these jobs. All proved unsatisfactory in comparison to the income and protections afforded by intimate connections to a powerful man in the local drug trade. A life built around narcotics trafficking proved a hard one to leave.

Nevertheless, existence as a drug dealer's woman remained fraught with danger and hardship for Lucia. Bandidos and donos were violent men who required total submission from their women, regardless of their own faithlessness and unreliability. Straying from that norm could mean death. Marcos, a powerful dono who occupies an important part of Lucia's narrative, several times threatened to kill her out of jealousy, once cut her with a knife, and on another occasion punished her by shooting her in the leg. For a dependent woman like Lucia, the insecurities of trafficker life meant sleeping in different locations night after night, threats from the gunslingers of rival factions, and abusive treatment from the police, all the while fearing the loss of her man's affections to another of "his women" and wondering when he would meet his inevitable violent end. Lucia's experiences taught her the seeming truth of Rogério's grim worldview— "there are two paths in this life: death or prison."

A strong-minded person, Lucia proved skillful in navigating through the perils of the world of narcotics trafficking. Nevertheless, once her brother Diago was imprisoned for drugs, she determined to get out of "that life." Her narrative moves from its focus on drug lords to her efforts to sustain her new life with her interest in Pentecostalism and with her new man Bruno, a well-educated former soldier who seeks to provide for Lucia and their new daughter. She sees the tribulations of the previous ten years as a form of destiny that she had to experience in order to "start over," one that taught her a great deal and ultimately gave her a new outlook. "I didn't study, and I'm here . . . unemployed," she tells Gay in a mixture of guilt and hope. "But I know that all is not lost . . . all is not lost. Because I have the will to learn everything . . . I will do better."

But real life is not a soap opera, and Lucia's story encounters formidable—perhaps insuperable—barriers to the achievement of a happy ending. Making a living outside the drug economy remains excruciatingly difficult. The burden on the female leaders of the household is enormous. Lucia's father is disabled, while her mother was dismissed from her last job as a domestic. Neither her sister's income as a waitress nor her brother-in-law's earnings from part-time employment provide enough. Diago's continued addiction to drugs renders him an emotional and economic burden. Lucia's work in a beauty salon suffers from low pay, barriers to advancement, and mistreatment by the owner. Bruno's past prison sentence for a narcotics offense continues to deny him any employment commensurate with his education, and he seems reluctant to accept anything less. Despite Lucia's determination that Amanda will study hard and lay the foundations for a different future, she has failed the fifth grade. As the story concludes, Bruno finds himself in jail in Brasília for driving a car he claims not to have known was stolen, Lucia is working part time as a maid, and a substantially completed three-room addition has appeared on the house. Sadly, Gay finds himself convinced that the family has gone back to the drug life. "I became angry and upset," he says. "But then, sitting in the comfort of my air-conditioned hotel room, I thought, who am I to judge? How could I possibly know what it was they were going through?"

Nevertheless, readers ought to form a judgment about Lucia's story, not a moral evaluation of her behavior, but rather an informed appraisal of her circumstances. Personal testimony has become a major means of documenting the lives of Latin American women in recent decades. "Testimonial literature can be compelling and immediate," notes one analyst, "allowing the reader the sense of hearing directly the voices of those recounting their lives. Because testimonies are the words of real individuals, they possess a flesh-and-blood authenticity lacking in the more abstract data of statistics and surveys."[1] The compelling quality of personal testimony with its apparent moral authority has raised serious questions about how readers should evaluate such texts. What should readers in the United States make of Lucia's testimony? Gay notes that her personal story is one of enduring conditions that most readers will find "simply unimaginable." It certainly contrasts with the images of Rio de Janeiro that those at a distance might derive from tourist brochures, imported Bossa Nova music, or films such as *Copacabana* (1947), *Blame It on Rio* (1984), or *Live from Rio* (2002). Yet, even then, aspects of Lucia's story may be "imaginable" to readers from afar. Viewers of *Black Orpheus* (1959) may remember the principal protagonist's ultimately futile struggle against an adverse fate. A verse from one of the film's songs laments that "Sadness has no end, happiness does." Those familiar with urban drug trafficking in the United States or with the impact of racial segregation upon American inner-city neighborhoods will find points of contact with Lucia's testimony.[2]

The authenticity of testimonial literature has remained subject to controversy, most particularly in the case of Rigoberta Menchú, the winner of the 1992 Nobel Peace Prize. Anthropologist David Stoll documented serious misrepresentations in the autobiography of this Guatemalan Mayan woman, setting off debates about testimonial truth that still continue.[3] Readers may ask how much of Lucia's presentation of her own life is true. Matters of gender and setting certainly raise questions about the completeness of her testimony. As Daphne Patai, a Professor of Brazilian Literature at the University of Massachusetts, notes, testimonial interviews require from people "the kind of revelation of their inner life that normally occurs in situations of great intimacy and within the private realm."[4] Could Lucia express deeply personal matters freely to a male interviewer? In an atmosphere of potential danger from other *favelados* and from the police, how forthcoming could she be? Gay considers that his long friendship with Lucia, her strong motivation at a time in which she was striving to "go straight," and various aspects of his interview methodology offer assurance as to the basic veracity of her story. At the same time, he recognizes the possibilities of distortion that exist, including deception on the part of Lucia to keep him "off track" on particularly sensitive matters. Oral history remains full of pitfalls. Readers should view Lucia's story as a self-portrait, important to her as she "started over." As Patai notes, "memory itself is no doubt generated and structured in specific ways by the opportunity to tell one's life story and the circumstances of the situation in which this occurs. At another moment in one's life, or faced with a different interlocutor, quite a different story, with different emphases, is likely to emerge." Given these complexities of substance and method, personal testimony does not "exclude the possibility of intentional misrepresentation, self-censorship, or unintentional replication of a given society's myths and cherished beliefs about the world, itself, or the roles that distinctive individuals or groups play."[5]

Readers with long memories will note that many of these issues over oral history testimony emerged in Brazil a generation ago in the case of Carolina Maria de Jesus, "a fiercely proud black Brazilian woman who lived in a São Paulo favela with her three illegitimate children (each with a different father)."[6] The publication of her diaries in 1960 with the assistance of a São Paulo reporter transformed her overnight into a literary sensation, one of international proportions as *Quarto de Despejo. Diário de uma Favelada* soon found its way into translation into thirteen different languages in forty countries.[7] Although her fame proved fleeting, controversies stemming from readers' a priori expectations of Carolina swirled around her until her death in 1977.[8] Many who first read Carolina's account wished to see in her an ideal representation of the world's urban poor. Critics found themselves offended when she exhibited intolerance for the behavior of her neighbors or when she failed to "lend her voice to calls for massive social change" in a "society that tolerates the most glaring maldistribution of wealth in the world."[9] Carolina, like Lucia, simply wished to escape a world of poverty and insecurity. Readers should be wary of casting their own expectations upon Lucia. Her story is an individual one, at once both ordinary and extraordinary in all its dimensions—and far from insignificant. At the very least, it should elicit empathy from those in more comfortable circumstances, underscoring the words of Nigerian author Chinua Achebe that "the world is not well arranged, and therefore there is no way we can be happy with it."[10] Lucia's testimony opens for its readers one window into the traumatic violence that surrounds the lives of the poor in many of the world's largest cities.

Latin American Urban Violence

Throughout their history, cities in Latin America have acted as the agents of change. For those who sought opportunity there, "the problem was to get to the city and immediately thereafter to integrate oneself into the mysterious social fabric of the city."[11] Today, however, endemic violence weaves itself through the "social fabric," making poor migrants and their immediate descendents "citizens of fear" within the enormous urban concentrations that have developed over the last several decades. "Imagine," asks urbanologist Jorge Balán, "cities of a similar size, but with a median income per capita as low as one-tenth that of Los Angeles, such as Mexico City, Bogotá, Caracas, or Rio de Janeiro."[12] The Latin American super-metropolis is a relatively new historical phenomenon. In 1950, barely one Latin American in four lived in a city of 20,000 people or more. Since then, as the population of Latin America and the Caribbean has tripled to more than 500 million, industrialization, rural-urban migration, and government policies have made the region ever more urban. Today, in the seven largest Latin American countries, at least 60 percent of the national population resides in localities of 20,000 or more people, at least half in cities of 100,000 or more inhabitants.[13] Brazil alone currently has twenty-three cities possessing approximately a million or more in their metropolitan areas, while São Paulo (18.5 million) and Rio de Janeiro (11.2 million) rank among the very largest urban concentrations in the world.[14]

The gigantic scale of contemporary metropolitan existence should not trigger any romanticizing of the past. Earlier generations of common city folk in Brazil experienced the burdens of racism and miserable living conditions. They suffered predatory public authorities dedicated chiefly to advancing the interests of the privileged. Nineteenth-century Rio's "modern police institutions buttressed and ensured the continuity of traditional hierarchical social relations, extending them into impersonal public space," argues historian Thomas Holloway. "The apparent contradiction is one example of the incomplete or discontinuous historical processes that help account for many of the characteristics of contemporary Brazil, including the divergence between formal law and the institutions ostensibly charged with enforcing it and socio-cultural norms guiding individual behavior."[15] Throughout the nineteenth century, servants and slaves in Rio engaged in a constant struggle with their masters of "street" versus "household." At the dawn of the twentieth century, the city's urban renewal brought an "explicit attack" upon the spaces inhabited and used by the lower classes, as the country's elite sought "to put an end to that old Brazil, that 'African' Brazil that threatened their claims to Civilization."[16]

Rio de Janeiro's first favelas appeared in 1898 when military veterans returning from northeastern Brazil constructed their own wooden shanties on the hillsides overlooking the city. Nevertheless, favelas did not surpass inner-city slums as the chief form of urban housing for the poor in Rio de Janeiro until the 1940s.[17] Despite considerable hardships, rural-urban migrants in Latin America after World War II generally fared better in the city than in their places of origin. "If far too many newcomers were required to work for very low pay, few were unemployed and even fewer were worse off than if they had stayed in the countryside."[18] Rates of formal employment growth in Rio de Janeiro and in other Latin American big cities did not keep up with the expansion of the urban labor force. Nevertheless, the city afforded unique opportunities for earning income in the informal economy, a grab-bag category of survival pursuits that includes small-scale workshops, nonprofessional self-employment, casual trade such as street vending, domestic service, and even illegal activities.[19] Studies over the years showed that favela residents labored in a range of occupations in both the formal and informal economies. Early impressions that favelados constituted marginal elements in urban life—variously depicted as either dangerous or apathetic—gave way to a more accurate appreciation of their existence. As urban expert Janice Perlman wrote in a famous 1976 study:

> Socially, they are well organized and cohesive and make wide use of the urban milieu and its institutions. Culturally, they are highly optimistic and aspire to better education for their children and to improving the condition of their houses. The small piles of bricks purchased one by one and stored in backyards for the day they can be used is eloquent testimony to how favelados strive to fulfill their goals. Economically, they work hard, they consume their share of the products of others . . . and they build—not only their own houses but also much of the overall community and urban infrastructure.[20]

Echoing this view, Gay notes that favela inhabitants were politically well organized and constituted a backbone of civil society efforts to bring to an end the military rule that governed Brazil between 1964 and 1985.[21]

But as is evident in Lucia's life, little seems to have gone well for Rio's favelados over the last two decades. In Brazil, as in much of the rest of Latin America, the advent of electoral democracy took the wind out of the sails of much of the popular movement, but it failed to provide effective representative institutions and services. Despite something as remarkable as the election of the former worker Luiz Inácio da Silva (Lula) as president in late 2002, the transition to electoral democracy in Brazil has done little to better the lives of favelados. Brazil's conditions echo those of the rest of Latin America—the irony of the establishment of formal democratic institutions accompanied by the negation of the benefits of citizenship for much of the lower ranks of society. In the words of a recent report by the Inter-American Dialogue, an "enlightened establishment" institution that brings together prominent figures from across the Americas: "Public opinion surveys consistently reveal disappointment with the performance of democratic institutions and elected leaders. Simply put, democratic politics are not delivering satisfactory results on a variety of fronts, including justice, personal security, and economic needs."[22] Present-day analyses of current public life in Latin America emphasize public distrust, weak governmental service institutions, corruption, and growing violence. "Common crime has become a nightmare for most Latin Americans, overwhelming the region's mostly under-financed, poorly trained, and often corrupt police and judicial systems," notes another Inter-American Dialogue report.[23] In Brazil, homicide has become the leading cause of death for persons between the ages of fifteen and forty-four.[24]

Residents of poor urban areas throughout Latin America, such as the favelados of Lucia's Jakeira, suffer an existence "embedded in structures of power that are often unpredictable and beyond their immediate control."[25] Extralegal violence, whether at the hands of gangs or police, holds sway over their lives. Latin America's transition to electoral democracy has taken place simultaneously with two other phenomena that have exercised negative social repercussions in the region, vastly amplifying its susceptibility to constant violence: the adoption of neoliberal economic reforms and the vertiginous rise in drug trafficking. The adoption of neoliberalism (often loosely referred to as "free market economics") originated in the debt crisis of the early 1980s when Latin America's post–World War II reliance upon inwardly oriented national industrialization reached a dead end. Pushed heavily by the United States and by multilateral agencies such as the

International Monetary Fund, neoliberal policies have emphasized stricter public finances, privatization of state firms, and a reduction in government programs of social assistance. Under neoliberalism, reduced state regulation has left labor, trade, and financial matters increasingly in the hands of unfettered market forces.[26] While these economic reforms brought international capital investment back to the region and reinitiated growth after the regression of the "lost decade" of the 1980s, they have achieved nothing that would remotely resemble prosperity or even stability. Economic expansion has proven both meager and unsteady. In Brazil's case, the per-person output has remained virtually stagnant over the last decade. The unsuccessful struggles of Lucia's family to gain an economic base outside the world of narcotics constitute a microcosm of Latin America's contemporary economic condition. While in some cases modest alleviation of poverty has taken place, as a whole neoliberalism has generated even greater social inequality and malaise than existed previously. As a recent study summarizes the matter:

> A shrinking formal working class and a stagnant or rising informal proletariat negate predictions about the capacity of the new economic model to absorb labor and reduce poverty. With the exception of Chile, most working persons in the region, regardless of where they are employed, receive wages that are insufficient by themselves to lift them out of poverty. The contraction of the state sector and of formal private employment has compelled substantial numbers of the intermediate and subordinate classes to search for alternative economic strategies. The new regime of open markets has, by and large, favored those with the resources to succeed in them, leaving the rest to fend for themselves. Micro-entrepreneurialism, marginal self-employment, violent crime, and accelerating emigration have accompanied the new model as adaptive strategies to its economic consequences.[27]

Over the same time period that neoliberal economic changes have exercised this devastating social impact in Latin America, the consumption of illicit drugs has become a truly "global habit," one that has multiplied the opportunities for quick if dangerous wealth.[28] Beginning in the mid-1980s, narcotics trafficking began its "incremental and destructive 'invasion' of

Brazil and the Southern Cone" of Latin America. "US-sponsored anti-drug enforcement operations [in the Andes] during the 1980s and 1990s unwittingly pushed the drug trade—its operations and consequences—further into the region, penetrating and undermining already fragile and vulnerable political, social, and economic conditions and institutions."[29] Rio de Janeiro became both a transshipment point for new markets in Europe as well as a market for local consumption. Lucia's testimony depicts in human terms the consequences of these changes for life in the favela. Gangs fill the void left by weak state institutions and insufficient economic opportunity, providing their "rule of law" in place of the independent community associations that earlier generations of favelados had constructed. The police, continuing their already established pattern of treating the poor as criminals, prey upon the favela and extort their profits from the narcotics traffickers. Permanent stories of rags to riches are hard to come by. Drug gang leaders—the donos—may be community heroes for a time, but their violent lives usually come to a premature end. Those engaged in the lower levels of drug trafficking—the bandidos—live no more well off than their neighbors—and even more insecurely.[30]

In the midst of this violent, male-dominated world, evangelical protestantism has exercised a significant and growing appeal. One well-regarded recent anthropological study suggests that "women are choosing religious conversion as a form of oppositional culture, one that resists male oppositional culture, namely, gang membership and participation in urban violence."[31] While Lucia has struggled with this question, her mother fully converted to a Pentecostal sect that exercised strict norms over personal behavior including drinking, dress, and dancing. Such conversions offer the possibility of some small measure of control over the terms of one's existence in a world of fear and violence that lacks any broader social or institutional alternative. Given the prevalence of these desperate sorts of conditions in large, rapidly growing urban concentrations of the Third World, mainstream multilateral agencies such as the Inter-American Development Bank and the World Bank have begun to redefine poverty. Their new research recognizes the significance of deep social inequalities of the sort that prevail in Brazil. It stresses that "social exclusion" underlies contemporary urban problems in the Third World. Income poverty, health and education poverty, personal and asset insecurity, and disempowerment constitute interactive elements that lock people like Lucia into an existence without exit.[32] As her case shows, barriers of class, skin color, and gender can frustrate the efforts at advancement of even the strongest-willed persons. Questions of social exclusion particularly affect women even as they have become a larger part of the urban labor force in Latin America and as the share of female-headed households has risen.[33] It remains to be seen, however, whether these new views of urban poverty will produce effective global and domestic policies capable of improving life prospects in large Third World cities, including those of Latin America.

Meantime, in the midst of the bleak conditions of Lucia's testimony, some analysts have begun to argue that

> [T]he evidence shows that local civic groups and social movements, networking with state actors, [can] play a crucial role in stimulating police reform and controlling violence. ... In Rio's favelas, where criminal groups are strongly connected to some civic leaders and governmental agents, networks provide the most effective way to extend democratic governance and protect citizens' rights.[34]

Active networks among cooperative politicians, police, domestic and international nongovernmental organizations, local community associations, and the press have proven effective in some cases in reducing violence. Particularly significant in this regard has been the ten-year-old nongovernmental organization Viva Rio that Gay mentions in his Epilogue. Viva Rio has constructed important networks in its campaigns for human rights, public security, community development, education, and the environment. Its programs have included reducing the supply of firearms, creating sports activities for youth, promoting job training, providing microcredit, setting up community computer centers, offering legal aid, and a variety of other activities.[35] Clearly, Viva Rio has not brought an end to the killing or solved matters of chronic unemployment, but it has enjoyed a measure of success, created innovative methods that others can adopt, and generated hope. Its incomplete victories parallel Lucia's longing to "start over."

Acknowledgments

I WOULD LIKE TO START BY THANKING Lucia and all the members of her family who have been so kind and welcoming to me over the years. My friendships with you are extremely important to me and it goes without saying that, without your participation, this book would not have been possible. I would also like to thank my many other friends in Jakeira who have for so long provided me with a home away from home and who have also greatly assisted with this project. I can only hope that some good will come of it and that the situation in Rio, which has deteriorated so rapidly, can be turned around.

I would also like to thank my many friends, students, and colleagues who shared their ideas, read and commented on drafts, assisted with transcription and translation, developed photographs and artwork, wrote letters of recommendation for grants and promotion files, entertained me when I was in Brazil, kept me from going insane, and were generally supportive. In this context I would like to say a special thank-you to Martha Huggins, Judy Hellman, Javier Ayuero, Geert Banck, Mike Delaney, Aidan Chapman, Neville Thorley, Fred Paxton, Sylvia Malizia, Jan and Alex Hybel, all my students in Soc 414 (you know who you are), my parents, James and Valerie Gay, who took me to Brazil in the first place, my brother,

Edward, Arthur and Adrianne Dudden, Fred Yeon, Alina Skonieczny, Mridula Swamy, Ed Cleary, Jon Shefner, Frank Graziano, Jeff Lesser, Paulo Sérgio Pinheiro, Desmond Arias, Bill Nylen, Janice Perlman, Linda Rebhun, Luke Dowdney, and Paul Horton. I would also like to say a special thank-you to the late Bob Levine who was very helpful and encouraging in the beginning stages of this project. Bob was also instrumental in convincing me that social science could be written in a different way.

Funding for this enterprise was provided by a timely and generous grant from the American Council of Learned Societies (thank you so much!) and a steady stream of travel support from my home institution, Connecticut College. It is difficult being an ethnographer of a far-off place when you have so many family and institutional obligations, so I very much appreciate the College's willingness to help me get to the field as often as possible. I would also like to thank Peter Wissoker and Arthur Schmidt at Temple University Press. I am delighted to be publishing with Temple again, and Peter and Arthur have both helped me immeasurably by answering my interminable questions and by moving this whole project along.

Finally, I would like to say a huge thank-you to my wife, Alexis Dudden, who has done all of the things I listed above—and a whole lot more—and my two daughters, Devon and Kirin. Without all of you, none of this would have been imaginable, let alone possible.

INTRODUCTION

I T WAS JUST PAST FIVE O'CLOCK on an oppressively hot and humid afternoon in mid-January. Lucia was perched beside me at the top of the concrete staircase that led from her mother's porch below to the living quarters that were being built for Lucia's sisters and their families. I remember sitting there, taking it all in, and thinking that it was a far cry from the cramped and makeshift three-room house that Lucia's grandmother, mother, father, two sisters, and brother lived in when I first made their acquaintances. It was still, however, a typical family arrangement in Jakeira, a typical shantytown, or *favela*, in the troubled and increasingly violent city of Rio de Janeiro.

    I first got to know Lucia while conducting field research in 1989. I had spent the previous three years documenting and writing about the different organizational types and strategies of favela neighborhood associations. I was introduced to Lucia by a mutual friend who worked for a nongovernmental organization (NGO) in Rio that funded programs for street children. Back then, I would run into Lucia once every two weeks or so when she poked her head in at the NGO's offices downtown or when I accompanied my friend to his house, which was also in Jakeira, a few miles from the city center. Then, a few years later, Lucia suddenly disappeared. I heard through my friend that she had taken up with a drug dealer and that she had also had a child. That was all I knew at the time and, understandably, her family was reluctant to talk about her, let alone admit publicly that she had chosen a life of crime.

About four years after her disappearance, Lucia suddenly reappeared. She had indeed been involved with what turned out to be a string of drug dealers, most of who were gunned down by rivals or by the police. And yes, it was true that she had a child, a beautiful and distracted young daughter who, according to those who knew him, was the spitting image of her long-since-dead father. But all that was behind her now. Lucia told me that she had grown tired of drug gang life and that she had decided to start over, to begin again. Returning to her home in Jakeira, she worked hard at restoring her relationships with her friends and her family and took her place at her long-suffering but forever-loyal mother's side.

Lucia's mother, Conceição, was seated in the front row of the congregation of fifteen or so people gathered on the porch beneath us. She too had gone through changes in her life. When I first met Conceição, she was a fun-loving, outgoing woman who smoked cigarettes and always had a glass of something in her hand. A few years ago, however, she converted to Pentecostalism. Now she no longer swore, smoked, or drank. And instead of tight-fitting spandex shorts and halter tops, she now wore the dark and somber below-the-knee-length skirts and outfits that are the trademark of members of the Pentecostal Church of God Is Love.[1] In fact, she credited her newfound faith for turning Lucia's life around and prayed constantly for the salvation of her only son, Diago, who was still heavily involved with the drug gang in Jakeira.

Diago had recently been released from prison where he served three years for illegal possession of drugs and firearms. It did not take him long to slip back into his old ways. In a matter of days, he was spending his nights with his fellow drug gang members mixing, weighing, repackaging, and selling cocaine and marijuana from the various selling points, or *bocas de fumo*, in the favela. Like many of his friends, Diago was also an addict, and working for the drug gang paid for his addiction. In the morning, I would stumble across him sleeping off his inevitable hangover on a mattress on the living room floor. Or, I would see him stretched out in front of the television in his sisters' bedroom. Everyone liked Diago, and everyone got on well with him. He was always quick to greet me with a handshake, a welcoming gesture, or a smile. He said nothing, however, of his life in the drug gang. It was his family's dirty secret.

During the last two years that Diago was in prison, Lucia made the one-hour plus bus trip from Jakeira each week to visit him. It was during one of these visits that she met and eventually fell in love with Bruno. At the time, Bruno was serving a seven-year sentence for smuggling drugs to Rio from a small town on the Bolivian border. Unlike Diago, however, Bruno was now attempting to turn his life around and, more immediately, to provide for Lucia and their daughter, whose birth was just a few months away. Things were not easy, however, as work was hard to come by and the ghosts of his recent past lingered close behind. Bruno knew full well that if he accepted the frequent invitations to become involved with drugs again, he would already have the house, the car, and the cash that he coveted, and that he had possessed before his incarceration.

Bruno was sitting opposite me in the far corner, his hands on his bible and his eyes fixed firmly on the pastor who was leading the prayer meeting, or *culto*, which was held at Lucia's house each Sunday afternoon. The pastor, himself a former drug dealer, was imploring his small but attentive congregation to resist the temptations of the devil and to devote their lives to the Lord. As the pastor's high-pitched voice reached a crescendo, a round of firecrackers announced the arrival of a police patrol car at one of the entrances to the favela. As the smoke rings from the firecrackers drifted slowly into the air, I watched as Bruno turned his head toward the neighborhood association building two hundred yards away on the side of the main road. "It's the struggle between good and evil," whispered Lucia in my ear.

What you are about to read is the product of a series of short but intensive visits to the field between the summer of 1999 and the spring of 2002. I first came up with the idea of the project following conversations I had with Lucia on her return home some eight years ago. As I sat listening, enthralled but at the same time horrified by what she was telling me, I could not help thinking that in light of all the changes I had witnessed over the past two decades, and all the killing and the violence that was going on around us, her story should be told.[2]

Since its transition to democracy in the late 1970s and early 1980s, Brazil has experienced a sudden and dramatic increase in the level of violent crime.[3] Between 1980 and 2000, for example, the number of homicides in Brazil rose steadily from ten thousand to forty thousand per year.[4] The majority of these homicides took place in and around Brazil's major cities and metropolitan areas, involved the use of firearms, and cut short the lives of predominantly young, male, poor, uneducated, and dark-skinned victims from the literally thousands of low-income neighborhoods, public housing projects, and favelas.[5]

Explanations for the increase in violent crime in Brazil run the gamut from the impact of globalization to changing attitudes toward work and leisure and the emergence—among the young—of a fetishism for high-priced articles of "style" that confer status and power. Three factors, however, stand out. The first is inequality. Since the 1960s, Brazil has become one of the world's largest industrial economies, and yet it competes with a handful of much poorer nations for the dubious distinction of being the most unequal place on earth. In terms of per capita income, Brazil is in the same league as countries such as Costa Rica, Malaysia, Bulgaria, and Chile. In terms of poverty rates, however, Brazil is much more like Panama, Botswana, Mauritania, and Guinea.[6] More significantly, perhaps, the past two decades of economic stagnation and recession have meant that the abyss that separates rich and poor in Brazil shows few signs of closing.[7]

The second factor has to do with what are often referred to as the "authoritarian legacies" of the previous regime. Under military rule, the Brazilian police acted with impunity to hunt down, torture, and, in some cases, execute political dissidents. In postauthoritarian Brazil, the police operate in much the same way, but with a different and much larger population in mind. Since the mid-to-late 1970s, the police have been engaged in the extermination of what are widely considered marginal, and therefore expendable, elements of Brazilian society. The brutal and cold-blooded murders of 111 inmates in Carandiru prison in São Paulo in 1992, eight street children outside Candelária Cathedral, and twenty-one inhabitants of the favela of Vigário Geral—the latter incidents both in Rio de

Janeiro in 1993—are but more heinous and well-known examples of what is standard police procedure. Protected, until recently, by military tribunals that dealt with complaints of human rights abuse, and since then, by an overburdened and ineffective civil judiciary, police involvement in crime, in general, and the summary execution of civilians, in particular, continues both unchecked and unpunished.

The third and by far most important factor in the increase in violent crime is drugs. Brazil is not a major producer of illegal drugs,[8] but over the past two decades or so the country has become an important transshipment point for cocaine that is cultivated and processed in the neighboring countries of Bolivia, Colombia, and Peru and exported to the United States and, more recently, expanding markets in Europe and the states that emerged from the breakup of the former Soviet Union.[9] A sizable portion of the cocaine that enters Brazil is, however, sold locally.[10] In fact, it is now estimated that Brazil is the second largest consumer of cocaine in the world.

In Rio, the majority of the distribution and selling points for cocaine—and, for that matter, marijuana—are located in the city's 600 or so favelas. Since the early to mid-1980s, whole areas of Rio and its hinterland have been controlled not by public authorities but by well-organized and heavily armed drug gangs.[11] These gangs purchase cocaine from intermediaries, or *matutos*, who bring it in from neighboring countries and states. The gangs then mix, repackage, and sell the cocaine to wealthy clients in surrounding neighborhoods and, increasingly, to users and addicts in their own communities. The struggle for control of the massive profits to be made from the cocaine trade has been, since the early 1980s, the basis for what are violent and deadly confrontations between rival drug gangs and between drug gangs and the police.[12] Indeed, as Lucia's testimony clearly shows, it is this combination of drugs, police violence and corruption, and savage and increasingly visible inequality that has transformed, not just a few select neighborhoods, but almost an entire city into what is effectively a war zone.[13]

In Rio, the increase in violence has seriously compromised, if not washed away, the foundations of what was an emerging and vibrant civil society. And violence—and, more to the point, the widespread fear of violence—represents, today, a significant threat to democracy.[14] When I first began doing research in Rio, I was acutely aware of the increasing availability of drugs and, more significantly, the growing presence of drug gangs in the favelas.[15] At the time, however, their influence was minor compared to that of neighborhood associations and other recently organized civic groups. And to be quite honest, like many of my colleagues, I was too busy imagining civil society to pay them much attention. With each subsequent visit, however, I noticed that the situation had changed. Fifteen years ago my friends in various favelas talked enthusiastically about organizing and attending meetings and their newly established democratic rights. Now all they talk about—in hushed voices and behind closed doors—is their reluctance to participate in public life and their strategies for surviving the undeclared civil war between increasingly violent drug gangs and the police.

Understandably, there are few accounts of what it is like to endure such conditions. Our knowledge of drug gangs and drug gang life is primarily through the grim reports and statistics that appear daily in the newspapers. Or, it is through the eyes and ears of ethnographers who have watched helplessly as communities they were intimately involved with have collapsed and disappeared.[16] However, Lucia's testimony provides something very different. First, it offers a detailed and intensely personal perspective on what it is like to lead such a life that is, by its very nature, far richer and more compelling than the occasional snapshot or secondhand account.[17] And, as a result, it forces us to deal with violence as she experiences and remembers it, as something that is not unusual or exotic, but very much a part of her everyday existence and humanity.[18] Second, Lucia's testimony offers a much-needed woman's perspective on what is, without a doubt, a male-centered and male-dominated world.[19] Women's roles and participation in drug gang life continue to be treated as sidelines and curiosities and, in this sense, Lucia gives voice to those who are rarely, if ever, heard and provides insight as to the ways in which women like her become involved.[20]

Finally, and perhaps most importantly, Lucia's testimony forces us to ask the question: "Who are the victims and the victimizers in this situation?" On the one hand, Lucia is an unusual and—some might say—unfortunate choice for a testimonial. After all, she is not an activist or a spokesperson for a protest movement or NGO.[21] Moreover, she has witnessed and, by nature of association, participated in what can only be described as a series of cruel and unusual acts. On the other hand, Lucia's story is about a young woman who has suffered conditions that, for most of us, are simply unimaginable, and who has struggled mightily, her entire life, to be treated with the minimum of dignity and respect. Unfortunately, like millions of other Brazilians, Lucia is a second-class citizen, if she can be considered a citizen at all. Laws, rights, privileges, and guarantees do not apply to her because, in truth, Lucia exists in a country, within another county, that we call Brazil.[22]

As you can imagine, this was never an easy research project to conduct. First, there were very real dangers involved. In most favelas there is a strict code of silence, or *lei de silêncio*, which prohibits anyone from talking about drug gang activities. It exists, primarily, to discourage local residents from passing information to rival drug gangs, or worse still, the police. The punishment for being an informant is usually a slow and painful process of torture, followed by execution. Because I was aware of this, my initial plan was to interview Lucia in the relative comfort and safety of my hotel room. Two or three hours of interviews each day would be sufficient, I thought, to cover the bases. It soon became apparent, however, that I was asking too much of Lucia who, at the beginning of the interview process, was responsible for managing her mother's household and, by the time I had finished, was looking after her two-year-old daughter and various other neighborhood children. More importantly, it became clear to me that Lucia's story only made sense in the context of her surroundings and her relationship with her friends, family, and neighborhood. Therefore, I spent most of my time shuttling back and forth from my hotel room and simply hanging out, observing and listening, and waiting patiently for the opportunity to tape-record interviews. On the rare occasion, we were able to steal away to Lucia and Bruno's makeshift bedroom in her sister's apartment for an hour or two. For the most part, however, the interviews were conducted in her living room in full view of everyone and anyone who cared to listen.

Lucia's family was more or less informed about what it was we were doing. Lucia's mother often joined in the conversation, or shouted comments from the kitchen, when she disagreed with something Lucia said or with her recollection of a sequence of events. Conceição herself was extremely forthcoming about aspects of her own life and, in particular, the hardships associated with the family's move from the Northeast of Brazil to Rio in the early 1960s. Bruno was also a willing participant, although I did not get to record interviews with him as often as I would have liked. I first met him a week after his release from prison. At the time, he seemed genuinely pleased that I was interested in what had happened to him, despite the fact that he didn't know me at all and the extremely sensitive nature of what it was we talked about. In fact, one of the most vivid memories of my fieldwork is sitting on the roof of Lucia's house, in plain view of everyone, tape-recording conversations about the seven long years he had spent in various state penitentiaries.

The only person I wasn't sure about was Diago. I believe he had a vague notion of what it was we were up to. But as long as I didn't bother him, he didn't seem to mind. There was always a pause in the conversation, however, when he emerged from his sisters' bedroom in the afternoon. On such occasions I would look across at Lucia as if to say, "Are you sure this is okay?" And Lucia would nod her head reassuringly and we'd continue. Lucia's friends and neighbors certainly knew what was going on, including one of the drug gang leader's women. We were sitting in a friend's house one day, watching over the kids, when this woman who I'd never seen before said, "Who's he? And what's he doing here?" Much to my surprise—and dismay—Lucia went ahead and told her. "He's an old friend of mine," she said, "and he's writing a book about my life." I expected the woman to, I don't know, get upset or something, but she said to Lucia, "Well, you make sure he gets it right. Make sure you tell him everything." Needless to say, I was a little nervous for the next couple of days.[23]

Whether it was because I was protected, or because I was just plain lucky, I never ran into any trouble, but things were not the way they used to be. A few years earlier, I could come and go whenever and wherever I pleased. Now, I made sure to call Lucia each morning before setting out from my hotel, just in case anything had happened overnight. And neither Lucia nor my other friends in Jakeira could be persuaded to take me to the places we used to hang out.[24] To be perfectly honest, however, I was far more afraid of the police. My greatest fear was that they would mistake me for a buyer from downtown or that they would get their hands on the tapes and transcripts that told of the innumerous instances of police violence and corruption. I felt a sensation of intense anxiety and then relief each time I passed a patrol car at the entrance to the favela on my way out.

The only time that I was really worried was in June 2002 when a well-known and respected journalist for the newspaper *O Globo* was kidnapped, tortured, and killed by a drug gang reportedly because of an article he had published on open-air drug fairs and research he was doing on public sex acts involving teenagers.[25] The reporter's brutal murder shocked even Lucia, who was otherwise unconcerned about the ramifications of our project.[26] I assured her that all the places, names, and identifiable subjects and objects of her testimony would be changed. And it was clear that my status as an outsider, who would eventually pack up and leave, was crucial to the project's success in that Lucia felt she could tell me things she had never even told her family. Lucia, in turn, assured me that the characters we were talking about were no longer around—that they were either serving time or buried in cemeteries and unmarked graves that were scattered around the state.[27] The way she saw it, if she were going to be killed, it would have happened by now. And as if to prove her point, she proudly displayed the scars from the bullet that shattered her left shinbone and the bullet that—to this day—remains firmly lodged at the base of her left buttock.

There is no doubt that the fact that I knew Lucia, and had gained her trust over the years, made the interview process easier. This does not mean, however, that it was easy.[28] As you will see, the initial conversations were hard work. This was primarily because neither of us knew where the interviews were going. In fact, I began this project with only a vague idea of what I would learn or how it would turn out. On the positive side, this meant that, at least initially, it was difficult for me to overdetermine the interviews. On the negative side, it meant that our early conversations edged, stuttered, and stumbled along. Eventually, however, Lucia grew more comfortable with her role and let her voice and her emotions take over, such that, by the end, I was acting primarily as a prompt.

The fact that I knew Lucia did not prevent her from employing what others have described as security measures and ethnographic seduction to keep me off track.[29] This was particularly true of our conversations about Bruno. I suspected, early on, that Lucia was reluctant to tell me exactly what it was he was doing. At one point, I even convinced myself that perhaps she didn't know. This was a critical issue for me because, in my own mind, it was because Lucia was "going straight" that the project was at all possible. In other words, it was Lucia's decision to turn her back on her past that provided me with the moral justification to continue. After all, this was no randomly chosen subject. I really liked Lucia and considered her my friend. And I believed in my heart that she was a good person. I had to be careful of these emotions, however, and had to constantly remind myself not to let my relationship with Lucia interfere with what I was doing.[30]

Fortunately, when it came to figuring out what was going on in her life, I held certain advantages. First of all, I had known Lucia for a long, long time, so it was much more difficult for her to conceal things from me. I had seen her when she was happy, and I had seen her when she was sad. And I had been present at all sorts of family events, celebrations, and crises. My second advantage was that Lucia wanted her story to be told. First, she was clearly interested in the money, and I had told her, in the very beginning, that if there were money to be made, it would be hers.[31] But more importantly, the interviews gave her an opportunity to relive and talk about things she had buried deep in her past. This was clearly important to her, and it provided her with a measure of relief.[32] There were times, however, when this was extremely difficult and painful for her to do. Her account of Rogério's death, for example, was followed by a flood of anguish and tears that left everyone in the room in a state of stunned silence.

My final advantage was that the interviews themselves were conducted over a long period. Between the summer of 1999 and the spring of 2001 we tape-recorded interviews about how she first got involved with drug dealers in Jakeira and about her relationships with the three most important men in her life: Rogério, Marcos, and, finally, Bruno. Then, between the spring and fall of 2001, Lucia and I read through each of the interview transcripts. This provided me with the opportunity to ask Lucia questions I had not thought of at the time, to clarify things that I had initially misunderstood, and to revisit certain issues.[33]

This second set of interviews also provided me with the opportunity to interview Lucia about her experiences at school and at work, her family's religious beliefs and practices, and her and Bruno's attempts at "getting out." In fact, the final tape-recorded interviews were conducted in somewhat surreal circumstances in the days immediately following September 11, 2001. I had flown out of LaGuardia on September 10, but because of bad weather, had missed my connection in Atlanta. I spent the next four days—like everyone else—glued to the television set, thinking the world was coming to an end. Four days later, however, I was back at Lucia's house in Jakeira amidst the violence and the squalor. It was, for me, a tremendously sobering experience. And I will never forget Bruno's comment to me. He said, "What did you Americans expect?"

The book is organized in the following way. Each of my conversations with Lucia is framed and linked to the next by a short discussion of issues as they are raised in the text. These discussions introduce the reader to the universe of the favelas, the emergence of drug gangs, issues of police violence and corruption, the prison system, education, the world of work and, finally, religion. These intermediary chapters were researched and written after the initial interviews were completed and represent my attempt to situate Lucia's testimony in its broader context without disrupting the flow and integrity of our conversations.[34] It was always my intent to tell Lucia's story from her perspective, but in a way that is, at the same time, much more than a story; in a way that attempts to bring faceless economic and political institutions and practices to life.[35] The book ends with an account of my last research trip to Lucia's house in March 2002 and an Epilogue that discusses what has happened in Rio since then.

I have attempted, throughout the book, to stay as faithful as possible to Lucia's own words. Inevitably, however, there are things that are lost in translation and in the process of transcription from the spoken to the written word.[36] I have also moved sentences from one part of the manuscript to another, in places, to ensure thematic consistency, and have edited, or edited out, a good many of the prompts and reiterative figures of speech that are an essential aspect of depth interviewing.[37] Also, as you will see, I have left my own voice in. Interviews are, by nature, conversational and involve a special form of collaboration and partnership between interviewer and interviewee. In other words, whether I like it or not, I was and still am very much a part of the production process.[38]

Finally, I have tried to make this book as accessible and readable as possible. There are two reasons for this. First, fifteen years of teaching have convinced me that when it comes to writing, it pays to be as simple and as direct as possible. Second, and more importantly, when we think about drugs and drug-related violence in Latin America, we do not tend to think of Brazil, and yet, the story you are about to be told is a direct consequence of more than three decades of U.S. foreign policy in the region. Since the 1970s, the U.S. government has been waging a "war on drugs" that has failed to stem the flow of narcotics and has succeeded, instead, in spreading the cultivation, production, sale, and consumption of drugs.[39] The war on drugs has also led to a militarization of conflicts that have cost the lives of literally hundreds of thousands of defenseless and innocent people and has generated billions of dollars in profits that have sustained guerilla, paramilitary, and criminal organizations and corrupted public authorities.[40]

In Rio, government officials continue to talk about their war on drugs in terms of "good versus evil" and the threat posed by a so-called "parallel state."[41] And they continue to favor heavy-handed, extralegal measures that threaten what is an already weak system of human rights. If Lucia's testimony tells us anything, it is that the authorities in Brazil are intimately involved with and, to a large extent, responsible for the drug trade at every level, just as they are for a system of exclusion and social and economic apartheid that has been in place for centuries.

CHAPTER 1

Getting In

——Let's start by talking about how you became involved with drug dealers in Jakeira.

——Well, it was mainly because <u>my brother wouldn't let me go out with anyone</u>. So I thought, okay...

——**What do you mean?**

——It's like I said, he wouldn't let me go out with anyone. So, I figured, I'll hook up with one of these *bandidos*... so he'll stop messing with me. So, I hooked up with one. I already had my eye on one of them. Do you remember Roberto, a tall skinny guy who looked like a gringo, remember? I introduced him to you on one of your visits, remember? He was shot in the leg during a raid on another *favela*... and then he was killed. You sent me a letter asking about him. But it was a childish affair . . . nothing serious. I was very young . . . and still at school at the time.

——Why wouldn't your brother let you go out with anyone?

——Because of jealousy. You see there used to be this group of guys who'd, you know, hang out together and call out as we passed by, "Ah, your sister . . . I'm going to get your sister. I'm going to get her and do it to her like this (gesturing with her hands). I'm going to do it to her today." You know . . . because around here boys talk a lot about what they do and don't do with girls . . . and then the girls' brothers feel the need to protect them. They try not to let this happen.

——How old were you and Roberto when you started going out?

——I was about fourteen or fifteen and he was eighteen.

——And where did he live?

——Down there, on the other side of the school. He was a friend of mine from school . . . but my mother didn't know anything about it. Then, after Roberto, I got together with Fábio . . . who was also involved with the drug gang. This time it was because my sister wouldn't stop following me around. Fábio robbed apartments and he dealt drugs.

——Did he rob apartments before or after he became involved?

——After he was involved. They don't have to . . . but some of them take advantage of their involvement . . . they take advantage of the guns to do this sort of thing.

——And how old were you by then?

——I was seventeen. When I got to know Fábio, I was still a virgin . . . and it was with him that I did it for the first time. I chose Fábio just for this . . . just for the first night. He turned sixteen on the same day I turned seventeen . . . on the first of March. So I said to him, "I'm going to give you a present." And the present was me! I wasn't going to fall for him though, because I had lots of friends who fell for guys and after they slept with them the first time, the guys didn't want to know. I just wanted someone to get it over and done with.

——Was he from around here?

——Yeah, he was from around here . . . and he was already involved with drugs. I had a way with him, so he gave me money for shoes . . . clothes and money to go out. And that's how it all started.

——Was it a big deal for you to have expensive clothes?

——Yes . . . designer clothes. It's always been like that. Women who are involved like to dress well and wear jewelry . . . and have all the things that rich people have. Now, young women these days aren't as concerned about this.

——How come?

——Because they're much younger, starting at the age of twelve or thirteen . . . starting real young.

——You're kidding, right?

——Young boys get involved these days at the age of ten!

——So, if they're not into clothes, why do they get involved?

——The youngest boys, for sneakers . . . for designer clothes. The young girls . . . no. They get involved to go out with guys with guns. They think they'll keep them safe. They think that no one will mess with them, or beat them up.[1]

——So, because Fábio gave you everything, you knew he liked you?

——Sure I knew. Because, in those days, I was young and tanned and had a great body. I was beautiful . . . I knew he liked me. But I didn't stay with him long because I chose him, you know, just for that one night. I stayed with him for only three months.

——Is he dead?

——No . . . he's in jail. He's served two years of a five- or six-year sentence. . . . Then after him, actually while I was still with him, we went to a *baile* at a bar in another favela where I met and danced with this other guy.

——What is a baile?

——I don't really know how to describe them. There's always sound equipment, with those big speakers . . . and a DJ who plays old vinyl records. And it's funk music, which is music from poor communities around here. Some bailes are organized by neighborhood associations. But mostly, they're organized by drug gangs. They charge money to get in . . . and they sell drugs.[2]

——Do people who live outside the favela go to bailes?

——Sure . . . even rich people. So, anyway, after the baile, I went back to the bar a lot . . . because I found this other guy interesting. So Fábio got really mad at me and asked me what was so interesting about this bar that made me go back there so often? So I told him that I was seeing this other guy. So, he went after him . . . armed and everything. Only that when he got there, he discovered that that this other guy was also involved . . . in Belém Novo . . . something that even I didn't know.

——Is Belém Novo a favela?

——Yes, except there the favelas are inside apartment buildings.

——What do you mean?

——It's like a whole mess of favelas inside an apartment building.[3]

——So you met this other bandido by accident?

——That's right, by accident. I was already a magnet for these kinds of guys. I had no idea, because he didn't say anything about this to me. So, when I found out that Fábio had gone there, I was kind of shocked, you know. It was then that this other guy—Maurício—told me that he was involved . . . and that if Fábio tried anything it was going to be really bad. So, I thought, oh my God, now someone's going to be killed because of me. So, I calmed the other guy down and left the bar with Fábio. And then I told him that it wasn't going to work anymore . . . I finished with him.

——Where did Fábio live?

——Over there (gesturing with her hand) near the bakery.

——Did he live with his parents?

——No, he didn't have a father . . . and he was adopted by his mother.

——Who was it that who took us to the market that time?

——That was Fábio. He was skinny and had very dark skin, remember?

——Yes, now I remember. What was his role in the drug gang?

——He eventually became a *gerente*. I only liked bandidos who were either *gerentes* or *donos*.

——And had he quit school by then?

——They are almost always out of school.

——And was Fábio the rebellious type?

——No, not at all. He was always a very calm person . . . a good person.

——So why do you think he got involved?

——Because it's the only thing that makes money fast . . . and lots of it . . . lots of it. Because if someone gets a job, any job, without an education, they will at most make minimum salary.[4] And they make minimum salary in one week.

——So you think it's because of this that young kids get involved.

——Yes. So anyway, this other guy was also involved in selling drugs in Belém Novo. I stayed with him for a year and a half.

——Did you go live with him?

——Yes, I lived with him there because I couldn't live here . . . because Fábio knew who he was . . . and that he was involved with another gang.

——What was your mother's reaction to all this?

——She tried many times to get me to come home. She was afraid that something would happen to me. But in those days, I did whatever I wanted . . . I wouldn't listen to anyone.

——And did Maurício ever come here to Jakeira?

——Actually, he did come here once. But by then Fábio had gone to prison. He also gave me everything. We went out to motels and restaurants a lot . . . and he gave me lots of presents.

——So, the police don't know everyone who is involved in the drug gang. I mean, you could still go out. You could still leave the favela?

——They only knew the donos and the more well-known people.

——And Maurício was a member of a drug gang that operated from one of the apartment buildings in Belém Novo?

——Yes . . . and it was during the time that I was with Maurício that I went on a trip to Vista Bonita . . . and got to know Amanda's father, Rogério.

——What do you mean?

——You know, a trip . . . to visit people. I got to know Rogério through his brother Edson, who was living here at the time. Edson also robbed apartments and was living here for a while because there were more rich neighborhoods around here than where he was from.[5] Edson and a girlfriend of his invited me to go to Vista Bonita with them.

——Did Maurício mind you going?

——He was very upset . . . very upset. But I just wanted to go on a trip. I didn't mean to get together with anyone else.

——Why didn't he tell you not to go? I thought *traficantes* told their women what they could and couldn't do.

——Usually they do. But I never let them . . . even though I am a woman. I never wanted to live . . . you know, live and take care of a house . . . no.

———So what happened when you reached Vista Bonita?

———When we got there, Edson took us to a house full of bandidos. Edson thought that I should get together with his brother. I guess I went there to pass the weekend with someone . . . and that someone was him. Then Edson left with his girlfriend and I was left all alone . . . there was just me and Rogério. So we talked and, when it began to get dark, his girlfriend arrived and saw us together. Nothing at all had happened but, even so, we started fighting . . . I fought with her. Then she slapped him across the face. So Rogério picked up his gun and shot her in the foot. And then he said, "Now I've done this to her, you'll have to stay with me."

———Weren't you scared?

———I was shocked, but there was no way out of the situation. I remember thinking there were few other houses to run to . . . and that it was too late to take a bus or a train. So I was sort of stuck . . . and all of this time he was pressuring me to sleep with him because of what he'd done to his girlfriend. So I tried thinking of the practical side of things. I thought, if I don't sleep with him, he'll kill me. So I'll sleep with him and then tomorrow I'll leave . . . I stayed there two days with him following me around wherever I went . . . because he told me he didn't have a car and there were no buses and that I had to sleep with him anyway. So, I played along with his little game. What was I going to say, no? I could already see that he was a violent, out-of-control person. Then, finally, I took him aside and spoke to him, you know, seriously . . . saying that I had to return home. After that, I spent two years without hearing anything from him. I hung out at various bailes, getting to know one guy here and another guy there. You know, I always liked to go out.

———And how old were you at this point?

———I was seventeen and about to turn eighteen.

———So we are talking 1992.

———Yes. I spent those two years far away from here, making friends with other people from other favelas . . . and making friends with various bandidos.

———Did you only hang out with bandidos?

———Yes, because we became kind of a big family. I got to know the bandidos' other women. And because those who aren't involved don't like hanging out with those that are. They like to talk with you. You know, talk with you and pay their respects and everything. But they don't like to hang out.

——So, people keep pretty much to themselves and everyone knows who is and who isn't a bandido or a bandido's woman?

——Right.

——So what about your old friends from here?

——They never said anything. I only came back here on short visits and spent most of my time with the bandidos' women from here. I lost all my old friends from school because the things we talked about were no longer the same.

——Were you ever scared?

——No, I was never scared. When I was young I had lots of courage. I was never too scared to visit other favelas . . . to get to know different people. I was never scared. In those days, women and children were spared when it came to killing members of other gangs. If a bandido came into a house, he let the women and children go. Today . . . no. Today things are different, you understand? Today women are very involved. There are women who deal drugs, women who carry and use guns, and women who are gerentes and donos. Today they are very involved . . . women are used to transport drugs, weapons, everything.[6]

——So, even though these guys were killers, you still weren't scared.

——If someone was going to be killed, they had to have screwed up. Screwed up and messed with things that belonged to the bandidos . . . like their money, women, or drugs. I was a part of all this. But I was never interested in doing drugs . . . I never did drugs. They were always close at hand, but I never used them.[7]

——And what about the bandidos. Do they do drugs?

——A lot.

——So, those who make money from drugs also use them?

——Look, those who are called donos, who are in charge of the drugs, are more in control. Because to oversee the business they have to be in control. What I mean is that the donos only use drugs when they are far away . . . when they feel they are secure. This is a business. The drug market is a business. It's the same in any business. If the owner of a hotel doesn't pay attention, you don't think his employees will take advantage?

———And what about the others?

———The others get involved almost exclusively for this reason. It's a way of paying for their addiction.

———**Is this how your brother got involved. He became addicted?**

———Yes, little by little.

———**And are there those whose abuse the privilege?**

———Absolutely. They do too much drugs and fall into debt. And when you are too deep in debt, you pay with your life.

———**Is this always the case?**

———There are some they don't kill out of respect for their parents . . . their families. Then there's a lot of talk, you understand, and an opportunity to pay off the debt. But if it's a person they don't know or don't respect then they'll kill them right there and then.

———**Who is it that kills these people? Does the dono tell someone to do it?**

———It's often an order given by the dono. Sometimes, someone is told to do the job . . . those who have the most courage . . . those who feel they have nothing left to lose in life.

———**So, there are bandidos who kill and bandidos who don't kill. In other words, you don't have to do it to show your loyalty . . . to show your courage.**

———You have to show it but there are bandidos who get by without killing anyone. For example, everyone in Jakeira likes my brother because he's more likely to try and save someone than to kill them, you understand?

———**And, do bandidos get used to killing?**

———There are those that do, yes.

———**Have you ever witnessed a killing?**

———No. I've found myself in situations where someone is about to die. But at this point I've always backed away. These were people who were sentenced to die. Personally, I don't believe that anyone has the right to take someone's life. So, I've always intervened . . . asked . . . you know? I've always asked them not to kill the person . . . I've always asked . . .

———**You mean you asked the bandidos not to kill someone?**

———Yes, the ones who were about to do the killing. But that's just me. I don't think everything should be resolved in this way.

——Do they have other ways of resolving things?

——No. That's the way it is. If they let a person live, the next day that person might get stronger and come back and get them.

——So, the sentence is always death?

——It's always this. Because that's the way it is. There are some that might have a chance. But they are few . . . and they go on to make the same mistakes.

——And what mistakes are these?

——Messing with drugs . . . and with their things.

——You mean messing with the dono's money?

——Yes. And sometimes it's because someone has informed the police. Here in Rio there's no chance of pardon for those who betray them to the police . . . what we call a *cagoete*. It's always death.

——Does this happen a lot?

——Yes, it happens a lot.

——So, are the donos afraid that someone in their gang will turn them in?

——It's all a game. Those on the lower levels are always looking to move up. They're always on the lookout. The big thing, you see, is to have all the money . . . to be in charge.

——And what about your boyfriends, did they kill anyone?

——Look, the father of my daughter was, you know, extremely violent and aggressive. Not with me, you understand. I have nothing to say against him. But, with his friends . . . he always made trouble. He wasn't a person who was always in control . . . and I think that this is because he never had a real childhood.[8]

——What do you mean?

——He was brought up in the street. He had a mother but his father died when his father was eighteen. He died young . . . they killed him. Rogério died at the same age as his father, you understand?

——Who killed Rogério's father?

——Bandidos.

——So, there were already bandidos in those days?[9]

——Oh yes.

——Where did Rogério live? In São José?

——Yes, in São José. That's where he grew up, you know, all rebellious. His mother took in another man to help her get by and her children didn't like him. And, in the meantime, all three children that Rogério's mother had with his father became involved with the drug trade.

——In São José?

——Not only in São José . . . also in Vista Bonita. They split their children up. Only one is still alive. He has a crippled arm and has been sentenced to thirty-two years of prison. He's been inside for what must be six years now.

——**Because of drugs?**

——He robbed apartments and banks and because he didn't know how to drive, on his last job he took his victim hostage and then killed him. Rogério's whole family was like that, you know. He was brought up in the street and was always rebellious. His mother also had three children by this other man. So she didn't have the means to raise him properly. And the little that she did have her children wouldn't take from her. So they decided that the easiest way to get by was to become involved. They wanted to live well but Rogério's mother had six children to feed and was in no position to raise them.

——**So Rogério never tried working for a living?**

——No. He told me that he used to make money watching over cars . . . and that one night, after watching over cars the whole night, he was returning home when the bandidos from the area beat him over the head with the butt of a pistol . . . he still has the scar from that. He said that one day, when he was all grown up, he was going to get his revenge for all the things that had happened to him . . . including his father's death. He started young did Rogério . . . and he died young too.

——**How many people were in his gang?**

——There were about fifteen of them.

——**And you knew all of them?**

——I knew all of them . . . and they died one by one.

W HEN I FIRST MET LUCIA, she was sitting on the front doorstep of her family's house in Jakeira. I had been led there via a labyrinth of twisting and narrow pathways that meandered back and forth from one of the entrances to the *favela* along the main road. On our way, we passed two churches, a key cutter's workshop, and a couple of roadside stalls selling cigarettes, biscuits, soda, and candy. Before we ventured in, however, I was reminded to keep my eyes fixed firmly on the road. I knew that there were two reasons for this. The first was to avoid unnecessary eye contact with the *olheiro* who was stationed at the first corner we came to. The second was to avoid the piles and smeared remains of dog excrement that littered our way.[1]

Sitting next to Lucia was her youngest sister Andrea and her mother Conceição. Conceição was born in 1950 in a small town in the interior of Paraíba, a poor agricultural state in the Northeast. She was one of ten children. Eight of these children, six boys and two girls, died of various complications and diseases before the age of two.[2] Conceição's family were farmers. In 1959, however, the family was forced to sell its only plot of land to pay off the debts of an alcoholic grandfather. Conceição was sent to stay with a family friend in the neighboring state of Pernambuco. She lived there, going to school and helping out around the house, until her mother returned from her travels, looking for work around the Northeast, when Conceição was fourteen.[3] A year later, in 1965, Conceição and her mother came to Rio and settled in a neighborhood that eventually became the favela of Jakeira. They were preceded, seven years earlier, by Conceição's father, who found work nearby as a laborer. Conceição's only surviving sister stayed behind in Paraíba. Then, four years later in 1969, Conceição married Carlos Alberto, and together they had five children, four of whom survived.

The first favela was established in Rio in 1898 by war veterans on the Morro de Providência, close to the city center.[4] Over the course of the next half century or so, both the number and the population of Rio's favelas increased steadily—and at times extremely rapidly—because of dislocations associated with urban renewal, two World Wars, the Great Depression, the eclipse of the local coffee economy, and substantial rates of national and international migration. During this time, the state either turned a blind eye to or engaged in heavy-handed attempts to organize and control the urban poor. In the 1940s, experiments were made with Proletarian Parks that required residents to present identification cards to enter, and were locked up for the night at ten o'clock.[5] Elsewhere, the state worked with the Catholic Church to organize neighborhood associations in the favelas so that the urban poor would make demands and voice complaints in politically and morally appropriate ways.[6]

Then in the 1960s, demands for the revitalization of local capital and real estate markets and the imposition of military rule led to a period of outright repression and wholesale favela removal. Between 1962 and 1978, an estimated 146,000 people were forcibly removed from approximately 114 favelas in the city.[7] The idea was to move them from illegally settled private and public land to public housing projects hours away from the city center. The policy was a complete failure, however. Many of the apartments ended up in middle-class hands or, more commonly, were abandoned because they were too expensive and too far from places of business and work.[8] In fact, the removal of substantial numbers of people did nothing to reduce the population of the favelas in Rio.[9] And, largely as a consequence, state policy toward the favelas since the late 1970s and early 1980s has changed from one of eradication to one of urbanization and consolidation.[10]

When Conceição and her mother first arrived in Jakeira there were ten houses, six on one side of what was then just a dirt road and four on the other. Conceição's mother and father lived in a rented shack at the entrance to the favela. Then in 1967, they decided that instead of paying rent they would build their own house. According to Conceição's mother, no one wanted them to build nearby, so they staked out a rectangular plot of land at the very edge of the settlement under the cover of a small copse of trees. A few weeks later, representatives from the Fundação Leão XIII—a church/state agency with a long history of intervention in the favelas—came by and tore down all the houses and evicted all the inhabitants, save for Conceição and her family. According to Conceição, it was God's will that the house was never found, and that four generations of her family have lived there ever since.

Lucia's house is small by any standards. The first room you enter is the kitchen, with a four-ring gas cylinder stove, refrigerator, sink, and an array of small glass-fronted cabinets. Beyond the kitchen is a similar-size living room in which there is a table, four chairs, and two rather tattered, cloth-covered couches. Between the kitchen and the living room are a bathroom and two small bedrooms. Finally, out back is a separate room that was built for Lucia's grandmother. This was the extent of the house when I first got to know Lucia and her family. In those days, her father and mother slept in one bedroom and Lucia and her brother and sisters slept head to toe in a queen-size bed in the other. Then, a few years later when Amanda was born, Lucia's father slept on a living room couch, Lucia slept with Amanda in her parents' bedroom, and her mother, Conceição, slept with her son and two daughters in the other. The house itself was very simple. The exterior walls were made of bricks and mortar but were unfinished. There were windows in each room, but no windowpanes, and the interior walls and floor were covered with a layer of coarsely laid concrete.

Fourteen years later, much has changed. With the consolidation of at least the formal trappings of democracy came a newfound confidence that the state had abandoned all plans to remove the favelas and would instead let them be. Once the threat of removal was gone, the residents of Jakeira invested what little money they had in their homes. Wooden shacks that once were very common almost completely disappeared. Residents finished interiors, installed windowpanes where once there were none, and added one, two, and sometimes even three stories to their original homes. Lucia's family's house was no exception. Bedroom apartments with small kitchenettes were built on top of the original house for Lucia's two sisters. The exterior of the house received a coat of whitewashed concrete that hid the somewhat precarious nature of its construction. On the inside, floors were tiled, walls painted, and new furniture and appliances bought and installed. Don't get me wrong, this was still very much a house in a favela. But it was now a very different house in a very different favela. Lucia's family no longer slept—out of necessity—on the living room couch or four to a bed. And, perhaps most importantly, Lucia's family members felt that the place was secure. They felt, for the first time, that it was theirs to pass on to their children and, who knows, perhaps their children's children.

In the mid-1980s, the state government of Rio even considered granting each of the 15,000 or so residents of Jakeira legal right of tenure. The argument was made that the inhabitants of the favela had been there for so long that they had earned legal right to the land. Plans were drawn up to compensate the original owners and, more importantly, to divide the favela into individual lots. The task of doing all this was given to the neighborhood association. Disputes soon arose, however, over exactly where one plot ended and another began. Neighbors and former friends were accused of moving fences and building additions in the middle of the night in an attempt to extend and stake out their territory. In the end, the project had to be abandoned. Among other things, the leaders of the neighborhood association realized that the regularization of property rights created a whole series of other problems, not the least of which was the prospect of having to pay local property taxes.[11]

Other than this, conditions in Jakeira have generally improved. When you turn on a light in Lucia's house, there is now a good chance that it will come on. When the favela was first settled, there was no electricity at all until it was tapped illegally from power lines alongside the main road. Then later on, the power company supplied electricity to a small number of locations in the favela where meters were installed. Electricity was then "sold" at elevated rates to adjacent houses.[12] Only recently has each house in Jakeira been supplied with its own line and meter. So the good news is that the power supply has been improved and regularized. The bad news is that everyone now has to pay for it, although I have been told that—for a small fee—there are people who will tamper with the meter, much like you would the odometer of a used car.

When you turn on a tap in Lucia's house, there is also a good chance that something will come out. I would not recommend that you drink it, but the house is supplied via one-inch-in-diameter plastic pipes that feed into a large water tank on the flat, concrete roof. The installation of a water tank was essential because the water supply in Jakeira remains intermittent. Some days water reaches the house, other days it does not. Nonetheless, this is a vast improvement on conditions that existed in the not-so-distant past. Lucia's mother and grandmother still talk about buying exorbitantly priced water from commercial trucks or collecting it in large plastic containers from water spigots down the road and carrying it home on their heads.[13]

Finally, and perhaps most importantly, when you flush the toilet in Lucia's house the contents leave via much larger plastic pipes through the floor to a ditch known as a *vala negra* that carries the waste to another, larger vala negra that eventually exits the favela.[14] In favelas that are built on steep hillsides, gravity ensures that the contents do not linger. In favelas that are built on relatively flat pieces of land, the contents of the toilet bowl empty into slow-moving rivers of untreated human waste that idle their way around corners and under buildings toward their final destination.[15] Once again, things have certainly improved over the years. More of the vala negras are now set in concrete, more are also covered, and more carry just sewage and not the runoff from what is oftentimes torrential rain. In the recent past, heavy rain would overload the system and send raw sewage spewing back from where it came.

Serious problems remain, however, despite a slew of public sanitation projects introduced by successive governments since the late 1970s and early 1980s. The pipes that carry the sewage are often blocked or punctured, partly because of their fragile nature and partly because of what is put down them. Trash is picked up in Jakeira every Tuesday and Friday by Comlurb, the municipal garbage collection agency. Many people cannot be bothered, however, and throw their trash into the nearest ditch. The trash then acts as a dam and you can imagine the rest. Indeed, I can count on the fingers of one hand the occasions I have walked to Lucia's house without having to tiptoe around a river of raw sewage where it was not supposed to be.

In conclusion, the quality of life of the residents of Jakeira has improved significantly over the past decade or so. The threat of removal has gone and the state has been working in conjunction with neighborhood associations, NGOs, and the like to transform favelas into regular neighborhoods. Part of this transformation in state-favela relations has no doubt to do with the return to democracy and elections. After all, the favelas are an invaluable and relatively cheap source of votes.[16] Part of it also has to do, however, with the threat posed by heavily armed drug gangs. In the 1950s, people used to say, "Climb the hills before the communists come down." These days they say, "Climb the hills before the *bandidos* come down."[17]

CHAPTER 2

Rogério

——When you were with Rogério, was he the gang leader . . . the dono?

——Yes, he was the dono. At the time, he had just invaded São José. When the *bandidos* beat him he left home for a while and lived in a *favela* in Vista Bonita. Then he came back to São José and invaded the place with some guys who were also from there. The idea was to go back to the place they grew up. So, he organized his gang and came back. After that, he came to Jakeira to visit his brother . . . and so I went to see how he was. I asked my friend to go see if he was still good-looking . . . and she said that he was. And he was! They told me he was at a party. So I got into a car with some friends who kept telling me, "Don't go, don't go." And when I got there, there was no party at all . . . it was all a lie. Then he brought me to São José and kept me there by force. He told me that I couldn't go out and that the police were looking for me. So I got all scared and stayed with him for a month. Then, after a month, I came home to Jakeira to let my family know where I was.

——Was your mother worried?

——She was very worried, but no one came to get me. And, after two months with Rogério I was already pregnant with Amanda.

——Did you plan for the child or did it just happen?

——It was because, you know, I didn't take any medicine. My mother asked me if I wanted to get rid of it . . . but I didn't. I thought that if I got rid of it, I might die. I'd heard people say that many times people die. So I said to myself, I'm going to have it.

——And what about Rogério, did he want the child?

——Yes, he wanted it.

——But you were you never married, right?

——No, things go very fast in this life. Money, for example. Money just flies. We never had time to think about anything. We only thought of today. We didn't have time to think of tomorrow . . . of the future . . . we just didn't. A person who lives this kind of life doesn't believe in the future.

——And did Rogério think this way too?

——We both thought the same way. He always said that there are two paths in this life: death or prison. And I knew this . . . I already had this perspective. And you think that, knowing this, you'll be ready. But you're not because no one knows the time or the day when it will happen.

——Can you describe for me a typical day with Rogério?

——Nothing was ever planned. Things just happened. During the day the *traficantes* always stayed at home. They only went out at night. During the day they slept, ate lunch, everything like normal . . . you know, slept in the afternoon, ate dinner.

——And what about you, what did you do?

——I went to the shopping center, you know, like normal. But at night I stayed alone . . . until a certain hour in the morning.

——And Rogério?

——He stayed out looking after his *bocas do fumo*.

——How many bocas did he have?

——He had one in Vista Bonita and one in São José.

——And is two bocas de fumo a lot?

——The drug market here in Rio is very competitive. A bandido who has two bocas already has a lot . . . if he one he has a lot! There are many traficantes . . . so he who controls one is doing well.

——Were there other bocas in São José?

——Sure . . . there were a lot.

——And these were controlled by other traficantes?

——Yes, by Rogério's enemies.

——And he sold primarily cocaine?

——Cocaine and marijuana.

——And he mixed it and everything?

——He mixed it, divided it up, and packaged it.

——Where did he buy it? Where did the cocaine and marijuana come from?

——It was brought to us by what are called *matutos*. Matutos are people who supply the bocas do fumo . . . who bring it from Bolivia and Colombia.

——Who are these people? Are they the police?

——They are all kinds of people. There are a lot of people involved . . . including the police and the military. They are mainly people of high status because ordinary people don't have the means, you understand? Those who have the freedom to move about can do this sort of thing more easily.

——And what sort of quantities are we talking about?

——If the person is well known, and a friend, he will leave the quantity that was asked for and set a date by which he is to be paid. If the person is not well known you have to pay one half up front and the other half by a certain date. This first half represents the cost of the drugs . . . the rest is profit. So then they buy the drug and mix it with powder.[1]

——Have you ever done the mixing?

——No, I've never done it. I've seen it done, but I've never done it. From one kilo they make two kilos. Then they put small quantities into plastic bags, count them out, and divide them between the *vapores* who sell them. Each of the bags that the vapores sell generates a certain amount of profit . . . for example, 30 or 40 *Reais*.[2] The more they sell, the more money they make each week, you understand? And so, they are given this task each week.

——And who do they sell them to?

——They have different customers . . . some from their own community and others from neighborhoods nearby.[3]

——Does your brother Diago sell drugs?

——No, because he's a user . . . he's addicted. So, it causes a lot of problems when there are drugs within his reach. They give the drugs to others who are less addicted. He's now working in another area. He looks after the firecrackers.[4]

——Was the money from the sale of drugs in Vista Bonita and São José always brought back to Rogério?

——Yes, the money was brought back to him and he divided up the profit and took his share. He was the dono and he controlled everything. He took a small part of the money to give to his sellers, but the vast majority of the money stayed with him . . . and from his share he took the amount that he owed so he could buy more. He always paid his debts on time so that even when he didn't have any money he could still get drugs.

——Was it a lot of money?

——If the person was a good dono then, yes, it was a lot of money. But back then, in our day, no. We were just starting out . . . and he spent a lot! We slept in hotels almost every night because he didn't feel safe where we were.

——Did he keep any of the money in a bank?

——No, he invested it in guns and more drugs . . . and in day-to-day necessities.

——And did Rogério also have *olheiros* and *gerentes* and the rest?

——When he was dono he had everything.[5]

——How many olheiros did he have?

——He had one on every corner . . . one on every corner . . . and they were always *menores*. They are always the youngest members of the gang and they earn very little . . . perhaps 20 or 30 *Reais* a week. That's to say when the money didn't end up back at the boca. There are always some that are addicts . . . they pay for drugs by working.

——What were the others positions in his gang?

——There's the gerente whose job is to collect all the money. Then there's another gerente who divides up the drugs. These gerentes have to count out and deliver the drugs very carefully. And then there's a *gerente geral* who is in charge of delivering the money to the dono.

——So this gerente geral is the person closest to the dono.

——Yes, it's a position of trust.

——Who was Rogério's gerente geral?

——A guy from São José called Bibi. And then there was also his right-hand man who was always with him . . . like a bodyguard.

——And did all his people carry guns?

——Everyone carried guns . . . including me . . . although we didn't all know how to shoot. There's no training school, you know.

——What type of guns did they use?

——All kinds of guns . . . from pistols to automatic rifles.[6]

——What type of gun did Rogério carry?

——When he started out he had various pistols and a small 12-caliber UZI submachine gun.

——And where did these guns come from?

——Mainly the police. The police are always involved with this. There's always someone who knows someone . . . a friend from another gang or something.

——So these friends buy guns from the police and then sell them to other bandidos. Do they always deal with the same people or do they change suppliers?

——No, they're always changing . . . because someone always knows someone else. They're always changing. They chose on the basis of price and quality.

——Did Rogério also pay the police to warn him about police raids?

——No, he didn't like to have this sort of relationship with the police. He knew they were untrustworthy.

——Did he have doctors and other people in the community that could help him out?

——There was an old guy here who helped us deal with the civil police . . . we trusted him. There was also a medical clinic that, in reality, was there just to attend to them.[7]

——And did you have to pay to use the clinic?

——We paid, but the owner of the clinic was a friend of ours. Anyone who got shot didn't go to the public hospital, they went straight to the clinic.

——Why did this guy do this?

——He lived there . . . in the community . . . and he had a girlfriend in Vista Bonita and needed to go see her . . . to stay at her house. You know, to get to know her parents. So he got involved too. Lots of people get involved for drugs too.

——Does the clinic here in Jakeira assist traficantes?

——Sure, sometimes. It's never happened with me . . . but with other people.

——Even though they know who they are dealing with.

——Because of who they are dealing with!

——And are they threatened if they don't . . .

——It's sort of like that . . . because they can't leave here to be treated at other hospitals. So they do whatever they can here.

——Can the doctors refuse?

——They can always refuse . . . but then who knows what will happen?

——I get your point. And were you always at Rogério's side this whole time?

——Always. He always said that when it was time for him to die, I would die with him . . . because I'd been with him through it all. Sometimes, when he was arrested, so was I.

——How so?

——When the police broke in while we were asleep, or when they got ahold of us in the street, I was always by his side.

——Tell me about one of these times.

——One time, on my birthday, my brother and sisters and friends were with us. And the police found out that we were all there. I had arranged for two cars to bring everyone to São José.

——How did the police know you were there?

——It all started with a fight between a storeowner and his wife who'd caught him with another woman. She called the police because he was being aggressive and beating her . . . and he was at my birthday party. Ten policemen invaded the party . . . that was full of traficantes and their women from different communities . . . different favelas. When we saw the police we all said, "Let's get out of here." And on the way out we heard lots of shooting . . . so I thought that everyone had been killed. Then, I returned later on, and the party was even more alive than before!

——So no one was killed?

——No, no one died. They didn't see anything at the party. There were lots of guns and stuff but they didn't see anything. They were too high. Then, another time, they caught us in a hotel. Then they put us in the police wagon and took us to a deserted hilltop and grabbed and threatened me. Then one of them said, "What have you got to lose?" They live like this, you see, risking their lives so that one day they'll have everything. Then Rogério said he didn't make deals with the police. So then they grabbed me and said, "You don't make deals with the police, but you will for her. And if you don't you'll see what we'll do to her!" Then they sort of threatened me and asked Rogério, "How much is she worth?" We had some dollars put away. All the money we made went like that.

——How much money did you have?

——I don't remember. At the time we had some dollars and two kilos of marijuana that we were going to sell . . . and a thick gold chain and a few pieces of gold. So we gave them everything. That is everything that we'd been given in exchange for drugs. This was sort of our investment. But when the police get ahold of you, you have to give them everything . . . for your life.

——And start all over again?

——And start all over again.

——Now, you said before that Rogério didn't have contacts with the police . . . that he didn't trust them. Is this common? I seem to remember that Fábio had contacts with the police. Am I right? Wasn't it Fábio's uncle the policeman we met that day?

——It was Guilherme's

——And wasn't he an informant . . . or did he sell them guns?

——He sold them guns. But Rogério didn't have contacts like that. He didn't because he didn't want to become well known. Because it's like this, there's no such thing as a policeman who's a bandido's friend. The police like to make out they're your friends . . . they want to know all about you. Sometimes a policeman, you know, won't take you in. But he'll tell someone else where you are . . . and then the money is divided between them. They appear to be your friends. But they're never really your friends. They're friends of money. They're on the side of whoever pays the most. If drugs are paying well, then they're on the side of the bandido. But if they decide they can make more money by holding a bandido hostage . . . so they always play a double game . . . you can't trust them.

——And are the police ever caught and punished?

——A lot . . . a lot. There are a lot of them in jail. The police are kidnappers. They are bandidos in uniform . . . bandidos inside the law.

——Was Rogério ever taken hostage while you were there?

——One time, Rogério lost control of the boca in São José because he was arrested in Vista Bonita. He had gone out with me to a nightclub, and then to a restaurant, and finally, to Vista Bonita. When we got there, a friend of his asked to borrow the car that we'd borrowed. So then the friend left and was so long in coming back that we had to stay the night. And, as it turned out, this was the night that the police decided to invade. The police had been told about the bocas and all the houses where the bandidos slept. Ours was the last house they found. When they found our house it was already morning and they surrounded the house with eight police cars. They told us not to react and not to do anything . . . and, as it turned out, there were no drugs or weapons in the house. Everything was clean. The police took all the men with them and left the women. They took the men to the local police station and it turned out that Rogério had an arrest warrant against him in São Aldeia. But before they found out about it they asked me for money to free him.

——How much did they ask for?

——Fifteen thousand.

——And did you have the money?

——No I didn't. I was going to collect it from friends of ours in the favela and put it together with the money we'd saved . . . so I could at least pay half. But when I got there, the police told me the deal was off, because they'd discovered the arrest warrant.

——What was the warrant for?

——A few weeks before, some members of his gang went to the police station in São Aldeia to free a friend who was being held there. When they got there, they discovered that this friend had already been transferred to another police station. So, not to waste the journey, they tied the police up, set the bandidos who were being held there free, and took all the guns.

———But Rogério was never part of this, right?

———Rogério was never part of this but it was assumed he was because he was a member of this same gang, you understand? But on the day that they went, Rogério did not go. Then, later on, one of the guns that were stolen from the police station was found in Rogério's grandfather's house. This gun condemned him, even though he had not taken part.

———So then what happened?

———Well, Rogério put his brother in charge . . . to look after things. But when a dono is sent to jail the whole favela is weakened. Because the dono is a pillar, like the kind you find in a house. So when the pillar collapses, the whole house falls.

———So, when Rogério was in jail, did he lose both bocas de fumo or just the one in São José?

———Only the one in São José. The boca in Vista Bonita was controlled by friends of his. He wasn't the only one who looked after it . . . he wasn't the only dono. There were five of them, all from São José. So there, the profit was divided between them.

———But in São José?

———It was just him.

———And were you already pregnant?

———I was already pregnant . . . I was one month pregnant.

———So when was Amanda born?

———In 1994.

———So, Rogério put his brother in charge to prevent him from losing the boca?

———Yes, but it took him a long time before he could get things under control because, you know, it's a lot of work. There's the finances, taking care of the money that's used for buying drugs and guns and stuff. You have to be on top of things . . . they work real hard. And his brother did not have much ability or control. He had been a bandido since he was young, but he didn't have many contacts. So a friend of mine put me in touch with someone who said they could provide us with cocaine. So we went there but nothing came of it. Then we went to Tajara and the comadre of a friend of mine got a hold of some for us. So then we packaged and mixed it.[8]

———What were you going to do with the money? Pay the police?

———The money was to pay for a lawyer.

——And did you ask for money here, in Jakeira?

——No, I had no contacts here at all . . . I didn't know anyone here.

——But what about all your friends from before, when you were with Fábio and Roberto?

——By this time, there were other people in charge . . . other people.

——You mean your friends were already dead.

——Already. But, in any case, our enemies, *os alemães*, found out that Rogério was in jail and decided to invade . . . so they invaded São José.

——Who was in charge of the money while Rogério was in jail?

——His brother . . . but we never had enough money. During the short time he was in charge we made some money but I spent it going to see Rogério and buying him things. I also gave half the money to the lawyer. But this lawyer did nothing, so I had to put another one on the case.

——Was this first lawyer incompetent or just after the money?

——The money! Lawyers just lead you along, saying that a person will soon be released. In reality they do nothing. But you don't know if they are working for you or not. And then there was this other woman Monica . . . a woman who was also pregnant and further along than me.

——Did you know about this?

——Of course I knew.

——So what did you think of the fact that you were with Rogério and he had another woman?

——But bandidos are like that. They never have one woman. They have one woman who's the mother of their children and other women around about.

——So they live with one woman and have many others?

——They don't live with any of them because they can't have a fixed address.

——So they constantly move around?

——Yes.

——And did this other women stay with Rogério?

——Rogério spent more of his time with me . . . we didn't get along. In fact, we wanted to kill each other. Our visits with Rogério only lasted fifteen minutes and we had to speak to him through a grate. We divided the visits between us. It was seven and a half minutes each. We traveled two hours carrying heavy bags to spend seven minutes inside. After a while it became difficult to pay the lawyer . . . lawyers are expensive you know.

——And you were living where, in São José?

——I was living in São José and then Vista Bonita. Then, when I was five months pregnant, I returned here to Jakeira.

——So, how was São José invaded?

——After two months of Rogério being in jail, they invaded.

——Did they kill many people?

——No, because everyone knew the entrances and exits. So, when they found out that they were going to invade, they managed to get out.

——And who were they?

——Comando Vermelho.[9]

——And Rogério and his gang were Terceiro Comando?

——Yes. But they weren't, you know, under their control. I mean, there was no dono in jail who gave orders . . . they were always in charge.

——Did the bandidos in Jakeira know Rogério was Terceiro Comando?

——Yes . . . it was a problem.

——So, where were you at the time of the invasion?

——I had already left. I was living in Vista Bonita because it was easier to get ahold of money.

——Where, in his house?

——No, Amanda has a comadre there who lived with Rogério's uncle.

——What type of house was it?

——It was a nice house, it belonged to the Army. Because Rogério's uncle was in the Army. It was on a large plot of land. There was Rogério's uncle's house and three others that also belonged to him . . . two of them he rented out. It was easier for me to be close to Rogério's friends. And, as I said, it was easier to get money so I could buy him things. But then, when I was four months pregnant, he got jealous of me and we had a fight. He said I was cheating on him and that I needn't visit him anymore . . . and that his other woman would visit him. It was a lie. This other woman told him that I'd been seen with another man. So I told him that I wouldn't visit him because he believed other people and not me. And then I said that the child I was expecting would be mine only . . . and that I was going home after all the sacrifices I'd made buying and selling drugs for him.

——Was it hard for you to come home?

——It was for me because it wasn't what I wanted. I wanted to get away and to come back here only to visit. I wanted to make my life somewhere else. But anyway, I started to take it a little bit easier and take medicines for my pregnancy. Then, when I was eight months pregnant I went to see a fortune-teller nearby. She told me, "I am seeing a baby and a young man close by." I said that's impossible, because my husband was arrested. And then I left because I didn't believe her. Then, after a few days, my neighbor said that a young man was asking for me. So I was worried because a few weeks before my husband had called some friends of his in Vista Bonita and told them to threaten me. So they came here and took me to Vista Bonita, saying that he would call me . . . so I went there.

——So what happened?

——When Rogério sent his friends to take me to Vista Bonita, I had no idea what they were going to do. Because he'd said I wasn't to visit him and that I wasn't to go out with anyone else. So when I got there, they started to push and shove me around. And so I asked them, "Have you brought me here to kill me?" "No Lucia," they said, "We wanted to know why you stopped visiting him. You know this isn't okay." It was then that Rogério called and told them not to lay a hand on me. He called every now and then. I don't know how . . . but he called. Then he told me that he would resolve all of this when he got out.

——Did he call from prison, or from the police station?

——From the police station. That was where he was to be tried. They go from the police station to what is called *triagem*. And from there they go to prison. So then I just waited. This kind of person believes that a bandido's woman cannot be unfaithful. A bandido has many women. But a bandido's woman can only have one man.

——And if she betrays him?

——She dies.

——Has this happened to anyone you know?

——Sure.

——Where, in São José?

——No, it happened to a woman in Vista Bonita. She told the dono she was no longer involved with traficantes. But in fact she had betrayed the dono with someone who worked for him. So they conducted a sort of trial. The bandido admitted that he had been with her, when he could have easily said that he hadn't . . . and that would have been the end of it.

——And the woman?

——The woman denied it.

——And were they both killed?

——No. The bandido didn't die. The woman died because she betrayed the dono and lied about it. He stayed alive because he told the truth. This is what I expected to happen to me. But then, as I said, my neighbor called saying there was a strange man asking for me. Then I began to get scared because I had no idea who it was . . . and it never crossed my mind that he'd be held for only eight months. I thought he'd be found guilty and would stay there for many years . . . I never expected him. I asked my sister to go take a look. When my sister came back she said it was Rogério. I was happy and, at the same time, afraid.

——If you are caught by the police with a gun how long are you put in prison for?

——For carrying a gun, it's not much. The worst is drugs, you know, dealing drugs and kidnapping people. Even murder's not as bad as that.

——And Rogério got out after how long?

——Eight months.

——How did he get out so soon?

——He got out because the mother of one of the bandidos testified on his behalf and convinced the police that Rogério was not there at the time. She told them that it had been her son.

——So she told the police that it was her son and not Rogério that assaulted the police station.

——She told the truth because they assumed it was Rogério.

——Instead of her son who'd already been killed.

——Who'd already been killed. So the bandido's mother confirmed that her son and not Rogério had been involved.

——And so then they set Rogério free.

——That's right.

——Did he have to pay anyone any money?

——No, he didn't have to pay anyone anything.

——And was it easy for him to return to Vista Bonita . . . to the same place . . . the same situation?

——Yes, because he was still the dono even when he was being held. He continued to receive money from there. He was the dono as long as his friends were there. Only if they all died . . .

——And Amanda had already been born by this time?

——No, I was eight months pregnant. And at this point I wasn't sure if I was happy or afraid. He had left some clothes and things here so I went down to give them to him. I knew that he wouldn't do anything here in Jakeira. He said, "Lucia, I came to see you." I told him he needn't have bothered because he'd already told me that he didn't want anything to do with me. He said, "I just wanted to see how you were." I said, "I am alive." He had brought my comadre Maria with him. So I walked down to the main road with them. Then he asked me to have lunch with him and I told him that he had to ask my mother's permission, because she was taking care of me and I was living off her money.

——You had to ask your mother's permission?

——Of course. I told my mother that we'd had a fight and that we were no longer together and that I was home for good. She'd already suffered enough. And now I was going to go right back?

——Did your mother like Rogério?

——It's not that she liked him. She had to put up with him because I liked him, you understand? So, my mother let me go, which made Rogério happy, and we went to Vista Bonita to show everyone my belly.

——But why did you go?

——Because I liked him. I wasn't worried because I figured he'd been a hothead back then because of so many problems that were beyond his control . . . like this other woman who told him she'd tell me—to my face—that she'd seen me with another man. It would have been her word against mine.

——What happened to the other woman?

——She continued visiting him at the police station on her own. He asked her to sell one of the houses he'd given her. So she sold the house. Then they made a sort of deal, that if she paid for his lawyer, he wouldn't come to see me anymore. Despite this, despite the fact that he was released, the first person he visited was me!

——Did you ever think of saying to him, "Stop seeing her or it's finished."

——No, never.

——So, you went back to Vista Bonita and . . .

——We went back to Vista Bonita where I stayed with him for a few nights. Then his other woman saw us together and we started fighting all over again.

——Did this other woman also live in Vista Bonita?

——She lived in the neighborhood but in another favela.

——So Rogério lived most of the time with you?

——No, he never had a fixed place. He stayed a little time here, a day or two there. I left there after a while because I was about to give birth. And from then on I spent most of my time here. I only went there to take Amanda.

——And did Rogério ever visit you here?

——Yes. He stayed in Vista Bonita most of the time with his other woman, whose son had already been born. He only found out about Amanda's birth twelve days after it happened. And even then he didn't call! It was around this time he was shot in the arm by the police.

——Where was he treated?

——He didn't even go to the clinic. He was treated right there by doctors from the clinic. It was after he was shot that my comadre came to get me in a car to go see him. I remember him holding Amanda in his arms . . . and from that point on I stayed there more than here. In fact, I stayed there with him until he was killed. He spent Christmas and New Year with us here. It was during Rock in Rio that he died . . . yes, it was just before Rock in Rio that they killed him.[10]

——Once Amanda was born, did you ever think of giving up this life?

——No.

——Because you liked the clothes and things that it brought you?

——Of course.

——So how was Rogério killed?

——We were visiting. We'd been here two weeks.

——And was Rogério here too?

——He was here for Christmas . . . no, he wasn't here for Christmas. I stayed here alone at Christmas with my family.

——But on that day, was he already here or had he just arrived?

——He was already here.

——And did he sleep here?

——Yes.

——Where?

——In the house. In that small bedroom in my mother's house. I slept there with Rogério and Amanda. It was a very small bedroom.

——So how then did it all start?

——The night before I'd gone down the hill with him because he wanted to call his mother. It was about seven o'clock at night, the day before he died. So he went to telephone his mother. The whole thing was already planned because, when we went down there, there was already a group of bandidos standing close by.

——Do you think they were waiting for him?

——I believe so. They didn't do anything because he had Amanda on his shoulders. So there was me, Rogério, and Amanda. He went to use the phone and then came back up with Amanda still on his shoulders. So they didn't do anything.

——So you passed right by them.

——We passed right by them and they were still talking to him. There were a couple of them that he already knew. But back in December he had come here with a friend. Another negão who came with him. So they thought that he was bringing people here to help him stay . . . to take over the favela. So the next day they called for him early, at about nine in the morning.

——Had you already had breakfast?

——No, we hadn't even had coffee.

——Were you still asleep?

——No, we'd woken up. We were giving Amanda a bath. We were all in the bathroom playing with her hair when they called for him.

——Did he know what was going on?

——There was a bus strike that day . . . there weren't any buses. So my grandmother showed up and said, "Rogério, don't go."

——Your grandmother!

——Yes, "Rogério, don't go. Go around the back and get out of here." So he stood there, not knowing what to do. And then he said, " I'll take my gun and be right back." So then I said, "No, don't take it because if they see that you're armed they'll think you're up to no good. But you've got nothing against them, nor have they anything against you." So he stood there for a while and said, "Yeah, you're right."

—(Conceição)—Make sure you tell the story correctly. It happened one Friday when he was here. I told him that it was very dangerous for him to be here because that night two men had come here wanting to talk to him. He didn't believe me. In the morning I warned him again and told him that there was still time to leave. Then, at about nine o'clock two men called for him. I told him not to go. He told Lucia to come with him to get some breakfast and I told him again not to go because he would be killed. He said, "I'm not going to die." Then he went down the path from the house with Lucia and a little later on I heard shots.

——How was he dressed?

—(Lucia)—He was wearing Bermuda shorts, a turtleneck shirt . . . and a pair of my brother's sandals.

——What color was his shirt?

——It was a sort of a rust color.

——And his shorts?

——Gray . . . and his sandals were black. So I said I was going to go down with him.

——And did they come to meet you?

——Yes. So I waited for a while and then left them together to talk. I went with him and said to him, "I'm going to my cousin's house," which was a little bit further away. So I went there and left him to talk, so I wouldn't get in the way.

——So you went a little bit further down the path to your cousin's house.

——Yes, I left him there to talk a little while before coming back up.

——Were you worried at all?

——No, no. They shook his hand to, you know, make it look like they were friends and said, "So Rogério."

——So how many of them were there?

——There were three. Rogério and the two gerentes.

——Did you know them?

——I knew them because they were from here. In fact, I'd already chosen one of them to be Amanda's *compadre*. And the night before he had held Amanda in his arms. So, I went down to my cousin's house and came back up pretty quickly. So then he saw that I had come back up and I stood there waiting for him to finish talking.

——How far away were you? Ten meters?

——No, I was really close . . . about three meters. So anyway, when I went down with him they shook his hand and said, "We came down here to see if you wanted a house here in the favela because you've been coming here a lot." He said, "No thank you" and that he only came here to visit. He said, "I only come here to visit because her mother lives here and I already have a lot of houses." Because he had houses in São José and Vista Bonita. Because when he came here he didn't get involved with them . . . he knew them but he didn't get involved.

——So he didn't owe them money or anything.

——No.

——Nothing. Nothing at all.

——His brother spent a good deal of time here. So he came here a lot because of his brother. But this time his brother wasn't here. Because his brother had fought with this Guilherme guy. What I mean to say is that it was done as an act of revenge.

——Revenge against his brother?

——Yes. I believe it was because his brother went out with Adriana. Yes, Adriana went out with Rogério's brother before she went out with Guilherme. So my brother-in-law had already . . . she'd already been with my brother-in-law. So after my brother-in-law finished with her, and she got together with Guilherme, they still fought. He even hit Guilherme one time, which caused a lot of trouble.

——This was Edson right?

——Yeah, Edson, my brother in law. So my brother-in-law left for Vista Bonita but his brother still came here because of me.

——You say Edson was your brother-in-law but you were never married to Rogério, right?

——No, we were never married. But I still thought of him as my brother-in-law. So anyway, after they finished talking they shook his hand and said, "Okay. Go in faith. We're going back up now." And he said, "I'm going back up too . . . to have some coffee." So I turned around, with Rogério close behind. So then he put his hand on my shoulder like this (gesturing with her hand). Then Guilherme fired a shot and he fell. There was only one shot. The bullet entered here (gesturing again with her hand) at the back of his neck. There wasn't even time for me to turn around . . . and I grabbed him and asked him to get up and said, "Phew, this guy's hard to lift." But the bullet had already killed him.

——So it killed him right away.

——It killed him. There was no blood, nothing . . . because he had a hemorrhage, and when you hemorrhage, there's no sign of blood. So then the other guy, Gustavo, came running towards me. I was a good friend of

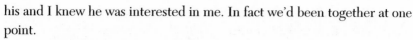

his and I knew he was interested in me. In fact we'd been together at one point.

——Who, you and Gustavo?

——Hey, he used to give me things. He gave me money, jewelry, clothes, and everything. He gave me everything that I wanted. But he had another woman. So, I said to him, "If you want to stay with me you'll have to let her go." He said that he wouldn't and that he'd set us both up with houses. But I told him that I wouldn't accept this. So I left him and he was thinking that, with Rogério dead, I would go back to him. But I didn't want anything to do with him . . . I think that's what he wanted. He kept saying that my daughter was his. When I was pregnant, Amanda's father was in jail. So he kept asking to listen to my stomach. He would put his head close like this (gesturing). I think he wanted him out of the way so I could be with him. By killing him I would be alone . . . I think that was what ran through his mind.

——So there was only one shot?

——No, Guilherme shot him once in the head. Then Gustavo shot him a few more times . . . not all over his body but here (gesturing) around his chest and thighs. It was done, you know, out of spite. It was when I saw Gustavo running towards me that I became desperate. It was then that I realized they were killing him. I realized what was happening and I ran. Because when Guilherme shot him, Gustavo was a good distance away. But then he started running and it was then that he started shooting. So I ran back up to the house to get someone . . . thinking that he was still alive. I wanted to find someone to help me take him to a doctor. And then Gulherme fired another shot. I was a long way away by then, but the bullet hit the ground and then it hit me.

——Was he trying to shoot you?

——I think so . . . but he was a long way away. It was supposed to hit me but because I was running it hit the ground and then me . . . it hit me somehow.

——Where, in the backside?

——Here (gesturing).

——Ouch.

——Can you see it. It's still in there!

——How did it feel?

——I didn't feel a thing. I didn't feel a thing because I was so upset.

——Was there blood?

——No, there was no blood ... I didn't see anything.

——So you ran back home and went inside and ...

——I asked my mother to go down with me but my grandmother and sisters said, "Lucia, don't go." I wanted to see if they'd taken him away. So my sisters went to see and they told me that they'd taken him. So then I was going to go up there and have it out with them ... but my family refused to let me leave the house and, eventually, my friends took me to the clinic where I took a sedative and was given an injection to calm me down. But I still couldn't sleep or stay calm. So I waited a while and then went up there to talk to them.

——What did you say?

——I asked them why they'd killed him. They said to me, "Oh, has someone died?" as if nothing had happened ... and that's when I saw the dono.

——Who was the dono?

——Rui, from Santa Clara.

——Did you like Rui?

——I had nothing against him at the time. But after what happened I began to hate him.

——Did he approve of the fact that his men killed Rogério without his permission?

——It wasn't done without his permission. He let it happen. He let it happen because he was told a very different story.

——So he knew it was going to happen.

——Of course he knew.

——So it was all planned beforehand.

——They weren't sent to do it. The one who liked me was simply waiting for an opportunity. Rogério was coming here a lot so he used his influence with the dono to say, "You know, he's coming here a lot." But he did this so he could kill him.

——But it still seems strange that he would let them kill Rogério when you and your family lived here.

——If it had been anywhere else, both us would be dead. That's the way it is. Because of her husband, a woman can die too.

——So, what happened when you saw the dono?

——At the time, Amanda's comadre lived near the bandidos ... and Amanda was there with her. So Amanda was crying and Rui picked up a bunch of money and handed it to me and said, "Here, buy some things for her." So I threw the money back in his face and told him to save it for his funeral. At that point, I was ready to go down to the police station and denounce them all . . . and leave. Then one of the members of his gang said, "Kill her quickly, kill her quickly." So I said (and at this point she begins to cry), "Go on, kill me. Go on, kill me . . . and my daughter . . . finish the job . . . because you're going to have to kill all of us . . . " So then I asked him, "Why did you have to do this?" And he said, "Because he was looking to take over. He almost . . . " So then the next day I left. They told me that my daughter could have everything and that they'd give me money each week. I didn't want it. I told them, "You're going to pay for his death. The money you'd give me won't pay for his life."

——And what did the bandidos do with Rogério's body?

——They dragged his body down to the main road and threw it in a dumpster. Then they put a sign around his neck that said, "Won't assault any more police stations."

——Why did they do this?

——Because they knew the story about when he was arrested. They put the sign there so the police wouldn't investigate. They knew that if the police found out that a bandido who assaulted police stations had died, they wouldn't investigate further. Because when someone dies who is not involved, the police will try to find out why. But when it is someone who is involved with drugs, they don't even care! It was simply a shoot-out, that's all.

——And what about when the police kill someone?

——They kill someone and say that it was a shoot-out. And that's it! Bandidos aren't real people you know!

——And did they leave Rogério's body in the dumpster?

——They left it there until the garbage truck picked it up about five hours later.

——And what did you do when you realized you'd been shot?

——I went to the local hospital.

——Where?

——Near the bus station.

——So what happened when you got there. What did you say to the doctor?

——When I got there I couldn't say anything about where the bullet came from . . . although the doctor did keep looking at me.

——Why not?

——Because they are in contact with the police . . . and there are police there. If I had told the truth . . . and there was a bandido there with me! The bandido took me there in a *kombi*. He stayed beside me the whole time. If I had told the truth something would have happened to my family. Anyway, the doctor told me that he couldn't do anything about the bullet, because my backside was extremely swollen. But he also said that it was no problem if I left it in, because it was well lodged . . . and that if I wanted it out in the future they would just have to make a small incision.[11] I told myself that I would only have it out when Guilherme and Gustavo were both dead. They told me not to leave the favela . . . but I packed up my bags and left. I packed up my bags and left Jakeira for a while. So then they sent people after me.

——Who?

——The bandidos. They thought I'd tell someone about them because I knew where they all lived. So I stayed with people they didn't know. My mother told me that they came to look for me here and that one day two women with guns showed up . . . and that they didn't even know my name. They called me the woman with the curly hair. Rogério's friends in Vista Bonita eventually found me a house that belonged to people they'd expelled from the favela. I slept there for a while but I was worried the whole time that the people they'd expelled would come back with the police. The whole situation made me very nervous. The only way I could sleep was to drink a ton of beer at night with my friends . . . the ones who were looking after me.

——Was Amanda with you this whole time?

——Amanda stayed here with my mother. Then, not long after, a friend of Rogério's found a place for me to stay in another woman's house. I had no right to ask anything from Rogério's friends anymore. Even his brother was helping me out. I remember thinking, "What am I going to do with my life?" So then one of Rogério's friends found us a place to stay. But it wasn't just me . . . there was also this friend of mine from Jakeira and two other women. One was my cousin's wife. The other was Rogério's uncle's wife. All of their husbands were bandidos and so we were all without a place to live. So they found a house where all of us could stay . . . with a woman whose husband was in prison. This woman said to us, "You are welcome to stay in my house, but you will have to help out." It felt good to be in that house, even though there was no place for us to sleep. You see the woman had her own family, her own children . . . so we had to sleep on the floor. She was very good to us, and told us that we'd only leave the house when we got married! So, we spent our time there helping her out and helping with the house.

——Did this woman buy things for you?

——No, she didn't work either. There were times when we all went hungry . . . even her children. Sometimes my cousin would give me money. Her daughter also prostituted herself so that they could put together some money. My friend also hooked up with a man she didn't really like just to help us with the house. At times there was nothing at all to eat. Sometimes we cooked up a *caldo de feijão com angu*, mixed it with an egg, threw the whole thing in a liquidizer, and split it between us.

——How long did this go on for?

——I stayed there for about three months. And by the end, Amanda was with me there too. Luckily, my cousin made sure she didn't go without. At the time, I wasn't on good terms with Amanda's grandmother on her father's side. They hadn't helped me out since the time that Amanda was born. And then, when they saw the situation I was in, they tried to take her away from me. They told me that they were going to take her away. I told them, "No. If Amanda has to go anywhere it will be to my mother's house. She's been here all this time and only now do you take an interest in her. I won't give her to you!" But I was so tired of being hungry, and without the things I needed, that I resolved to go back home . . . even if I couldn't ever live there again.

——Why couldn't you live there?

——Because after I left, after Rogério's death, I went to Vista Bonita . . . and from that moment on I couldn't go back there. I could no longer go back there to my house. I had been kicked out. Well, I mean I wasn't actually kicked out, but I left. They told me not to go. I made the decision to go away but, as a result, I couldn't come back . . . because I went away without talking to them . . . without asking their permission.[12] There were days when I got as close as the supermarket opposite the entrance to the favela and stood there thinking of the day when I could return home. And when I finally did return home, the bandidos all looked at me, shocked and surprised. Then, a few days later, the dono paid me a visit. He said that he was very sorry for what had happened and that he would give me money each week . . . so I could look after Amanda. I refused and told him that no amount of money could pay for the life of my husband. I told him that I just wanted to be left in peace . . . to live my life. I wanted nothing to do with them . . . I wasn't going to talk to anybody.

——So who was the first of them to die?

——Gustavo. He died eight months after Rogério was killed. They set a trap for Rui, so the police could catch him. They betrayed him . . . they told the police where he was staying.

——Who?

——Guilherme and Gustavo . . . Rui's own gerentes. So the police came and took Rui away and they became the new donos. Guilherme, Gustavo, and another guy called Antônio. It was what they'd always wanted. So then Gustavo left Jakeira to take his family on a trip . . . and he only came back here to collect money . . . and so they set a trap for him as well. When Gustavo arrived he sent someone to get his money . . . and they sent someone to kill him. It was a whole bunch of people . . . it was Guilherme.

——You mean Guilherme had him killed?

——He had him killed . . . there was a bunch of them. It was right over there on that stairway. They shot him a bunch of times. And so then Guilherme became the only dono.

——And then he died too?

——He died too. There was this guy who was Antônio's brother . . . except that he was a bit disturbed . . . you know, a little bit mad. He was a Comando Vermelho fanatic. It was forbidden to give him weapons . . . because he was so crazy. He did a lot of drugs, so no one liked to see him with a gun. So anyway, they said to him, "Maluco,"[13] which was his nickname, "Guilhereme wrote the words 'Comando Vermelho' in blue." And the words 'Comando Vermelho' always have to be written in red. And so then, he got real mad . . . and they gave him a gun with 12-caliber bullets, which are the worst, and they explained to him, when you get there give this piece of paper to Guilherme and ask him to read it to you. And when he begins to read it to you, shoot him in the head. So this Maluco went to find Guilherme and gave him the piece of paper, you know, all innocent like. And when Guilherme took the piece of paper, Maluco shot him in the face . . . right in front of his woman and child. It was horrible . . . he killed him right there. There's no getting out of the way of one of those bullets.

——How did you hear of all this?

——My sister came into my bedroom and said, "Lucia, guess who died?" And I said, "Not Guilherme!" So then I woke up Amanda and grabbed her in my arms and started jumping up and down.

——And what about Rui?

——Rui stayed in jail for about two years. Actually, you know what, it wasn't much more than a year. It was a year and a few months. He escaped from jail through a tunnel. He went to Santa Clara to look for help so he could take over here, in Jakeira. And he was here for a while. He was a different person though . . . he was really rebellious . . . full of hate.

——And so how did he die?

——He went to Santa Clara to ask for help so he could take over here. But the guys here had made things very difficult for him. They'd left him with lots of enemies . . . and so they killed him in Santa Clara.

DRUG GANGS

THE BRAZILIAN MILITARY'S withdrawal from politics in the late 1970s and early 1980s was accompanied by a groundswell of popular mobilization and protest. Hundreds of thousands of Brazilians took to the streets to demand a return to competitive and open elections and participated in what was described, at the time, as the "resurrection of civil society." For many, the proliferation of grassroots church groups, labor unions, liberal professional organizations, and neighborhood associations across the country signaled the dawn of a new era. The hope was that these so-called new social movements would undermine support for elitist and authoritarian parties and sweep the democratic Left to power.[1]

The population of Rio's *favelas* was very much a part of this process. Throughout the 1950s and 1960s, neighborhood associations in the favelas were organized and fairly closely controlled by the state. Social services and public works were made available on a sporadic and piecemeal basis in the understanding that government candidates would be rewarded with support at the ballot box.[2] Then in the late 1970s, a group of leaders emerged who challenged the nature of state-favela relations. Instead of begging for social services and public works as favors, they demanded them as rights. And, by the early to mid-1980s, the so-called favela movement in Rio was a political force to be reckoned with.[3]

Over the course of the next decade, however, the situation changed dramatically. First, the return to democracy took the wind out of the sails of the favela movement and just about every other movement that protested military rule. Second, divisions emerged within the leadership of the favela movement as political parties and state and municipal administrations sought to establish their influence and control. A large contingent of presidents and directors of neighborhood associations accepted positions in local government and more than a few ran for political office. Finally, it became increasingly common for presidents and directors of neighborhood associations to be accused of favoritism, incompetence, and corruption.[4] In other words, neighborhood associations ceased to be autonomous and communal spaces and were perceived instead as yet another administrative layer between the population of the favelas and the state.

Far more significant, however, was the threat posed by drug gangs. Between 1969 and 1975, the military government in Brazil housed political prisoners who were engaged in armed struggle with common criminals in a prison on the island of Ilha Grande, off the coast of Rio. The political prisoners impressed upon a small group of their fellow common-criminal detainees the importance of organization, loyalty, and discipline and instructed them in the art of urban guerrilla warfare. The product of this unlikely encounter was the Comando Vermelho, the first of what was to become a handful of powerful criminal organizations based in Rio's penitentiaries.[5]

Initially, the Comando Vermelho sought to impose its control over Ilha Grande and other prisons in the system. It took out rival factions, introduced strict codes of prisoner conduct, and negotiated for improved conditions with suddenly besieged prison officials. Eventually, however, the reach of the Comando Vermelho extended far beyond the prison system's walls to well-organized and clandestine cells that conducted bank robberies and, later on, kidnappings to finance the purchase of weapons and what were oftentimes the spectacular escapes of their colleagues.[6] Then around 1982, the decision was made to fund the Comando Vermelho's activities through the drug trade.[7] Since the late 1970s, Rio de Janeiro had become an important entry and exit point for cocaine produced and processed by drug cartels in Colombia, Bolivia, and Peru.[8] However, Rio also became an important market for cocaine consumption, and it was this multimillion dollar market for cocaine—and to a lesser extent marijuana—that the Comando Vermelho sought to capture and control.[9]

The decision by the Comando Vermelho to finance its operations via the drug trade led to a period of intense and bloody civil war for control of the favelas. By the end of the 1980s, the Comando Vermelho profited from the sale of marijuana and cocaine from an estimated 70 percent of all the selling points, or *bocas de fumo*, in Rio.[10] Many of the leaders and rank-and-file members of the Comando Vermelho were from the favelas and so the relationship between such areas and drug trafficking naturally followed. Those that resisted were forced out, kidnapped, or killed. Or they turned for help and protection to one of the Comando Vermelho's rival factions, the Terceiro Commando or the Amigos dos Amigos.[11]

The ability of the Comando Vermelho—and its rival factions—to operate the drug trade depended on the relationship between each drug gang and the surrounding community. Drug gangs rely on the local population to provide cover for their activities and to protect them from the police. It became increasingly common, therefore, for drug gangs to provide social services such as free medical treatment and transportation and to finance public works such as day-care centers and recreational facilities.[12] It also became increasingly common for drug gangs to take advantage of the absence of public authorities by laying down the law and punishing—oftentimes quite severely—those who disobeyed orders or who caused trouble.[13] In the early to mid-1980s, drug gangs coexisted fairly peacefully with neighborhood associations that continued to play an important and independent role in favela life. By the end of the decade, however, the vast majority of neighborhood associations and other social and political actors in the favelas were either directly controlled by or under the influence of drug gangs.[14]

When I first got to know Lucia, the neighborhood association in Jakeira was already in trouble. The association was founded in 1958 but existed in name only until it was resurrected, in the early 1980s, by representatives from the Pastoral de Favelas and the Federação de Associações de Favela do Estado do Rio de Janeiro (FAFERJ), the state federation of favela neighborhood associations. In 1983, a new president and board of twelve directors were elected for the first of what were to be seven consecutive two-year terms of office. And in the beginning, the leaders of the neighborhood association were at the forefront of efforts to improve conditions in Jakeira. They held weekly open meetings, sent delegations of local residents to occupy the time and offices of state and municipal employees downtown, and organized countless *mutirões* to clean up the favela and to make improvements to the facilities that were administered by the neighborhood association.

By the early 1990s, however, much of the initial enthusiasm and support for the neighborhood association was gone. It became increasingly difficult to persuade people to participate in the association's various projects and activities, and, more importantly, to run for office. One by one, former presidents and directors grew tired and disillusioned and ultimately withdrew. Those that remained were accused more and more frequently of favoring friends and family with the jobs and positions that were allocated by the neighborhood association and with the location and even the scheduling of public works. They were also accused of allowing their own political biases to influence neighborhood association policy and, worse still, of squandering the resources that the state and nongovernmental organizations passed their way.

The difficulties experienced by the neighborhood association in Jakeira coincided with the emergence of a drug gang. At first, the drug gang went quietly about its business and stayed away from the neighborhood association's affairs. Over time, however, its presence gradually increased until eventually it assumed complete control. This was partly due to the incompetence and lack of resources of the neighborhood association. Increasingly, it was the drug gang and not the association that sponsored cultural events and invested money in the community. It was also, however, due to an escalation in the level of conflict between the drug gang in Jakeira and gangs in other favelas and the drug gang in Jakeira and the police.

In 1988, Jakeira was invaded by a group of *traficantes* associated with the Comando Vermelho. For the next two years, members of the drug gang in Jakeira participated in raids to take possession of other favelas in the area that were not yet under the Comando Vermelho's control. Then in 1994, Jakeira was invaded once again by the Comando Vermelho. Except that this time it was to physically remove what was perceived as a disloyal and ineffective *dono* and his *gerentes*. The order for the invasion was given by the real dono who was serving time in prison. Then, three years later, traficantes from the gang that was driven out in 1994 returned with reinforcements to take possession of the favela once again.

The struggle for possession of Jakeira involved fierce and prolonged gun battles that were covered in detail by the local press. The perception was that, little by little, the authorities were losing control of whole areas of the city. So, every now and then—and especially before elections—the police or, on occasion, the Army would be sent in to keep the peace.[15] On one such occasion, the leader of the drug gang in Jakeira called the president of the neighborhood association to complain that the twenty-four-hour police presence at the entrances to the favela restricted his ability to do business. So he ordered the president to draft and sign a petition asking the police to leave.[16] After much deliberation, the president of the neighborhood association refused, despite the fact that he had been told that if he did not sign the petition he and his family would be killed. The president told me this as we were walking through the favela inspecting the latest round of public works. He also told me that, much like the dono, he was spending each night at a different friends' house. A month later, the president of the neighborhood association packed his bags and left.

Then, in 1997, the perhaps inevitable happened when the drug gang marched into the neighborhood association and told the last in a long line of democratically elected presidents to go. The president was replaced, a few days later, by the first of what was to become a long list of drug gang appointees.[17] The drug gang needed the neighborhood association to represent its interests and communicate with the outside world. What this meant was that, in effect, the fourteen-year-long experiment with democracy in Jakeira was now over.[18]

CHAPTER 3

Marcos

——So what did you do after Rogério died?

——After Rogério died, I thought to myself that I didn't want to be involved in this life anymore. So I started going to *bailes* with my friends and brother and sisters in a town nearby. And it was there that I met Celso, from the *favela* of Papagaio. But we were never serious. In fact it was kind of dull. We never did anything on weekends . . . and I like adventure! Then, one night, after he'd told me he wasn't going out, I caught him at a bar. That was the final straw for me. So, the next time we all went to a baile, I found myself another boyfriend. This guy was from Novo Horizonte.

——Was he a *bandido*?

——No, this guy was a *trabalhador*. I got together with him at a baile and we stayed together for a while . . . and I even went to his house to meet his parents and all that.

——How did you get together with guys?

——I found this one at a baile . . . you know, flirting and messing around.

——So, one dies and then . . .

——You replace him with another. If you don't, you start thinking . . . you know, you get old, you start to give up. It was about this time that Jakeira was invaded and a bandido that I'd been with before appeared again. The first person that this bandido looked for was me! It had been many years since I'd seen him, because he'd been expelled from the favela. But then, one beautiful day, I ran into him again. I told him what had happened to my husband and that now I had a child. He asked me what I was doing so I told him I was working and that I was seeing someone from Novo Horizonte. So then he asked me, "How much time do you need to get rid of this guy?" But I didn't want to get rid of him. I wanted to stay with him. So then he told me that all he needed to do was to send someone to Novo Horizonte to kill him. So, to save the guy's life, I went with the bandido . . . I stayed with him. He told me that he didn't want me to work anymore. He wanted to look after me here . . . and, if truth be told, he gave me everything. I mean really, he gave me everything.

——So, you stayed with him because you didn't want him to hurt the other guy?

——I stayed with him because that's what he threatened to do.

——So, apart from Rogério, your relationships with bandidos weren't that serious.

——They were serious for me! A bandido's woman cannot be unfaithful. A bandido can betray his women and there's nothing they can do. So, for me, they were very serious. You had to be serious with bandidos or else you ended up dead!

——So, if a bandido likes a woman, there is no choice but to go with him?

——It's not quite like that, but since I'd already been with him, he had a sense of who I was. It's not that he forced me, you know, it's just that he kept running into me.

——You mean, he made it difficult for you to say no.

——Exactly.

——And when you say he gave you everything, how much did he give you?

——In one day I received what I would usually earn in a month. I spent it all on clothes and shoes. I never thought of saving anything. I used to take Amanda to really expensive stores . . . I bought fancy soap and shampoo. I went to *pagodes* here in the favela and spent money on all my friends . . . I bought clothes for them too. Then, one time, Amanda got sick, and he refused to give me money for medicine. So I decided that I wasn't going to stay with him anymore . . . because if I'd still been working, I'd at least have the money for medicine. So I went back to Vista Bonita to find another lover.

——You don't like being alone do you?

——No, I hate being alone. So then I got together with a guy called Eduardo. All his friends said, "Eduardo, you'd better go talk to Marcos," who was the *dono*, "because Marcos likes Lucia a lot and is sort of a father to her." So, Eduardo went to talk to Marcos who told him that he better take good care of me . . . find me a house and look after my daughter. But the guy was very low on the ladder and knew he couldn't afford all this. So he stole stuff from other people's houses in the favela.

——So he could give you money.

——Yeah, he stole a new stove from one of the houses. I told him that I didn't approve of that type of thing. I wasn't about to take other people's things so that, later on, I could be turned in to the police. So I broke up with this guy. So then everyone told me that Marcos liked me a lot and was passionate about me. I said, "Are you kidding?" But, you know what, he gave me everything I asked for. I asked him for new contact lenses, and he gave me them. If I wanted to go somewhere, he took me there. . . . And another thing, he was with Monica. She got together with him after Rogério's death. At the time, I said to myself, wherever she goes, I will go too. Whoever she gets together with, I'll get together with too. So, whenever she was with him, I would make sure I was there too. You know, I'd kiss him and all that.

——Why?

——To make her jealous, I wanted her to be really jealous. I asked him for money and he gave me money. She asked him for money and he wouldn't give it to her. All this made her really angry. So, anyway, I noticed that he treated me really well and that he was up to something with Maria, my *comadre*. So then he asked me to do him a favor by bringing some of his clothes to another favela near Vista Bonita. You see he was the dono of six or seven other communities. When I got there, he told me that I couldn't leave because there were police everywhere. The problem was that it was already late, so I asked him if there was any way he could take me home. He said that no there wasn't and that we could stay at a friend's house and go back home in the morning. So he took me to the house of a couple he knew who spread out a sheet on the floor for me to sleep on. I rolled back and forth on the ground until, finally, I saw him lying next to me. I thought to myself, what's all this? Then he kissed me. Everyone told me to stay with him because he was dono and all that. So I decided to stay with him. Then, the next night he took me to Minas Gerais,[1] to a house of another dono.

——Where was Amanda during all this?

——Amanda was here with my mother.

——And what did Marcos look like?

——He was tall and dark-skinned . . . and very strong.

——And did you like him from the beginning?

——I liked him . . . he was my friend. We had known each other for a long time. But, as a woman I didn't really like him, because he was very aggressive . . . very excitable.

——Did Marcos have any children?

——He had about ten children . . . which was a lot.

——And all of his women knew about each other.

——Of course they knew. But Marcos was like this. Once he had a child with a woman he didn't want anything to do with her. He gave her money, that's all. And, in return, she couldn't be with anyone else, you understand?

——And what was the relationship like between Marcos and his community?

——He was a good person to the community . . . a very, very good person. Lots of people liked him. He did a lot too. He paid for medicine, he bought gas tanks for people's stoves, he bought ice cream and cakes for children's parties and paid for a new soccer pitch. Whatever it was, he'd help out.

——And what about his family? Did he have a father and mother?

——His whole family was from São José. He didn't have a mother and he lived with his father. But his father turned him in to the police because of a suitcase of dollars he'd stolen. After that he hated him.

——Did he have his father killed?

——No, he didn't. But he never saw him again and had nothing more to do with him.

——So his father turned in his own son!

——He was desperate, you know, seeing his son in that sort of situation. Because no one who has children wants them to get involved in this kind of life.

——And was Marcos a member of the same gang as Rogério?

——Yes. I got to know him on the same day that I got to know Rogério. Marcos was the oldest member of the gang and so people called him ... Marcos was sort of a father figure.

——How old was he?

——At the time he was around twenty-one or twenty-two ... and Rogério was sixteen.

——And how old were you when you got together with Marcos?

——I was twenty-one.

——So, getting back to the story, then what happened?

——So anyway, I stayed with him in Minas for a whole week. And, by the time we came back, all of his women knew we'd been together. One of them was a friend of mine. We got on well and sometimes I helped out with her children. I told her what had happened so she didn't think I was going behind her back. She said to me, "Lucia, can't you see that he's not nice to us and that he'll treat you well at first and then ..." I told her that it was okay with me that he didn't have anything to do with any of his other women. The only women he slept with were me and Monica. The other women, who had given birth to his children, he only gave them money. He also arranged for each of us to have a car ... but the others couldn't get together with anyone else. I was the only one who did everything with him. I traveled with him, fought with him ... and with Monica of course. I went through hell with him as well. He was a good guy and a really bad guy at the same time.

——How so?

——When he killed someone he never used drugs. He killed them in cold blood. When he used drugs, he wouldn't hurt a fly. He was different from the rest.

——**Did he like to kill? Had he killed many people?**

——He'd killed a lot of people. When I'd been with him for four months . . . he put on a lot of bailes, you understand. Because by putting on bailes, he could sell a lot of drugs. A lot of people go to those you know. Anyway, he told everyone at each baile that he didn't want any fighting . . . and that, if there was any, he'd shoot. So, of course, the first person to start a fight was me . . . and Monica. She'd been provoking me . . . getting under my skin. So naturally I wanted to kill her. So I started to run after her and, as luck would have it, we ran right into Marcos. So he picked us both up by the hair and pulled out a 380. He fired at the muscle but the bullet hit and crushed my bone.[2]

——**And what about Monica?**

——She was also shot in both legs . . . me too.

——**Where did the bullet go in and come out? (She points out the locations) Did it hurt?**

——It only hurt a little bit because I'd already drunk a lot of alcohol. In fact, we carried on running for a while and then I fell to one side, and Monica the other. Then he said that anyone who went near us would be shot as well. He looked at us and said, "You don't want to fight? Go ahead and fight!"

——**When people fight, do they usually have to report to the dono?**

——Sure. Because when things happen in other communities, they call the police. In communities where there are *traficantes*, people are unable to call the police . . . the traficantes are the law. So then a little boy came towards us to take a look and Marcos got even madder and swiped him across the back with the butt of his pistol, and told him to go away. If he didn't, he said, he'd mess with him too. By this time we were losing a lot of blood. But he didn't want to call for a doctor because he wanted to watch us suffer. So we had to sit there and listen to him talk about how he was going to clean house. No one dared disobey his orders . . . because if he had the courage to punish his own women, he'd punish anyone. Then, after a while, he sent someone to take us to the hospital in Vista Bonita. But he didn't even leave us at the door . . . he left us at a square nearby until someone came to help . . . and all the while we were losing lots of blood. Then this guy walked past and we told him that we'd been shot at a baile, and that we needed help. We had to lie because we couldn't say who'd shot us. So, when we got there, the doctor said that he had to take an x-ray but that the technician was asleep. I mean, we were losing precious time. So the doctor lifted my leg into the wash basin and threw a liter of ether over the wound. I cannot possibly describe the pain . . . an incredible pain . . . it hurt like hell! Then he put both of us in casts and sent us to the Emergency Room.

——How long did you stay there?

——Monica stayed only one night because the bullet went through her muscle. I was supposed to stay fifteen days. I only stayed three though. I was questioned a lot by the police. There were lots of police there so I had to lie a lot . . . but always tell the same story . . . along with Monica . . . so the police would believe us. I couldn't say that Marcos had done this to us and he told people that no one was to visit us or he'd kill them.

——Why?

——Because he gave the order . . . he gave an order. My family could visit me because they were from another favela. But people from the community where he was dono couldn't. You had to do whatever he wanted. In any case, some of my friends came to visit . . . to bring me things like blankets. But they couldn't stay. My comadre, who was like a sister to him, visited me almost every day. But the nurses told me that I had to get myself transferred, because the doctor didn't have the right dressing, and it was becoming one huge clot that could infect my entire leg.[3]

——What do you mean the doctor didn't have the right dressing?

——I don't know. They just left me there without dressing the wound or anything. There were times when I couldn't go to the bathroom because my legs wouldn't support me . . . and other times when a young man who was visiting his mother would hand me a wastebasket to pee in. I had to take off my clothes because my leg was in a cast and the nurses never came by to help. "Don't get upset my friend," he said, "We are nothing on this earth . . . and don't worry, I won't look at you." When they moved me from the Emergency Room they put me way up there. I don't even know what floor it was on. I felt completely abandoned because

nurses never went up there. They only went there to give me injections.
They wouldn't even tell me what the injections were for. It was horrible
being left up there. Then my comadre came to visit me and I said, "Maria,
please take me out of here. I can't stand it anymore and if you don't, I'll
throw myself from a window." She told the doctor that she was going to
take me out but the doctor told her that she couldn't because my
condition was too serious. So Maria told him that I wasn't happy there and
he told her that she would be responsible for whatever happened to me
and that she should think very carefully about what she was about to do.
But I was already smelling really bad because I had been wearing the
same clothes every day . . . the same underwear! So she took me to the
clinic and Marcos said to her, "Maria, you brought her back from the
hospital so you can be responsible for paying for all her treatment and
medicine." So she told him that she would and because of this I think of
her like a sister. Then the doctor told me that if he didn't do something
soon I was likely to lose my leg, because the clot had become infected. So
he cut it out right there by making a hole with a pair of scissors. I stayed in
the clinic for two nights. On one of these nights, Marcos came by to visit.
I was drugged and a little bit out of it, so when I woke up I started
screaming because I thought he'd come to kill me. He told me that he
loved me and I asked him how he could possibly love me if he could do a
thing like that to me . . . and I started to scream even more. Then the
doctor came in and said that I couldn't have this sort of visit and that I was
still drugged up. So then, the next day I told Maria that I wanted to go
home and the doctor told me that I could only go if I kept the leg
stretched out and a nurse accompanied me to change the dressing. So
then, he started visiting me and sending me presents. So I treated him
nicely so that when I got better I could kill him.
    ——Really?
    ——Really! I thought that if I didn't treat him nicely, he might do
something to me. That was the way he was. And then I wouldn't have
accomplished anything. I was going to poison his drink or kill him with
one of the guns he always went to bed with. Then he came and paid for all
my medicine because, in the end, it was all very expensive. All in all, I had
something like forty injections. Then the doctor told me that I wouldn't
be able to walk properly and that I would always have a limp in my left

leg. The doctor also told me that I had to go on a diet. My daughter always held this against him. Amanda was still young . . . only two years old. But she told me that she didn't like Marcos because he'd killed my leg. So I never took her there. Whenever I came back from one of my trips I always brought her a present. Then one day I went there and told him that it wasn't working out and that this should have never have happened to me. So then he gave me a bunch of money wrapped up in a towel . . . and it was a lot of money. I told him that I was going to put it in a savings account for my comadre . . . which I went and opened. He thought I'd forgiven him. Then, close to my birthday, I asked him to throw me a party. So he threw a huge party for me with two pagode bands, two kegs of beer, and a barbecue. Except that I had to stay sitting down the whole time . . . and Monica was already fully healed. But then, after the party, I changed my mind about killing him. Then he took me and another dono and his girlfriend on a trip.

——Where did you all go?

——Well, first we went to São Paulo and then to Volta Redonda.

——Did you go by bus or by car?

——By car. So anyway, one night Marcos, myself and a cousin and a friend of mine went to dinner. During the meal my cousin and I went to the bathroom. On the way, this guy came up to us and gave me his telephone number. Marcos saw all this happen and when I came back to the table he got really mad. I told him it was nothing. Then he started messing with the waiter who was serving us. So then I got upset and didn't want to eat or drink anything. So I told him that when I got back to Jakeira I would put on a really small bathing suit and go to the beach . . . because I knew he didn't like to. He got so mad that he hit me and split my mouth open, across here (gesturing). The waiters all crowded round, shocked at what had just happened. Marcos told them all not to worry and that it was all quite normal . . . you know, a fight among family. He's the type who destroys things and then patches them up.

——What do you mean?

——He likes to break things, you know, he breaks things like this (gesturing). Then he puts it all back together. He used to tell me this. He broke things then put them back together. So, if he beat someone up and broke their arm, he'd pay to get it fixed. So he brought me to a clinic in

Volta Redonda and I had to have six stitches in my mouth. The doctor at the clinic started asking questions so I had to lie about it, saying that I'd drunk too much and hit my mouth on the table. At this point, Marcos had to leave the room because the doctor was asking so many questions.

——So this wasn't a clinic you were familiar with.

——No. So anyway, afterwards he took me to a hotel and started to snort cocaine. He asked me why I was always talking about leaving him. And that if I continued in this way he would have to kill me . . . and that he didn't want to have to do this. And then, the next morning, he didn't want to take me back . . . they had rented a house in Volta Redonda.

——Did he bring lots of money with him?

——Lots.

——And did he always carry money with him?

——Yes . . . and he always sent someone back to get more money and more drugs. So anyway, I had to stay in this house with him and the other dono and his woman.

——Couldn't you escape?

——My leg was still bad. Every day I took what they gave me for it. So I stayed there until my mouth healed. Then Monica called when he wasn't there, because he and the other dono had gone back to Rio to get more money . . . and to keep an eye on things. So when Monica called she spoke to the other woman and told her that he was in Vista Bonita and wasn't coming back that night. Then, in the early morning, someone rang the doorbell. We didn't want to open the door because this house was in the middle of nowhere . . . and we couldn't open it for just anyone. So we took our time opening it, and when we did open it, it was them. They asked us what took us so long so we told them that Monica had called and told us what was going on. So the next morning Monica called again and he threatened her, saying he was going to beat her up. Then that same morning four police cars showed up.

——Did you hear the cars pull up?

——We heard them and we saw them.

——And was there a lookout there?

——No, just us.

——So then what happened?

——There were various things in the house like drugs, guns, and a computer with a list of a lot of people's names. Because this particular house was not far from where the *matuto* delivered the drugs. The matutos were always influential people and so it was much easier for them to make contact this way.

——What do you mean influential people?

——Rich people . . . influential people from the city. The sons of mayors and people like that. Most of those involved were in the Navy or the Air Force. You know, influential people, important people. It's not poor people from favelas that do all this.

——So Marcos would buy drugs in Volta Redonda and then bring them back to Rio?

——He brought them back to Vista Bonita . . . and he also set up *bocas de fumo* in bars in and around Volta Redonda . . . because the price of drugs there was much higher.

——You mean the price of cocaine?

——Yeah. Here they sell it for five to ten *Reais*. And there for twenty to thirty.

——So then what happened with the police?

——They wanted to know about lots of things and took the women to one side of the house and the men to the other. The other dono's woman led me into the kitchen and, in desperation, took all the little bags of cocaine and started tucking them under my blouse . . . because she was pregnant. That made me even more desperate. So I went into the living room and told the police that I was menstruating and needed to go to the bathroom . . . and they let me! When I got there I threw all the bags in the toilet and flushed it three times.

——And what about the guns?

——There was only a 38-caliber pistol. When Marcos went on trips he didn't take big guns with him. They only used those when they went to war. The police took the gun and then they took hold of Marcos and the other dono. They tried to force us to call all the people on the list and to tell them to come. But I said no . . . I refused to do it.

——Why?

——Because they would have arrested them all once they reached the house. The other dono's woman got scared and actually called one of them. He came over and they tied him up and tortured him with electric shocks.

——Why did they do this?

——So he'd confess. It was a form of torture. I couldn't deal with all this so they warned me that if I kept coming into the room they'd do the same to me. They were there from eight in the morning until five o'clock in the afternoon.

——Were they looking for money?

——Of course. They took Marcos and the other dono to the police station, and then sent the other dono back to Vista Bonita to collect enough money for their release.

——Did they do anything to you?

——They hit me and pushed me around. So I told the guy who was in charge that they had no business mistreating us. He said he hadn't given anyone the order to beat us. So then they went through all our jackets and shoes and took everything. I managed to save only some gold chains and a few dollars that I had hidden under my blouse. They told us that they were going to call some reporters they knew because we were involved with international drug trafficking, drug gangs, car theft, and a whole mess of other things. They asked me if I was aware that I was involved with all this and I said no. Then they called the other people on the list and told me to tell them to come to the house. But when they called I shouted, "It's a trap, the police are here." That was when they hit me . . . because the guy I'd warned called everyone else and told them too. So then they took us all to the police station and asked for money. It was five thousand to free all of us. So then they let the other dono go back to Vista Bonita to get the money. I stayed in that house alone for a week because I had to go and visit Marcos. After this, the other dono came back with the money to get Marcos released. Once he gave them the five thousand everything was okay . . . and from there we went to Minas Gerais, where we stayed two weeks, and then on to Barra do Piraí, which is nearby Volta Redonda.

——What did you use for money?

——We didn't go right away. We went at the end of the week.

——So you had time to go back to Vista Bonita and get more money.

——Drugs sell really fast. There's always more money to be made. Then, after we stayed in Barra do Piraí for a few days, we returned to Vista Bonita. And, after all this, I continued to stay with him and he was less aggressive than before. He was the sort of person you have to know how to handle.

——What do you mean?

——He didn't like anyone challenging him. But I was the only person who would call him names and make fun of him in front of others. It was at times like these that he really wanted to hit me, you know, kill me.

——Weren't you ever scared?

——I was never afraid of him . . . and, after he shot me in leg, I was even worse. Then I really made fun of him. But, as far as the people of his community were concerned, he was an excellent person.

——What do you mean?

——If someone needed a new bottle of gas, a bus ticket, or some medicine, he would pay. He also paid for a new soccer pitch for the samba school.

——Was there a neighborhood association in his community?

——Yes, there was. In one of the favelas under his command, he elected the president and directors of the neighborhood association. He controlled various favelas . . . but he dominated only one. In the other communities there were presidents of neighborhood associations that were elected by the residents but that weren't associated with Marcos. But even so, they had to do things a certain way and had to follow his orders if he wanted something done.

——So, even if the president of the neighborhood association is elected . . .

——He has to maintain a good relationship with people in the community or he'll get into trouble with the traficantes.

——So, Marcos only elected the president of the neighborhood association in the community he controlled.

——That's right. The president of the neighborhood association was my comadre, Maria. People thought of them as brother and sister. She was sort of his right-hand man.

——So she was involved with everything.

——Everything . . . and in this community a politician had to ask Marcos' permission to go in. Only those who helped the community in some way were allowed to enter.[4]

——What do you mean?

——Around election time, politicians go looking for votes . . . primarily in favelas. But to get into a favela you need to know someone. So, Maria took advantage of this to get politicians to help out.

——What sort of help are you talking about?

——Like, when Marcos had the soccer pitch built. If a politician paid for the paving, that was helping out. They only let two or three politicians hold rallies in the favela. So she arranged all this . . . they all received a lot of votes because of this.

——How do you know?

——Because it was our community that elected them.

——And were these politicians from one party or from lots of different parties?

——Different parties . . . lots of different parties.

——And were they primarily local-level politicians, like town councilors and state deputies?

——Primarily politicians who were at the beginning of their careers.

——So, Maria campaigned for them?

——Marcos controlled almost all of the communities in and around Vista Bonita. Maria took these politicians to almost every one. Maria didn't just look after her own community . . . she looked after them all. Everyone liked Maria. She visited them all. I also received a little money each week from politicians because Maria put my name on the list of people who had to be paid.

——What do you mean?

——Because we worked for them. We went with them in their cars to visit various favelas. We helped organize rallies and got people together to throw parties for them. You know, we went with them from favela to favela and because everyone knew who I was there was never any problem. It made them feel more safe . . . more secure.

——Did you do this a lot?

——A lot.

——And these politicians were never worried about the situation?

——No.

——And were these politicians well known? Were they from around there?

——No.

——And this relationship between neighborhood associations and traficantes, is this something new?

——It's something new . . . since about six or seven years ago.

——What about before then?

——Before then, everything was normal. The representatives of neighborhood associations were elected by the people. The traficantes always had their way, but not like this. They weren't "their" people. They were regular folk . . . you know, residents. Now, the majority of neighborhood associations are linked to traficantes . . . because they take care of everything in the favelas . . . and because no one trusts the police.

——And you trust them even though they are killers?

——What else are we to do? The police are also killers and they remain free!

——And at least you know the traficantes.

——We know them and we feel more comfortable dealing with them.

——Did the police know who controlled the neighborhood association in Vista Bonita?

——They knew about it but they could never prove it . . . and our neighborhood association was relatively unknown and didn't have a relationship with any state authority or organization. They had no idea who was in charge of the neighborhood association.[5]

——And what about here, in Jakeira?

——They might have an idea, but they really don't care.

——Okay, getting back to Marcos . . .

——The residents of his community liked him a lot. I put up with him . . . I had to.

——Did you cook or clean for him?

——No, I hardly ever cooked or cleaned for him. I only saw him and went out with him at night.

——And what about Amanda . . . how often did you get to see her?

——I made the trip back here every week.

——Even though it took two hours by bus.

——I used to take a special bus that only took an hour . . . even though he didn't like me to come back here.

——What's the favela like there? Is it hilly like here?

——No, it's on flat land. Most of the houses were built by COHAB[6] . . . but in the favela of Vila Rica the houses are simpler . . . much poorer. Now they've urbanized it a bit . . . they've built a square and a road.

——So, you mean in the favela of Vila Rica, the houses were built by the residents themselves.

——It was a real favela. He liked to stay there more than other places because it was easier to hide.

——How many houses were there, more or less?

——There were a lot. There were many entrances and exits. There were lookouts all over the place. It was much bigger than here.

——How many people did he have working for him?

——There were only a few. At most eleven or twelve. But he had a lot of people working for him, if you put all the people together who worked for him in different favelas.

——Did he have problems there with the police?

——He had problems with the police a couple of times but even the police were scared of that place. He told the police that they could come and go during the day but at night they would be shot at. He was the kind of guy who never missed!

——What do you mean?

——He never missed his target.

——So he was a killer.

——He had to . . . and he was like that until the day he died. So I could never tell him that I wanted to leave. One time I did try and tell him that I wanted to finish with him.

——Why?

——Because you can't trust these traficantes . . . I was tired of it all. They go out with women behind your back. I've had a lot of boyfriends and I knew that the moment I left he would find himself another. So one night, after he'd called for me at two in the morning, I told him that I wanted to finish with him. I could tell by his eyes that he was about to get really mad and he took out a knife that he kept in his bag and told me that if I didn't stay with him, I would stay with no one else. So I asked him what he was going to do with me and he told me he was going to kill me. I begged him not to because I had a daughter to raise. Then he began to cut me . . . and I pleaded with him to stop.

——Was he holding you down?

——No, he was making small cuts with his knife like this (gesturing) and I was pleading with him . . . and crying, saying that I no longer wanted to leave him. Then my *compadre* came in and asked him what he was doing. He pleaded with him to stop and told him that he must be mad. Marcos told him that I'd asked to leave and that he wasn't going to harm me . . . even though the blade of the knife was against my chest. Then Marcos told me to go back to the house and take a bath, because we were going to go out. He asked me if I was afraid of him. I told him no. He said that it was good that I wasn't afraid of him.

——But surely, you must have been afraid?

——No. When I got back to the house another of my comadres saw me all covered in blood and began to cry. I told her not to be worried. I only told her that if I didn't return that night it was her job to inform my family. Then, when I went back, he told me that we weren't going to go out but that we were going to sleep at a house nearby. So, we went to sleep and in the morning I came home to Jakeira and left him asleep there in Vista Bonita. I had to take some medicine because my body was very sore. Then he told me not to come back and to stay there a while. I had to pretend that everything was all right after that because I was afraid he might do something. I didn't like him much after that and we only went out once in a while. So then he got together with another girl, who was younger and prettier. I fought with her and Monica fought with her as well. Then Monica got pregnant by him. So then he started paying less attention to her, just like he had with all the others. At times she would wait in the hot sun all day for him because she needed money . . . but he wouldn't come. She would call and speak to him . . . but he wouldn't come. He didn't even call her. Then I got pregnant by him too. So I asked another dono if he would give me money for a sonogram . . . but it was really to have an abortion.

——Where?

——I went with a friend of mine to a clinic in Agua Santa, and had it done there.

——But isn't it illegal?

——It was done by a doctor who works at a public hospital but does this on the side. You know, for the money.[7]

——How did you find out about the place?

——Through friends, who had already had it done. What you do is call and make an appointment . . . it's a front.

——**But how do you go about doing this? I mean, you can't just call up and say "I need an abortion."**

——No, what you do is call and set up a time. Then you tell them what it is you want . . . and that you were referred by a friend who has already had it done.

——**But aren't they suspicious?**

——No, because they know the person who's already had an abortion. You can only get it done if you are referred by a friend. Now that I've had it done, if I wanted to refer someone, it could be done. But it's all a front because they have prenatal and childbirth clinics there. It's a childbirth clinic . . . but in reality they get rid of babies too.

——**Is this common?**

——No, it's difficult and well covered up . . . but you can get it done.

——**And is it expensive?**

——It usually costs between 900, 1,000 or 1,200 *Reais*. They even do micro-Cesareans for about 1,600. A micro-Cesarean is when someone is already six months pregnant . . . they perform a Cesarean.

——**And in your case you were three months pregnant?**

——Yes . . . at the time, this was a lot of money for me.

——**Who paid?**

——I saved some money from when I was working with my mother in a private home. I earned a good salary in those days. Then the next time I went there my comadre told me that if I showed my face Marcos would . . . ! So I came back home to Jakeira and went with a friend to the clinic. I was three months pregnant. They got me to lie down on a table and gave me a general anesthetic . . . but it was a weak one so I just felt drowsy the whole time. When I woke up, they had already finished and they gave me a prescription to buy medicine . . . which made me nauseous. Then I came back home to Jakeira and stayed here for about fifteen days. When I arrived back in Vista Bonita, my compadre asked me what I'd done. I told him that I'd gotten rid of it. He told me that he'd been ordered to kill me if I'd done anything . . . but he told me that he didn't want to have to do this because he liked me. So he told me to run so he could shoot and miss me and that, at least that way, the others could hear. So he told me to run . . . but I didn't want to.

——Why not?

——Because I wanted to stay. I mean, he already had ten children.

——**By how many women?**

——There were only two women that he took responsibility for . . . me and Monica. But there were many more that he didn't.

——**Did he at least give money to these women?**

——Some of them.

——**So there were children that he didn't support.**

——Some he claimed weren't his . . . he wasn't sure. In these cases, he didn't give them anything. I saw how these other women suffered . . . after they gave birth to his children. He wanted nothing to do with them and forbid them from having relationships with other men . . . they became one of his objects. I didn't want to end up like that. When I got there it turned out that he'd been kidnapped by the police. He didn't tell me though. He told me he'd gone to a swimming pool nearby. In reality, the police kidnapped him and took him to a house with a pool. They didn't want to arrest him. They just wanted money. So he stayed there with them until the money was delivered.

——**Did the police do this to him a lot?**

——Only a few times.

——**How much did they want?**

——In this case they wanted 100,000 *Reais*. But then, after a while, they lowered the price to 50,000 *Reais*. So we gave them part of it in cash and the rest in jewelry and electrical appliances . . . you know, televisions and refrigerators . . . whatever they wanted. So then, while all this was going on, he called me to say he'd be there soon and that I wasn't to leave. But then he took so long that I went to a baile and got really drunk. Then, all of a sudden, they started letting off firecrackers to celebrate his return. I was wearing a very tight-fitting and revealing outfit. And when he saw me we immediately got into a fight and that's when he pulled out his revolver. So then my comadre came over to me and begged me not to say another word for fear he might do something. But I told her I wasn't frightened and that I wasn't some whore he'd picked up in some bar. Then, after a while, I decided to go back to the house. Then, in the

morning, a boy came by to get me but I refused to go see Marcos for
another whole week. I told him that I'd been extremely tired that day and
that I'd lied about losing the baby . . . he sort of believed me.

——So he didn't do anything to hurt you?

——He didn't do or say anything to me.

——You mean he left you in peace.

——Yes.

——So how did he die?

——So, when I got to his house there was another woman there. But
I decided not to pick a fight with him, to antagonize him . . . and when he
saw that I was there he sent the other woman away. Then we went on a
trip to Minas . . . but after a while I came back because I didn't like him
anymore. I told him that I wanted to get away and it was then that a
woman I knew told me about a traficante she knew from another favela.
She told me to leave Marcos because this other guy would give me
everything. Unfortunately, a friend of mine overheard all this and told
him. Marcos was livid and told everyone that today was the day to pay off
old debts. He got together all of his women . . . with me in the
middle . . . and all of the gays in the favela . . . and told us that we would all
pay . . . and he meant it. He was going to shoot someone. Then he told us
that someone had told him that I was going to leave him. So I said that this
was what the other woman had told me to do and that I wasn't going to
get together with the other guy. Then the other women there said they'd
heard the woman say the same thing. So he sent someone to get her so he
could kill her . . . and he sent someone to get black plastic bags to throw
the body in the river that ran by there. So then I got scared, because he
said that if the woman could prove that I'd agreed to see the other guy, I
would be killed along with her. So I got really scared and was asking God
to not let them find her because I had told her that I wanted to get to
know the other guy. But this woman was a prostitute who worked in a
nearby town . . . so she didn't get home until very late. We stayed there
until three or four in the morning . . . and the whole time he was playing
games with my mind, telling me to go get sodas. There was no way I could
run away. All I wanted to do was to run away and escape. When I looked
behind me he was standing there with his gun pointed like this
(gesturing), so I couldn't do anything. Then he sent me to buy other
things. Then, finally, when he was tired of waiting for the woman he

ordered his gang to be split up. One half stayed with him and the other half went with his *gerente* from another favela.

——Why did he do this?

——Traficantes have to be split up. They can't all stay in one place. They have to be split up to take care of the different areas.

——Where was this other guy from?

——From a housing project nearby. So then he asked us, "Who do you want to go with. With him or with me?" There were many who decided to go with the gerente because they knew what Marcos was like. Then he asked me and I said I would go with him because if he was going to do anything to me, at least it would be him. I suspected that the other guy, who hardly knew me at all, was capable of anything. Those who went with the other guy were beaten up and shot . . . and those that went with Marcos were set free. He didn't beat us up or anything. It was a test. He just gave us a warning.

——Was it Marcos who punished the others?

——No, it was his gerente. He shot them all in the foot . . . not to kill them but to, you know, mark them. He told us that we were all free to go . . . but that if anyone betrayed him again, he would make them pay.

——How many people did the gerente shoot?

——There were lots of them . . . lots of them. So then this woman never showed up. I think someone must have told her. She disappeared . . . and from then on he didn't trust me and wouldn't let me come back here in case I got together with someone. That's when I got tired of all this and my grandmother asked me to go away with her. I didn't want to go at first but my grandmother told me that it would only be a short trip. So I went to tell Marcos.

——Was your grandmother trying to get you to go away on purpose?

——Of course. Marcos was in Cabo Frio, where he'd been for some time. A policeman friend of his found out that I was planning to go away, and told him.

——How did he find out?

——One of my friends must have said something to him.

——Where, in Jakeira?

——No, in Vista Bonita. So, anyway, the policeman told me that he'd sent for me in Cabo Frio. I told him I wasn't going because he'd kill me.

The guy said that Marcos was calm and that he wouldn't do anything to me. So I went there. When I got there he took me to a bar where we sat talking. I told him that I wanted to leave that day. He told me no and said that he'd take me back the next day. But, before I went away, I'd sent him a letter saying that I wanted to end it with him. I could never tell him to his face because he'd get so mad. So he wanted to talk to me about this letter . . . so I had to lie about it.

————Were you afraid he'd do something?

————Sure I was afraid. I couldn't tell if he was serious or if he was joking but he kept asking the guy behind the bar if he'd finished my headstone. The next day I wanted to leave but he wouldn't let me. He was playing games with my emotions, saying that we were a long way away and that my mother wouldn't be able to hear my screams. Then he grabbed an enormous knife and took me to the top of a hill. He asked me if I liked the view and I said yes. He told me that this would be where I'd stay. He said that part of me was going to be kept in a room in Vista Bonita and the rest on top of that hill. I asked him if he meant it and he said that he did. He was not going to let me go away and that if I didn't stay with him I'd stay with no one else. After a while I tried to get out of it by saying that I was upset when I wrote the letter and that I still liked him . . . and that I was only going away with my grandmother. He let me go and told me that I had to be back in a month, at the latest. But I only did this to trick him. So, after a long time, he let me go. It was already very late. It was Monday and I had to leave on my trip on Tuesday. So I left there and went away to Fortaleza. I stayed there for more than two months and I called my sister to tell her not to let anyone go to Vista Bonita so he wouldn't know where I was . . . because I'd left there without anything . . . without leaving an address or anything. After I'd been there for two months my mother told me that he'd died. I was sad, because I didn't want this to happen to him. I hoped he'd leave this life and have a family like normal people . . . but he never had the opportunity.

————It seems that not many do.

————It doesn't happen very often. It's very difficult once a person has a taste for this kind of life.

————You mean like you?

————I wouldn't say that. I always thought I'd have a house . . . a family. I got involved for many reasons . . . because I wanted more than I could have. But now, I think my head's in the right place. Things changed when my brother was shot and sent to prison.

——Was that here in Jakeira?

——Yes, my mother didn't say anything to me about it. I ended up staying four months in Fortaleza. Then I started working so I couldn't visit him.

——Did Marcos want a normal life?

——I think so. He always talked about it . . . but he was involved with many women. He didn't want to leave any of them . . . to choose only one.

——But he wanted to leave this life behind?

——I think so.

——And did Rogério want to quit too?

——When Rogério died he'd already changed a lot . . . he was completely different.

——Were you at all relieved when Marcos died?

——I was more sad than relieved . . . because he was very easy to lead. I messed with him a lot you know.

——How did Marcos die?

——It happened during a raid by the police . . . he was in a house and the police invaded.

——What about the *olheiros*?

——He only told one or two people where he slept. He didn't trust anyone so he only told one or two. And when he went to sleep, he never took anyone along with him.

——He always slept alone.

——Always.

——But you often slept with him. Right?

——Only with his women . . . because we always went to sleep in some family's house. You know, regular folk.

——So he'd just knock on a door?

——These were people he already knew . . . who liked him. They opened their doors to him.

——So he changed where he slept each night.

——He kept changing.

——So how was it that the police found the house he was sleeping in?

——Someone told them.

——Are you sure?

——Yes. Before the police killed him, a policeman who was in Marcos' pay told him he'd been turned in by Monica. His own woman! And one of his gerentes.

——Come again?

——One of the policemen involved in the operation, before the others killed him, told Marcos. He said "Marcos, before you die I'm going to tell you who betrayed you . . . Monica turned you in," who was one of his women, "and one of your gerentes . . . Ronaldo."

——You mean the policeman told Marcos this before he died.

——Before he died.

——But how did he do this? Did he enter the house with the other policemen or did he send a message?

——No, he came in on his own. This policeman came in on his own first.

——And he said, "You're going to die." Why didn't Marcos escape?

——The house was already surrounded . . . and his gerente had taken the bullet clip off his gun. Because if he'd had his gun and its clip . . . Marcos was a very good shot. He would have died for sure . . . but he would've killed as well. He wouldn't have died alone because he was a very good shot. The whole thing was planned by his gerente and Monica.

——So he was surrounded by the police without a gun.

——They brought him his gun without its bullet clip so he had no way to react.

——Did they kill him with a lot of bullets?

——No, they shot him twice with 12-caliber bullets in the chest . . . one on each side.

——How do know this?

——My comadre told me. Then they took him to the hospital.

——Was he still alive?

——No, he wasn't alive. Twelve-caliber bullets are enormous. They use them to kill elephants. It's a real thick bullet (gesturing). When they hit the body they explode. They have metal pieces that explode inside the body . . . they make an enormous hole. They killed him like that. He had no chance.

POLICE

O N MAY 13, 1996, President Fernando Henrique Cardoso unveiled Brazil's first Human Rights Plan. The Human Rights Plan was the product of eight months of intensive negotiation between the Ministry of Justice, non-governmental and human rights organizations, and representatives from various other groups in civil society. The Human Rights Plan called for Congress to introduce more than 200 separate measures to address a broad range of human rights issues in Brazil. Perhaps the most pressing of these issues is the widespread and unpunished practice of the summary execution of civilians by the police.[1]

The police force in Brazil is organized and operates at the state level. A small federal force monitors interstate and international drug trafficking and protects Brazil's borders. The vast majority of the 500,000 or so policemen and women, however, serve in the civil and military police forces that are administered by each of the twenty-six state governors. The civil and military police in Brazil are split along functional lines. The military police are reserve units of the Army that patrol the streets, maintain the peace, and respond to and investigate crimes in progress.[2] The civil police, on the other hand, investigate crimes that have already been committed and oversee the operation of the various police precincts, or *delegacias*.

Since the mid-1980s, the Brazilian police have waged an all-out war against what they maintain are criminal elements. In 1992, for example, the police in São Paulo killed a staggering 1,428 civilians, more than three times the number of people who were killed or "disappeared" during fifteen years of military rule. Most police victims, it turns out, have no criminal record or any involvement with crime. They are simply the wrong "type" of people at the wrong place and at the wrong time. Occasionally, as in the mid-1990s, international outrage over police brutality in Brazil has forced state authorities to intervene to reduce the number of police homicides. In recent years, however, the number of civilians killed by the police has once again been on the rise.[4]

A number of factors make the investigation and prevention of police homicides difficult. The first is that the initial investigation of the crime scene is in the hands of the police. In other words, the first people to arrive on the scene are oftentimes the perpetrators of the crime itself. The second is that the police always claim that they are acting in self-defense, or in defense of others, and that extrajudicial killings are in fact the result of shoot-outs with dangerous and well-armed criminals.[5] The third factor has to do with the widespread use of unregistered and unauthorized guns. It is common practice for police in Brazil to plant guns on their already deceased victims to corroborate claims of a shoot-out. And finally, bodies are often removed to local hospital emergency rooms to create the impression that the police tried to help their victims and to compromise any investigation of the crime scene.

There are also institutional factors that make the investigation and prevention of police homicides difficult. Until recently, the military police in Brazil were encouraged by their superiors to eliminate—as opposed to detain—criminal suspects. In the mid to late 1990s, for example, the military police in Rio de Janeiro were given pay raises and promotions for acts of "bravery" and "special merit," which, in essence, meant killing urban youth.[6] Also until recently, military police tribunals investigated crimes committed by the military police. Obviously, these tribunals could be counted on to determine that civilians were indeed killed in acts of self-defense.[7]

If the Human Rights Plan has achieved anything in Brazil, it has been to transfer oversight and jurisdiction of police homicides to civilian authorities. Even so, it is up to the police to determine what is and what is not a homicide, and the military police retain the right to "oversee" such cases. Furthermore, civilian witnesses of police brutality are routinely threatened and discouraged from testifying, and few prosecutors have the time, resources, or political will to conduct their own investigations. For many, the execution of criminal suspects by the police is simply not a priority. And because the judicial system in Brazil is so overburdened and inefficient, changes in the oversight and processing of police crimes have had little, if any, effect.[8]

Finally, and most significantly, there is also widespread support for extrajudicial police action among the general population.[9] Death squads composed of off-duty and retired policemen are often hired by local merchants to clear the streets of "undesirables" and are responsible for killing a large number of Brazilian youths each year.[10] More importantly, there is even support for extrajudicial police action among those elements of the population who are most likely to be affected. It is not uncommon, for example, to hear relatives of innocent victims of police violence call for even more heavy-handed and extreme measures.[11] This should in no way be seen as an endorsement of the police—far from it. Few Brazilians trust or make use of the police, who are perceived, quite rightly, as untrustworthy and violent.[12] It is, however, an indication of how far the situation has deteriorated and the desperation of the population of Brazil's major cities.

In recent years, drug-related violence has spilled out beyond the low-income neighborhoods, public housing projects, and *favelas* into all areas of city life. There is now no safe haven in Rio. Government offices, supermarkets, and hotels have been targeted with gunfire, bombs, and grenades. Banks, businesses, and schools have been ordered by drug gangs to close their doors in protest of state policy or, more commonly, in honor of fallen comrades.[13] Buses are routinely held up at gunpoint and burnt to the ground. Cars and trucks on Rio's major roads and highways are pulled over and shaken down by armed men who are often dressed as police. There have even been instances of heavily armed gangs literally invading public hospitals, police stations, and even prisons to "liberate" their colleagues. It is within this context of generalized violence and fear and the breakdown of public law and order that calls for the extension of human rights to police victims have fallen on deaf ears.[14]

Part of the problem is the widespread availability of guns. There are an estimated 20 million illegal firearms in Brazil, and firearms are now involved in approximately 70 percent of all crimes. The vast majority of these firearms are manufactured in Brazil and bought—or stolen—from private citizens, the military, or the police.[15] Others are sold legally to dealers in other countries and then smuggled back in. In July 2001, the state government in Rio destroyed more than 100,000 guns in a public ceremony that was part of a weeklong demonstration and appeal for peace. Unfortunately, neither the apprehension nor the destruction of large quantities of guns has made much of a difference. The drug gangs in Rio continue to be well armed and, in many cases, even better armed than the police.[16]

Part of the problem also has to do with the police. First, the police in Brazil are extremely poorly trained. Not many receive instruction in the basics of criminal investigation and, consequently, the few cases that are solved are solved because the perpetrator is caught in the act, a witness actually agrees to testify, or a confession is literally beaten out of a suspect.[17] Second, few police receive instruction in the use of firearms. It is small wonder, then, that so many people—including the police—are caught in the line of fire.[18] Third, the police are also badly paid. Many of the forty thousand or so military and civil police in Rio supplement their incomes by working second shifts, more often than not as private security guards. Thus, while a career in the police provides certain elements of the population with opportunities for advancement, it is in general an unattractive and extremely dangerous proposition.[19] And finally, the police are—for good reason—subject to widespread mistrust and hatred. Police who live in drug-infested neighborhoods are forced to disguise who they are and what they do for a living. Otherwise they are likely to be expelled or, worse still, executed.[20]

The worst problem by far, however, is police corruption. The newspapers are full of reports of police involvement in all sorts of illegal activities, including the drug trade.[21] When the police go into a favela, they are more likely to be after a share of the profits than the individual members of a drug gang. When they do manage to get ahold of someone, they have little intention of making a formal arrest. They are simply out to make money.[22] When the drug trade is going well, there is enough money to go around. In fact, drug gangs often budget for the amount they need each week to pay off the police. The system breaks down, however, when business is not good and the police go after what they perceive as their fair share.[23] This is not to say that all drug-related violence can be explained in terms of conflicts between drug gangs and the police. It does mean, however, that the issue of police involvement and complicity needs to be taken far more seriously.

Occasionally, when things get out of hand, steps are taken to reform and clean up the police. In recent years, the establishment of an anonymous hotline and the appointment of an independent police ombudsman have meant that police operations are subject to much closer scrutiny.[24] It is far more usual, however, for police or specially trained antinarcotics units to be sent in to occupy drug-gang controlled areas of the city and to temporarily keep the peace. It is invariably the case, however, that if they leave it is business as usual and if they stay they too become involved.

When the drug gang assumed control of the neighborhood association in Jakeira, the newly appointed president was given the job of paying off the police. The deal was that if the police got their money they would leave well enough alone. The drug gang always tried to pay up because, if they did not, the police would cause trouble. And if the police caused trouble, it made it hard for the drug gang to operate. And if the police made it hard for the drug gang to operate, the drug gang had a hard time coming up with the money, and so forth. When the police got ahold of someone, they called the dono of the drug gang on his cell phone and began to negotiate. The higher up the person on the drug gang ladder, the higher the asking price.[25] Occasionally, if the asking price was high, the dono asked local merchants and residents to make a contribution. And it was not unknown for the dono in Jakeira to ask another dono for help. The police knew most of the members of the drug gang and where their girlfriends and family lived. So if they could not get their hands on a member of the drug gang, they would take a family member hostage instead. The only time this system broke down was when the police were under pressure to make arrests or when a particularly despised member of the drug gang member was taken in and killed. Otherwise, drug gang members seldom made it as far as the *delegacia*.

1980 - 2000 - exponential increase
in police murdering civilians
- most victims have no criminal
record or any involvement
w/ crime

CHAPTER 4

Bruno

——So, when you left Marcos and spent four months in Fortaleza, what did you do?

——I don't know . . . I just passed the time.

——**Did you enjoy your stay?**

——Yes . . . well not really, no. There was nothing to do. My family there are all *cristão*. I couldn't really go out. The friend I made there also didn't go out, you know, to other places. So I just stayed there. I went to the square, I walked around the square . . . which is very small. And sometimes I went to the river or someone's *sítio*.

——**So you weren't a cristão back then.**

——I'm still not a cristão. I go to services and I believe, but . . .

——Did you attend services back in those days?

——I've always gone to church.

——Catholic church or . . .

——No, cristão.

——So, was it while you were there that you decided to leave this life behind?

——No, it wasn't while I was there because after I came back I got involved again. You know, I didn't give it up completely. I didn't go out with *bandidos* any more, but I still went to *bailes* . . . I still went to Vista Bonita.

——To see Marcos' friends.

——Yes. I only really left after my friend Anna Paula died. Until then, I went there every weekend. But after Anna Paula died I was really sad . . . I was watching everyone die.

——How did she die?

——The police, again. She was at a *pagode* that I used to go to.

——This was after Marcos died?

——Well after . . . her husband had already been killed.

——So who took over after Marcos?

——It was another guy. I didn't know him . . . because the other *dono*, Ronaldo, was in prison. So there was no one left. My cousin had also died. So another guy took over who we didn't know. He took command.

——So he wasn't a member of the same gang.

——No. Only after this other guy . . . his name was Cabo. After the police kidnapped Cabo, he disappeared. He never showed up again. I believe they killed him . . . both Cabo and his woman disappeared. His woman had gone to hand over the money and never came back. So then another guy took over after he was released from prison. This other guy was around at the same time as Rogério. I already knew this guy . . . a *negão* with glasses . . . I already knew him.

——So, getting back to your friend . . .

——Every weekend my *comadre* would go a pagode near her house. I used to go too . . . I liked it there. And I already knew this negão with glasses. We'd get there and there would be a barbecue . . . he would give us all money.

——So the dono organized the pagode.

——He organized the pagode, the barbecue, the beer . . . and so I always used to go. He was a good person. I always went at the weekend.

But on this weekend when my comadre died I couldn't get the money together for the bus. This was on a Saturday. The pagode was on a Saturday. On Sunday her mother called me and told me that the police had killed her. They also killed the negão with glasses . . . who was the bandido from there.

——How did this all happen?

——The police were hiding behind a wall . . . a wall close to the pagode. Everyone was at the pagode. The police watched Anna Paula go back and forth to get money from the bandidos. It all started when this negão with glasses got up to leave. The guys who were his bodyguards got up too and it was then that the police came out from behind the wall . . . there were a ton of policemen. They came out shooting all over the place. They didn't kill more people only because . . . they took aim at my comadre when the negão with glasses went down. Everyone was running trying to get away and getting shot. The negão with glasses and two other guys died . . . two of his men died with him. The police kicked him in the face, and jumped on his stomach, and dragged him around the *favela*. Anna Paula tried to run inside a bar. They shot her in the head . . . a bullet right in the head. She was still breastfeeding. Her baby was eight months old . . . her youngest. There was also another guy, a transvestite who, in desperation, tried to help. He was there with her and tried to lift her up to help her. They shot him too . . . in the head.

——And he died too?

——He died too.

——So five people were killed . . . and you were on your way there.

——I was going to go there. I went there a few days later and she was already in her coffin. I was also there for her burial a little while later.

——And then?

——Then it hit me that everyone I knew was dead.

——Except for you.

——Thank God. Me and Maria. Maria was a cristão. She left but then returned to the church. And then they were divided. The part where Maria lived and the part where I used to go, this other favela—where Anna Paula lived—were enemies. They were friends when Marcos was there because he was in charge of everything. But after Marcos died it was invaded and became the enemy of the public housing project where Maria lived. So I couldn't go where Maria lived anymore. I stayed where

Eliane lived, my other comadre. But I couldn't visit Maria . . . after this I never saw Maria again.

———Is she still alive?

———I think so.

———And you still can't go there?

———Now I can, but I'm scared. Now I'm scared . . . because I don't know who's there . . . because at the time, her sister was there. Her sister became a bandido. Her sister became a dono.

———Her sister!

———She made a deal with the police and took over. They even came here to my house. Maria's sister brought Maria and two policemen here to see me.

———Why?

———Maria's sister said that I had a bag of money that Marcos had stolen from a robbery . . . and that I'd kept the money. They wanted to take it from me.

———**Getting back to Diago. You told me that you couldn't visit him when he was in prison because you were working. Where did you work?**

———In a hairdressers salon . . . so I couldn't visit him. It was only when he was transferred from the police station to prison that I began visiting him. Everyone here worked and so no one could visit him. He had a girlfriend, but she wouldn't take his things to him. Someone had to take the things we bought for him twice a week.

———**And are there prisoners who don't receive anything.**

———Sure. It depends on the family. So anyway, I quit my job so I could visit him. And because I quit my job my family gave me some money each month so I could provide for my daughter. I began visiting him in September and it was on one of these visits that I met Bruno. And so each time I went to visit him, my brother would say, "Speak with that guy there, he's intelligent." Sometimes I spoke with him, and sometimes with others. Then there was a Christmas party there, which he organized. So he said to me, "You have a daughter, don't you?" I told him yes I have a daughter. So he told me he was going to give me a present for her . . . because around here everyone gives presents. So then he brought two dolls for her. So the next time I went there my brother said that Bruno was tired and had asked if he could rest against my legs. And he really was tired! It felt kind of strange. Then I went to the bathroom and when I came back he gave me a kiss, you know, in front of everyone. Then he went up to my brother and told him that from this day on they were brothers-in-law. I already had a boyfriend on the outside. But whenever I went there he treated me well, and my sisters.

——So your sisters accompanied you there?

——Sometimes. So anyway, I told him that I wanted nothing to do with him. But I became more and more attached to him. I visited my brother for two and a half years. After this, my brother got out and I continued to visit him. He was there another year. From there he was transferred to another prison where he stayed for eight months. Then he returned to a maximum-security prison that made it more difficult to visit him. I couldn't visit him twice a week . . . but I visited him at least once a week until he was released.

——Even though you knew he had also been involved in drugs.

——I always thought that he was different from the others. I thought that perhaps he would leave this business . . . because what happened to him was really bad luck. He didn't grow up in a poor environment. He didn't go without like me. He studied. So I thought that he'd learned a lot these seven years he spent there. He'd seen a lot. So I thought he'd live a normal life. That's why I decided to give him a chance. Because I was tired of this life. Because life that is today, may not be tomorrow. I was more afraid . . . because before, I wasn't afraid of anything.

——Also because of Amanda, right?

——Yes, also because of her. My daughter was already big and had no father. I didn't want her to follow the same path. Because my mother had always given everything she could to us . . . but we always wanted more.

——You mean in terms of clothes and things . . . and money.

——Money to go out, jewelry . . . but everything was difficult because she had so many children and I didn't really try that hard, at school or at work. So the only way I could put together any money was like this. (Turning to Bruno)

——So Bruno, tell me about the day you were arrested. What happened?

——I was stationed at the border . . . in a small town on the border between Brazil and Bolivia. And there, it's real easy to become involved.

——Why's that?

——Because 50 percent of the population makes money from drugs.

——That come across from Bolivia.

——There are people who transport the cocaine. They don't sell it, they just transport it across the border. Then there are people who transport it from there to other cities, in Rio, Minas Gerais, São Paulo, and Recife. It's a huge business. But to get involved you have to know someone. You have to have a partner. And when I was in the Army I got to know people who had a lifestyle that was incompatible with their salary.

——Did you earn a good salary?

——I earned a reasonable salary and it was enough to live on in that city.

——But you had friends who had much more.

——They had big houses, cars, motorbikes, jet-skis . . . things like that. They made a lot more than I did. There were times when I couldn't afford to go home to Belém on vacation. When they had fifteen days off they just took a plane . . . because they were already involved with narcotrafficking.

——And these were all Army people?

——Some were in the Army and some weren't.

——So, all your friends were rich.

——It's not that everyone was rich. But a large part of the population was involved with this business. Obviously, a lot of people worked at other things having to do with import and export. But it was obvious that there was a lot of money laundering going on. There's a lot of commerce across the border. It's a business that involves a lot of money . . . obviously it involves a lot of money. But the money to be made from drugs is incredible. I estimate that about five tons of cocaine crosses the border per month . . . and is sent to various places.[1]

——How does it get in?

——Various ways. By truck, by car. And I'm only talking about the small amounts that we call *tráfego de formigas*. So anyway, it was there that I got to know people who were looking for someone to transport drugs . . . from there to São Paulo. And, given my position, it was easier for me to get past the roadblocks . . . because I knew all the roads. Because there are various ways of getting out of there. There are various roads . . . various routes. Because that part of Brazil is wide open.[2] So, while the police paid attention to the main roads, there were other ways. There are hidden airstrips and ranches, some of which belong to the government. And so, it's like a vicious circle. Because you do it once and you make money. And then you do it a second time and on and on like that.

———But what about your career? Weren't you taking a huge risk?

———But I thought I'd only do it once, without anyone knowing. I wanted to buy a house and a car and continue my career. Except that things are more complicated. You do it once and you don't want to stop. You realize that money is everything and that you can do everything you've always wanted to do.

———Did you transport large quantities of cocaine?

———No, small. Then afterwards I began transporting large quantities.

———How much did you make?

———It varied from seven hundred to a thousand dollars per kilo.

———In profit.

———In profit. The smallest amount was five hundred dollars but it was a thousand dollars if you wanted it sent anywhere in Brazil. There are certain places, such as Suriname, that can cost as much as five thousand dollars.[3] So then I got to know someone else from my town, the owner of a hotel, who wanted someone to transport drugs to Rio de Janeiro.

———In a car?

———In a truck.

———What was it hidden in?

———Inside a washing machine, as if it were part of a move. It was as if someone was moving to another place. So I did it, I arrived here and delivered it to a place in Barra.[4]

———Just you?

———Just me.

———Weren't you afraid?

———No. I've never been afraid of anything (laughs).

———Did you know the person you delivered it to?

———No, and I still don't know who it was. Until then I had never been involved. I collected my money, caught a plane, and got out of there. I took a plane from Santos Dumont to São Paulo. I got to São Paulo, spent the night in a hotel and, the next day, I went to a car dealer and bought a car. Then I drove back home in my new car (laughs). When I got home I bought a house on the border and threw a party for my friends, who were all *traficantes*. They told me how smart I was and that I should be moving a lot more. Because I was doing very little. So I invested part of the

money I'd made in drugs and sought out the guys in Rio de Janeiro and
sold it here.

——So you started buying drugs.

——Not just buying drugs, but transporting and selling them too.
Because many people say that Rio is violent. Many people are afraid to go
there. So they needed someone who could get along with the
vagabundos ... because the vagabundos from this city are really strange.
And then there's the factions. There are favelas that are controlled by the
Terceiro Comando and the Comando Vermelho. It used to be said that
the Terceiro Comando killed people so that they wouldn't have to pay.
But this happened a long time ago and today things are different. They
pay as little as possible in order to buy more. It happened maybe a couple
of times ... and this is what made people afraid. Very little used to come
through here. So I brought it and delivered it here. So that's how it all
started. And I got to know some of the favelas here ... only favelas that
were controlled by the Comando Vermelho. It was easier to deal with
those guys.

——So how were you arrested?

——It was by chance. The police were looking for a *cativeiro* and
found us in this house with the drugs. And that's when things fell apart. I
was expelled from the Army and sentenced to seven years in prison. I
spent a year in an Army jail. Then I was turned over to the civil police
and transferred to another prison in Rio. It was when I got to this other
prison that I realized how far I was involved ... I saw that the situation
was far more serious. I was in prison ... with common criminals ... I was
nothing. I saw things going on in there, but I couldn't say anything to
the guards. I couldn't tell them that I was intelligent and that I saw they
were doing things they weren't supposed to: violating human rights, the
laws.

——What do you mean?

——Beatings. The prison system in Brazil is pure evil, you know? It's
the poor, the blacks, the illiterate. The garbage of the garbage is in the
system. And there's a lot of innocent people there too. The police get
ahold of them and they don't know how to react. The fear generated by
the police keeps the poor population down ... in fear. Because the police
are meant to help people. But for the poor they are there to mistreat
them ... to judge them.

——So how did you survive?

——In this prison there was a cell block that was Comando Vermelho and a cell block that was Terceiro Comando. And there were other, smaller cellblocks, for people who weren't involved and for crimes of passion.

——What's a cell block like?

——It's a corridor with various cells. They are placed side by side to prevent fights. Because before there were a lot of deaths. Now they've separated them. And when I got there, there was already this division. And when you arrived you had to choose which cell block you wanted. Inside the prison you have to choose sides.

——So which side did you choose?

——The side of the Comando Vermelho is more united. Everyone's more united. Here, in Rio, what the government doesn't give the prisoners is provided by their families. But all my family lived in Belém. So I was going to really suffer. So I had to choose a side that would help me because I didn't have family nearby. And they needed someone intelligent to plan escapes and things.

——So you mean you were accepted by them.

——Without any problems. Then, the year after I asked to be transferred to another prison. Because a prisoner came by—he wasn't even a prison official—asking who wanted to go to another prison. Because there were too many prisoners in that prison. They told me that in the prison I was going to the prisoners lived in harmony and peace. And that was good for me.[5]

——So what was this other prison like?

——The prison was controlled by the Comando Vermelho and everybody obeyed their rules. The prisoners were united as if they were all brothers. They shared their toothpaste, soap. And the prisoners that mistreated others and were considered rapists were taken out. There were some deaths in that prison and the Comando Vermelho family was created.

——And you were part of all this?

——Yes, because I saw that they did things the right way.

——And most of them were from the favelas?

——Most of the leaders were from the favelas. Their philosophy was peace, justice, and liberty. Justice because justice was done. If someone was really poor and needed a lawyer we'd get together and help the person from the kitty that was created by this group. If a family couldn't afford to visit we'd send them the money for the ticket. And then this spread to the favelas. It spread to the neighborhood associations and they began to help. They did things that the government wasn't doing, either in the prisons or in the favelas. So then the prisons began to command more respect and the leaders of the favelas were nominated by the leaders of the prisons.

——**Even here?**

——Everywhere. If there wasn't someone who was nominated by someone they would certainly get rid of him. They would invade and take them out.

——**In Jakeira the neighborhood association used to be strong, but now it's controlled by . . .**

——It's very common. Because occasionally the government takes charge but they only do this with an eye to how many votes they can get. Because the whole thing's a farce. They begin a public work and then stop. Then someone from the outside comes in and they show them what they're doing and then they forget about it.[6] Sometimes the vagabundos don't even come up with the money. But that's capitalism. There's always someone in need of medicine. Sometimes even the doctor at the clinic says he's not coming in because it's too violent . . . but he still makes his money. That's how it works.

——**So how long did you stay in this second prison?**

——I stayed there for two years.

——**And then?**

——I tried to escape. But I was recaptured. And then I was transferred to another prison.

——**Was this one worse or better?**

——No, it wasn't any worse. It was a maximum-security prison. I dug a tunnel there with some other friends. But I also helped teach the other prisoners. Because many of them don't know what it's like to be part of society. They only know the favela and the prison. I taught them about Brazil. I tried to pass on what I'd learned.

——**And what about the tunnel?**

——We were almost at the wall. But there was a failure in our security system. Because we needed guys from other cell blocks. So we sawed through a grate and stuck it back up with soap. Except that when a friend of mine came through to work this grate fell down. So then the guard saw it and got suspicious and we were all caught.

——Were you punished?

——Yes. I spent thirty days in solitary and was transferred to another prison. And when I arrived at this other prison there were thirty in each cell.

——How big were the cells?

——Four by three meters. There was a toilet.

——Windows?

——No, only grates. Everyone was suffering. Sometimes, a prison guard would come in and get everyone to take off their clothes to beat them. They beat us with baseball bats. I have a scar here on my hand (gesturing). So I sent a card to the governor and was transferred again. This time I was in a cell with eight people . . . but I had already been through almost four years of this suffering. The cells in this prison were divided up because some leaders had been killed. There was a split within the faction so the prison was experiencing many problems. There were a lot of young people. So when I got there I became one of the leaders.

——How long were you there?

——Almost two years. Because there were no mattresses and other things. And they didn't know how to ask for them. They didn't know how to exercise their rights. All they knew was violence. So a group of us got together and explained that we could demand our rights without violence between us and the guards. Because violence was giving them an excuse to come in and kill us. So a friend of mine suggested we write a card and send a representative to talk to the director to demand our rights. The prisoners thought it was a good idea and elected my friend leader. We all became involved to save our own skins and those of our friends. Because if we'd have left it to the others, it wouldn't have done . . . because they're ignorant.

——So did you and your friends have to make difficult decisions?

——We had to make difficult decisions. But every decision we made was on the basis of psychology.

——So you never had to have anyone killed.

——No, we didn't have anyone killed. Even when the order was given for someone to be killed we said that we would lose the contract we'd made with the director. So we had to find a less violent method. We wanted to show them that we could run the prison in a reasonable way . . . without all these connections with the favelas, and cocaine. We organized parties on mother's day, on New Year's day, and for children. We got donations of pencils, books, and erasers from universities. We gave lessons in computing and physical fitness, because I had been in the Army. We held sports competitions . . . anything to improve day-to-day life. We created a library, because there wasn't one. Because this country is like this, if you want something, and you have the will, you can get it. It's not difficult. It's just that there are people . . . for example, the director of a prison. If he is someone who's educated, he can run the prison no problem. But if on the other hand he's stressed out and hasn't the talent for it, and is just doing it because he has no other options, it's logical that . . . especially in a country where corruption is never ending.

——**And that's where you met Lucia, right?**

——Yes. Because I was far away, only a few persons visited me. Only a few friends when they remembered me. So it was there that I got to know Diago, Lucia's brother. It was at a party in December that he presented her to me. And when I saw what her life was like, I realized that her life was more or less the same as mine, you know? We'd made mistakes. So we met and we helped each other . . . I changed her life and she changed mine.

PRISON

THE PRISON POPULATION in Brazil has more than doubled in the past decade. Rising crime rates, harsher criminal sentences, and mounting public pressure for a tougher stance on crime have filled the prison system to well beyond its already limited capacity.[1] Consequently, almost all of Brazil's 500 or so prisons and jails are seriously overcrowded.[2] In fact, in many facilities, petty thieves, recidivists, murderers, and even prisoners awaiting trial are thrown together and forced to sleep on cramped cell floors, in bathrooms next to the hole in the ground that serves as a toilet, tied to cell bars, or suspended from the ceiling in hammocks.

Overcrowding means that already meager resources are stretched to the limit. By law, prisoners in Brazil are entitled to various types of assistance, including food, clothing and bedding, legal aid, medical care, and opportunities to work and to attend school.[3] In reality, few of these resources are made available. A minority of Brazilian prisoners work or are in school, qualified medical personnel are in short supply, and legal assistance is provided—oftentimes for a fee—by prison employees or, occasionally, by visiting teams of outside lawyers.[4] In most facilities, clothing, bedding, and sometimes even food are provided not by prison authorities but by friends and family or are purchased from other inmates.

The worst conditions, by far, are to be found in the police precincts and lockups. In theory, when a suspect is arrested he or she is taken to a police precinct for booking and initial detention. Within a few days, if he or she is not released, the suspect is transferred to a jail or house of detention to await trial. Then, if the suspect is convicted, he or she is sent to a facility for convicted prisoners. In reality, however, the lack of available space in the prison system means that up to a third of all prisoners awaiting trial and even many convicted prisoners are held by the police in Brazil for months, even years.[5]

The long-term detention of criminal suspects and convicted prisoners by the police is a major contributing factor to the very serious problem of police brutality and torture. According to Human Rights Watch, many police stations in Brazil have special rooms set aside where detainees are stripped naked and subjected to beatings, electric shocks, and near-drowning. Unfortunately, few incidents of police brutality are investigated despite the enactment in 1997 of an antitorture law. And the relative powerlessness of the inmate population means that few people care if abuse against prisoners goes unpunished.

By far the worst case of police violence occurred in October 1992 when the military police were called in to quell a riot in the Carandiru prison complex in São Paulo.[6] By all accounts, the police made no attempt to negotiate or diffuse the situation, forced prisoners to strip naked, and shot many of them at close range in the back of the head. One hundred and eleven prisoners died that day. It was not until July 2001, however, that the military police colonel who ordered the invasion was sentenced to 632 years in prison.[7]

It was the Carandiru massacre, as it became known, that gave birth to the Primeiro Comando do Capital, a criminal organization—much like the Comando Vermelho—that subsequently took on the prison authorities. The Primeiro Comando do Capital shocked the nation in February 2001 when it organized and coordinated a simultaneous uprising by forty-three thousand inmates in twenty-nine different prisons and police lockups in São Paulo.[8] The Primeiro Comando do Capital took seven thousand hostages, to prevent a repeat of the 1992 massacre, and demanded the return of five prisoners who had been transferred to prisons in other parts of the country and the resignation of the state secretary for prison administration.[9]

The prison authorities in Rio have been dealing with criminal organizations since the early 1980s, and until recently, they have been relatively successful in keeping the peace.[10] They have been wholly unsuccessful, however, in breaking the back of the criminal organizations themselves. In 1988, a brand-new maximum-security facility was opened in the neighborhood of Bangu in Rio to house and isolate the leaders of the Comando Vermelho, Terceiro Comando, and Amigos dos Amigos. All three organizations continue to function and thrive, however, as orders for drug and weapons transactions, the invasion of enemy territory, and the torture and execution of debtors and informants continue to be made from the inside.[11]

Orders are made in a number of different ways. Sometimes they are passed along by friends and family. Sometimes they are passed along by the prisoners' own lawyers.[12] Most of the time, however, they are given directly via cell phone.[13] It costs about 5,000 *Reais* to get a cell phone on the inside, and until now, the prison authorities have been unable to cut off the supply.[14] Many of the cell phones, weapons, explosives, drugs, and other materials are smuggled in by visitors.[15] The vast majority, however, are sold to inmates by prison workers and guards. Prison workers and guards also have been known to accept money to facilitate escapes and even the murder of prisoners from rival gang factions.[16] The problem is that it is often difficult—and dangerous—for prison guards and workers to do otherwise.[17] In September 2000, for example, the director of the Bangu prison complex in Rio was executed on her front doorstep by what were rumored to be either drug gang members or the police. The director had been attempting to clamp down on the use of cell phones in Bangu and a system of bribes and kickbacks that totaled an estimated 1 million *Reais* per month![18]

CHAPTER 5

School

——I started school when I was seven years old . . . right here in Jakeira. It was the only school there was in the favela. There was also a private school nearby, but it was really expensive. It's a private school, so . . .

——So, only a few kids from the favela went there.

——Only a few . . . and these were children of people who worked there. In general, children from here went to the public school. When you are in first grade you go in the morning.

——And before this you stayed at home?

——I never went to a day-care center. They give you lunch there in the morning . . . a small lunch.

——What time did you start school?

——Seven in the morning. At about nine they give you a snack of biscuits or crackers with coffee or Nescal . . . which is chocolate powder and milk. Then at midday I would go home. The children that go to school in the afternoon are the children that have the most difficulties. There's first grade but there's also different groups. There's 101. When there's a 101 it's always the best group in the school. When the last number is one it's the best group . . . 101, 201, 301 . . . always the best students. Then there's group 2 . . . 102, 202 . . . which is a lower level. It's still good and there's an even lower level, which is 3. That's how the children are divided up.

——So in the school there are different levels . . . and in first grade you were already divided up.

——It all starts in first grade. They decide where you're going to be placed. If you're going to 101 or 102. It depends on the ability of each child. If the child has learned a lot, learned to read . . . if the child has learned a few letters. So the children that already know this go into a stronger group.

——So the children who are in 103, for example, go to school in the afternoon and those in 101 or 102 go in the morning.

——That's right. This way they already know something about the ability of each child. If a child is in 103, they need more attention . . . they need to study more.

——Do these children stay in school longer?

——No, they don't stay in school any longer. They stay the same amount of time. But the teacher has to pay more attention to the students that are in this group.

——So, school hours in the morning are from seven until midday. And in the afternoon, from . . .

——Midday until five.

——Are they the same teachers?

——No, they change them. They are different teachers.

——Were you in group 101?

——I was never among the best. I was always in 102 or 103.

——And all of your friends from here started school at the same time?

——All of us.

———So you knew everyone in your class.

———I knew them all. You got to know everybody.

———**Did children from other favelas from around here go to different schools? For example, children from Santa Clara?**

———The children from Santa Clara went to their own school . . . near where they lived. Jakeira is one favela, Santa Clara is another. The children who went to my school were from Jakeira . . . and Vila de Liberdade . . . which is the favela right next to us.

———**What do you remember about your experiences at school?**

———It was very difficult. At the time, my mother had four children . . . and everyone was at school. Diago and Andrea were already at school. Then I started as well. So my mother had to get us all ready. She had to buy supplies for school . . . everything was difficult for her.

———**Was she working at the time?**

———In a motel.

———**And did you all go to school in the morning or at different times of the day?**

———At the time, I think I was the only one who went in the morning. The others went in the afternoon. If I remember, when they got there they gave them lunch.

———**At school?**

———It was always something like rice and fish, or macaroni and sausage . . . and a fruit. An orange or a banana. Lunch was always something like that.

—Conceição—I was working so hard I got sick and had to go see a psychiatrist. There was so much going on in my life. I worked at night and took care of the kids during the day. My husband worked but he drank a lot too. He broke everything in the house . . . everything in the house. It was a very difficult time. I had to live life basically on my own.

———**What time did you work?**

———From ten until seven in the morning.

———**So what time did you leave here?**

———I left here at nine or nine thirty.

———**Where was the motel?**

———It was about twenty minutes by bus from here. The children stayed here sleeping. I left a bottle ready for Camilla.

——And your husband?

——He worked as a carpenter. When he left for work in the morning I was coming home . . . with bread and milk.

——**You must have been exhausted.**

——All I did was work.

——**What did you do?**

——I cleaned rooms for truck drivers who left early in the morning . . . at around two. Then the next group arrived an hour or so later . . . so you had to get all the rooms ready. I worked there at night for six years.

——**And during the day you looked after the children.**

——I looked after them. I hardly slept. But even so, I got through it . . . thanks to God.

——**This must have been a difficult time of your life.**

——Yes it was. It was a difficult time when they were children. I was on my feet all day and had no help in the house.

——**Did your mother work?**

——No, but she had her own life.

——**But she was living here with you, right?**

——Yes.

—Lucia—All I remember was that from fifth grade on things became more difficult because there were more teachers. Until fourth grade one teacher taught us all the subjects . . . Portuguese, mathematics. From fifth grade on you had a different teacher for each subject . . . but the teachers were not very good. The most dedicated teacher was the one who taught us Portuguese.

——**What do you mean?**

——Because you could see that she enjoyed what she was doing. She wasn't just there to pass the time. Both the Portuguese and the science teachers were very good.

——**Why? Were these teachers particularly good or sympathetic?**

——Because they taught us . . . they taught us. The math teacher . . . if you didn't pay attention and learn right away, you didn't learn. I was terrible at mathematics . . . because if you learned it when he first taught it, you got it. But if you didn't, the teacher didn't have the patience to explain it to you again.

——Did you still graduate to the next class even if you didn't learn anything?

——Yes. It was rare that anyone repeated a year. They did everything they could to make us pass.

——But there are people who don't graduate, right?

——There are people who don't pass when they are terrible at all subjects. But if you are behind in only one subject, they let you pass. Even if you are really not very good in that subject, even if in trying to catch up you don't, they let you pass. Because you are behind in only one subject. The child who doesn't pass is the one who does badly in two or three subjects. Then there's no way they can pass.

——So, which subjects did you like the most? Portuguese, right?

——Yes. I liked Portuguese. I liked science. But I didn't get on well in math.

——And so it was from fifth grade on that you lost interest . . .

——That I lost interest in school. In sixth grade I only wanted to study so I could pass as quickly as possible . . . so I could finish primary school. All I wanted to do was finish primary school. I didn't want to study anymore.

——So you don't have to finish secondary school. I mean, it's not compulsory?

——No, it's not compulsory. But now I wish I had. Because before, employers accepted anyone with a primary school education. Not any longer. So then in seventh grade there were already no physics or chemistry teachers. I've never studied chemistry or physics. There were always teachers missing in this school . . . math teachers, art teachers rarely made it to class.

——And were these teachers who lived here, or were they from somewhere else?

——Somewhere else . . . they were all from somewhere else.

——And were they mainly women?

——Yes, they were mainly women . . . but there were men teachers as well.

——And were they teachers who knew about the community . . . the poverty and the difficulties you faced?

——They didn't care that much. There were some that cared . . . some who taught us well . . . who gave us support. Then there were those who taught us and, when we didn't learn, were only there to pick up their wages at the end of the month.

——**Can you say something about conditions at the school at the time?**

——The school itself was very clean. It was a clean school. The food, while it may not have been of the best quality, was good food. The lunches were well prepared. There were tablecloths. You could eat . . . have second helpings. During my time there it was like this.

——**Even so, after finishing primary school, you decided to quit.**

——I quit. I wasn't liking school anymore and wasn't interested in studying.

——**How old were you?**

——Fifteen, sixteen years old when I stopped going. I was never really interested in anything. I liked to go out a lot . . . to go to *bailes*. Studying wasn't for me.

——**So, you never went on to finish secondary school later on. Andrea finished, right?**

——She's finishing now . . . after how many years?

——**And Camilla?**

——She's finishing as well.

——**And what about Diago?**

——No. Diago dropped out in fourth grade.

——**Isn't it compulsory to finish primary school?**

——No, it's not compulsory. But it gets difficult to find work. It's compulsory in stores . . . in business. But in the old days you just needed to know how to read and write.

——**When you were fifteen years old, what did you imagine your future would be? What did you think you'd be doing ten years down the road?**

——I imagined it like this . . . that I'd find a rich man and that would be it . . . without working, without having to do anything.

——**And was it during this time that you started going out with these guys.**

——Yes. I loved going out.

——And when you were fifteen and no longer went to school, did you stay at home helping your mother or did you go out?

——I stayed at home. I helped out in the house . . . and I worked at the neighborhood association with young kids.

——At the day-care center?

——Yes. I earned very little there, something like half a minimum salary. For a whole day's work with children!

——Did you ever think that an education was important, you know, for a career . . . a good job . . . to make good money?

——No, I never thought about it.

——How come?

——Because I never had anyone who would . . . now that I am older I tell my daughter all the time that she has to study, study, study.

——And what about Fábio and Roberto? Did they also quit school at an early age? Are *bandidos* usually guys who don't study . . . who don't finish their studies?

——In general, they don't finish.

EDUCATION

O

OVER THE COURSE of the past decade or so, the Brazilian education system has undergone what many claim is a "silent revolution." Enrollments in primary and secondary school are up and the proportion of the population that is illiterate continues to decline.[1] The Brazilian government also has taken steps to raise the level of teacher training and preparation and has introduced a system whereby schools in the public and private sectors are evaluated and accredited on a regular basis. And finally, new and innovative government funding and assistance programs have made resources available to those who are most in need.

The most heralded of these government funding and assistance programs are Fundef and Bolsa-Escola. Fundef is a federal program that subsidizes states and municipalities that spend the federally mandated proportion of their budgets on education but cannot afford the federally defined expenditure of 315 *Reais* per student.[2] Fundef has reallocated significant resources to the poorest regions of the country, raised educational expenditures in general, and generated new jobs. Bolsa-Escola is another federal program that pays families that earn less than half the minimum salary a stipend for each child under the age of fourteen who stays in school.[3] As of December 2001, the program had distributed 105 million *Reais* to 7 million children and their families in more than five thousand municipalities.[4]

The education system in Brazil remains an embarrassment, however, and compares unfavorably with almost all others in Latin America. The Brazilian government continues to spend too much on higher education, which is the almost exclusive domain of the middle class and the rich, while primary and secondary schools in general are in a state of physical disrepair and lack basic resources such as libraries and computers in the classroom.[5] Furthermore, huge discrepancies exist in terms of the quality of schools and education that are available in different parts of the country and even in the same city or state.[6] In fact, the recent push to increase primary and secondary school enrollments has only made matters worse. Increased enrollments have meant a decline in standards and, until recently, higher rates of grade repetition.[7] Students in Brazil are supposed to begin school at age seven and finish primary and secondary school at ages fourteen and eighteen, respectively. In September 2000, 20 percent of students in Rio repeated a grade, and 66 percent of the children in primary school and 75 percent of the children in secondary school were older than they were, theoretically speaking, supposed to be.[8]

The trend toward greater repetition has only recently been addressed by a policy of automatically promoting students from one grade to another and by enrolling those who fall behind in acceleration programs. There is no doubt that the older the student vis-à-vis the rest of the class, the more likely he or she will become discouraged and drop out.[9] Furthermore, repetition is also extremely costly to the school system and takes scarce resources away from other areas. There are those who argue, however, that the policy of automatically promoting students before they are ready does the student a disservice and that, as a consequence, many Brazilians who graduate are barely, if at all, literate.[10]

Of course, there is also no necessary relationship between education and higher wages, or education and greater equality.[11] Many of those who are returning to school, including Lucia's two sisters, are doing so because the jobs they used to get with a primary school education are no longer available.[12] When Lucia was in school, she needed just a few years of primary school education to get a dead-end job earning a minimum wage in a restaurant or supermarket. Now she needs to have completed secondary school. Much the same goes for teachers. A good friend of mine who works in one of the four day-care centers in Jakeira has been informed that to continue in her position she has to have a college-level diploma. She will still be paid the same low wages, however, and will be forced to endure the same miserable and overcrowded conditions.

Finally, one of the goals of the recent changes that have been made to the school system in Brazil has been to keep children and young adults off the streets.[13] Unfortunately, most of the schools—particularly those in the poorest areas—are in session for only a small part of the day. This means that many children and young adults in Brazil are left unoccupied and unattended.[14] Increasingly, however, it is not the school system's inability to keep children in that is the problem, but its inability to keep drugs out.

An increasing number of schools in Rio are hiring private security guards as more and more schools are affected by the violence associated with drug gang life.[15] In many areas of the city, schools have been forced to close their doors as a show of respect for a recently deceased drug gang member. And in at least one case, a school director who initially refused to do so was told that ten children from her school would be taken up the hill and executed.[16]

CHAPTER 6

Work

——I've already worked at almost everything . . . in shops, in supermarkets. I've worked in people's houses. I've worked in Laundromats . . . but always for a short time . . . never at a fixed profession.

——Is it difficult to find work?

——It's not that difficult . . . because most of the jobs I've had have been through friends.

——Is that how the system works?

——It's hard to find a job if you don't know someone. The world is so violent that you can only find work if someone has recommended you.

——What was your first job?

——With children at the neighborhood association.

——And how old were you?

——I was sixteen . . . and I earned half a minimum salary. And then this contract came to an end . . . it was with Mobral.[1]

——How long did you work for?

——One year.

——With other people from around here?

——Me and Anita and some others.

——Who was it that paid you? The neighborhood association?

——Mobral paid us. Mobral was an institution that helped disabled people . . . illiterates. They also helped children . . . and paid our wages.

——And this was in the neighborhood association building.

——Yes, on the first floor.

——And after this?

——After a while this project came to an end . . . so then the president of the neighborhood association asked me if I wanted to work as his secretary. My handwriting has always been very good . . . very legible . . . very pretty. So he invited me to work as the secretary of the neighborhood association. But I didn't really like it. You sat the whole day attending to people. It was really boring. Some days no one came by at all. I was often there all alone. So I started eating and putting on weight. I started to get fat! It was good there though because I earned minimum salary. For me it was a lot of money . . . but then I quit. I didn't want to continue.

——You say that for you, you earned well. What could you do with a minimum salary?

——Since I didn't have children at the time, it allowed me to buy . . .

——Did you give any to your mother?

——No, my mother always . . . she never accepted money from us. She told us to use the little we earned to buy clothes. At the time, my mother was working.

——Was she making a lot?

——More or less.

——So, how long did you stay there at the neighborhood association?

——I stayed there very little time . . . a few months. So then they called my mother . . . because it was my mother who signed me up, what with me being a *menor*. So I quit. I didn't want to work anymore.

——When you are under eighteen, some one has to sign you up for work?

——They have to give their permission. We couldn't do anything ourselves. Nowadays it's different. Now, you can work after you turn sixteen. But before . . .

——So what did you do once you left the neighborhood association?

——It was a while before I worked again. Then I went to work at Pão de Açucar.[2]

——What was your day like there?

——I started at nine o'clock . . . from nine to six.

——Did you have to wear a uniform?

——No, I wore my own clothes. Then, when I got there, I put on a uniform. They had a changing room there. Everyone had their own . . . their own. So I changed clothes and left my own clothes there. The uniform and the shoes were theirs.

——Did they wash your uniform for you?

——No. We had two uniforms. When one was dirty I'd bring it home, wash it, and take it back.

——So, you'd get there, change clothes, and . . .

——Go to work.

——Doing what?

——I bagged groceries. I bagged them so they could be sent to clients' houses.

——From nine until six.

——On my feet the whole time. We only had an hour for lunch.

——But you told me before that the manager wouldn't let you have . . .

——Lunch. He gave us fifteen minutes . . . because everyone has the right to a break for lunch.

——So you spent from nine until six working with only fifteen minutes break for lunch.

——By the end of the day our legs would be aching . . . and by the time I got home I couldn't bear to even stand up.

——And did you like the job?

——No. I earned very little.

——How much?

——I earned minimum salary. I took a job there because Amanda was about to have her first birthday . . . and I wanted to throw her a party. So I took the job. I stayed there three months. I stayed so I could put together enough money for her party.

——That's all?

——Because I also had an argument with the manager. He was arguing with a friend because she wanted to take an hour for lunch, and he wasn't letting us. So I went to complain too and he told me that we could both leave.

——You mean you were both fired.

——Yes.

——Was it easy for him to find other workers?

——It's easy because there are lots of people unemployed . . . lots of people.

——So, you couldn't stand it, quit, and the next job?

——From there I went to a store that sells things made of plastic . . . cups, plates.

——How did you get this job?

——I was walking around looking at shop windows. It was late in the afternoon and there was this sign saying "Wanted: Shop Assistant." So I went in and spoke to the manager. He told me to take a simple Portuguese test. I took the test, and did okay and talked the job over with the manager and . . .

——Did you need any references?

——No, he didn't ask. He didn't even ask about my work experience in other stores. He was pretty desperate. Some other women had already applied for the job . . . but in any case, he told me to start the next day.

——Who looked after Amanda?

——My sisters. Andrea and Camilla weren't working at the time.

——And how long did you stay there?

——I stayed there very little time . . . perhaps three months. Because they were using me to wrap things and as a saleswoman. I wrapped things and sold things. I was a saleswoman. I sold things as well . . . together with the other saleswomen. So, in truth, I was taking sales away from them . . . because, if I am attending to a customer, I am taking a sale away from another saleswoman. And this money was being passed on to them, to the store.

——So, from your perspective, you should have also been paid as a saleswomen. You worked as a saleswoman but were paid as a cashier.

——I earned minimum salary and they wouldn't pay me for the things I sold.

——How much did the saleswomen earn?

——A lot. If today the minimum salary is 180 *Reais*, they would earn something like 450.

——Why didn't you say to the manager, "Look, I'm working as a saleswoman . . ."

——I did. I said, "Can't you see that I am selling really well? Sign my *carteira*[3] so I can earn my commission." I was always complaining . . . because all the money I earned went to the store. Because if I sold something and I wasn't a salesperson, my name wouldn't appear and the store got the money. I spoke with him . . . I was selling well . . . I was making money . . . I treated the customers well. I asked him to make me a saleswoman . . . to give me my due. But he wouldn't. They didn't want to change my carteira. They were using me one way and paying me another.

——What sort of person worked there? Were there other women who lived in *favelas*?

——The manager earned between 1,000 and 1,200 *Reais* . . . enough to pay rent outside of a favela.

——Was there a big distinction between those, like you, who packaged things, and the saleswomen?

——There's a big difference . . . but only in terms of salary. Many of the saleswomen lived in favelas . . . many of them lived in favelas. But there's a big difference in terms of salary.

——So the saleswomen were poor as well?

——They just earned more . . . because they had more experience in other stores. They were used to it. So they didn't want to give someone else the opportunity. Anyone could do what they did. It's easy . . . anyone could learn. So they didn't want to give me the opportunity . . . and I didn't want to waste any more of my time . . . wearing myself out earning minimum salary. I worked two jobs and earned minimum salary. I felt exploited. So I decided not to stay any longer and quit . . . after three months.

——Did you take that job immediately after working at the supermarket or did you take time off?

——Soon after working at the supermarket. I'd quit and stay home, or else in Vista Bonita. Then, once I got bored from staying at home, I'd look for another. Because I liked walking around looking at stores. So I got a job just so I could do this. But whenever I found a job there was always something that annoyed me.

——So where did you work after that?

——I worked at a clothing store in the shopping center.

——Doing what?

——The same thing . . . packaging things. The pay there was just as bad, even though it was a store that sold designer clothes. I earned the same salary . . . minimum salary . . . even in that high priced store.

——Was there a big difference there between you guys and the rest of the staff?

——Very different. They'd finished school . . . they were very different. Then there was me from Jakeira and the cashier, who was from Santa Clara. She took the money and I wrapped things up in pretty boxes and bags.

——So they were really from a different class.

——From a different class.

——And did they talk to you?

——They talked to us, but only when necessary.

——Did you make any friends there?

——No. There were a few who messed around. The others were very serious . . . got on with their work and that was about it. The best thing about the job was that at the end of the week, on Saturday, they would give us a meal voucher . . . for us to spend on whatever we wanted at one of those restaurants.

——Did you like working there?

——I liked the place. There were lots of beautiful people. But it was the same deal. The manager was a very demanding person . . . a person who was always stressed out and who got upset about the smallest of things . . . but always with the *faveladas* who are "uneducated."

——So the manager got upset with you but not the others.

——With me and the cashier. Whenever something was wrong it was always us, our fault. So you see, I spent long hours on my feet for minimum salary while she earns a thousand times what I earn . . . and they always want things done fast. They throw the clothes at you and it's me who has to take off that alarm thing, fold them, wrap them in tissue paper, and put them neatly in a bag. I work and they earn. There was one customer who told us to go fuck ourselves . . . right there in the store.

——Why?

——I don't know. I brought her bag and she pulled it away from me and told us to go fuck ourselves. But as they say, "The customer's always right." One of the girls, one of the saleswomen said, "Lucia, she told you to go fuck yourself." What could I say? I couldn't say anything. The customer's always right!

——How long did you last at that place?

——A few months . . . three or four months.

——And you earned?

——Minimum salary.

——And did you quit that job or were you fired?

——I quit from there as well.

——What did you say to the manager when you left?

——I asked for my money. I told her I didn't want to stay.

——And what did she say?

——Fine.

——And what about your friend, the cashier?

——No, she earned more than me . . . about 300 or 400 *Reais*.

——Why?

——Because she's the cashier. The cashier always gets more. The cashier has more responsibilities. She deals with money. She still earns very little . . . because the saleswoman who doesn't do anything earns piles of money. Because a store that sells designer clothes makes a lot. Things are very expensive . . . and they earn good commission.

——Was there any chance you could work there as a salesperson?

——No, because they never give you the opportunity.

——How do you know?

——Because I've tried already. They wouldn't give me the opportunity. That's what upsets us the most. There are people who work for years at the same job and earn the same thing. It really annoyed me . . . because I always liked to dress well . . . and to look good . . . and all I saw were these salespeople who dressed worse than me. So I quit . . . after this I worked in a Laundromat . . . I worked there for nine months.

——How did you find this job?

——My sister knew an elderly lady and she said that she had a friend who owned a Laundromat, who was looking for help. I was unemployed so my sister took me there. So I went there and I stayed there working.

——From nine to five?

——From nine to five . . . from nine to six!

——So you washed and ironed clothes . . . all this?

——Yes, but there it was the same situation. It was a lot of work. There was only me and the owner's sister. The owner of the Laundromat only came in the morning . . . then at about midday she left us in charge.

——Did you help with the clothes or were you just the cashier?

——No, I helped mark the clothes . . . because there, all the clothes were marked with a thread. So, for example, if a customer was assigned the black thread we would mark all of that customer's clothes with black thread. All the customers clothes were washed together. So each customer was assigned a thread . . . a colored thread. Each piece of clothing that was marked with a thread belonged to a certain customer. For example, Senhor João . . . black. Dona Maria . . . white. Then we put all the clothes together . . . all together. Then we put them in to dry in those enormous dryers . . . and then, after all that, we had to separate the clothes.

——Did you have to iron them as well?

——No, we only ironed for customers who asked. There was a different price for this. For those who didn't ask, we would fold their clothes neatly and place them in a bag with their name on and leave them there until they came by and picked them up. For those who paid to have them ironed, I ironed them. But it wasn't part of my regular job. I wasn't hired to do this. I was hired to work at the counter. I was hired to take the clothes from customers and to weigh them . . . just this . . . but I had to iron.

——So you were supposed to pass the clothes on to someone else.

——Exactly, there was supposed to be a person at each station. One person to wash, one person to iron . . . but me and her sister did all this . . . to save money.

——How much did you earn?

——Minimum salary. So then I didn't want to stay there any longer because she wanted me to do delivery, which meant traveling a long way carrying a bundle of clothes . . . on foot. I didn't . . . I don't know how to ride a bike . . . and she wouldn't give me the money to take the bus. There were too many clothes and too far to go to do.it on foot. Sometimes customers called up and didn't pay a thing. Whether they gave you a tip or not, they took the clothes from you and locked the door without so much as a thank you. So I told her that it wasn't working. I told her that she had to pay someone from the outside to deliver, or pay me a little more, or give me money to take the clothes by bus. But she felt uneasy about it, because she was afraid of losing customers.

——Did you like it there?

——I liked it because the owner was a very good person. She wasn't rich so she understood people's problems . . . a very good person. But, even so, it wasn't good enough. I already had Amanda and I had to buy her things.

——Did you get to know any of the customers?

——Some. There was an elderly lady who always asked me to stay for lunch at her house. Sometimes I would take lunch to work with me . . . I didn't have enough money to buy lunch out. I'd buy a pastry or something. I'd often go from early in the morning until nighttime on just a pastry and a soda.

——You didn't have money to buy lunch?

——If I bought lunch every day, it would cost more than my salary.

——And you had to pay for bus fares too, right?

——That too . . . and so it was through delivering clothes that I got to know this woman . . . who was wonderful.

——Where did she live?

——Near the square. See, I had to walk that far. To give you an idea, I walked from the Laundromat to the square . . . from the Laundromat to take her clothes. She was a wonderful person. When I got there, she always told me to rest . . . to sit down. I always stayed there a while. They gave me fruit . . . some sort of fruit. They also gave me a little bit of money. So I explained my situation to her. They took pity on me and told me they would help me. So every month they'd give me four tins of milk . . . they gave me biscuits, fruit, and money. For example, at the time they gave me 15 *Reais*, which helped a lot . . . because I earned very little.

——What was the minimum salary back then?

——Very little. I don't even remember.

——I think it was around 40 *Reais*.

——I got paid weekly. It was around 42.

——So 15 . . .

——15 was a lot . . . it was almost half my salary that she gave me.

——**Did she give you 15 *Reais* each week?**

——No, each month. She gave me a bag of groceries . . . you know, milk, cornstarch, and biscuits . . . to help me out . . . and she gave me these 15 *Reais*.

——**And then after nine months, you left.**

——I left. I was exhausted. I couldn't stand it. More and more customers wanted their clothes delivered. They didn't want to leave the house to pick up their clothes. They'd rather have someone bring them for free. After this I worked in various other places. I worked as a *diarista* cleaning houses. It paid very little but I needed the money.

——**When you say diarista you mean you were hired on a daily basis. Some days there was work, others day there wasn't. And you were paid by the day.**

——Exactly.

——**How did you get this job?**

——My aunt worked there and told me about it.

——**Did you like this kind of work.**

——No, I hated it. It was a lot of work . . . a lot of work. At one apartment I ironed clothes every fifteen days. There was a ton of clothes. I ironed clothes from first thing in the morning until night.

——**How much did you earn?**

——I don't remember . . . but today, with the minimum salary at 180 *Reais*, I would earn 30.

——**Twice per month.**

——Exactly. I worked that job without a carteira assinada. Day work is like that.

——**You mean you are paid under the table.**

——Yes.

——**What's the difference between a job with a carteira assinada and one without?**

——With a carteira assinada you have rights . . . you have unemployment, which pays you money if you are fired . . . and then there's your pension.

——**But you still don't earn much, even with a carteira assinada.**

——No, very little.

——**And after working at the Laundromat?**

——After this I worked in a beauty salon.

——**How long did you work there?**

——Not very long. I earned minimum salary there.

——**What did you do?**

——I served coffee . . . water.

——**So you didn't cut hair.**

——No. I wasn't really interested . . . and, looking back, I should have signed up then for the course I'm doing now. If I'd started working in a salon back then, I'd have money now . . . because working in a salon opens many doors. You are never without work. Once you've worked in a salon you'll never be unemployed.

——**Was it after this that you worked with your mother and sister as a maid?**

——I only worked three days.

——**Was it a big house?**

——It was an apartment that took up an entire floor.

——**Where?**

——Near the shopping center. There were lots of maids working there. The house wasn't dirty so the work was easy to do. Our job was to keep it clean. Sometimes, when the nanny was real busy with the children, we'd help out. Sometimes, when the nanny couldn't make it to a birthday party, we'd go along instead. I worked there three days each week.

——**But you earned good money.**

——I earned a minimum salary each week.

——**Even though you only worked three days.**

——Yeah, and I worked there without a carteira assinada.

——**What about your mother?**

——The same. She worked there for two years without a carteira assinada. After two years she got her carteira assinada but they didn't pay her for the previous two years.

——**And so why did you leave there? Was there no more work or were you making money doing something else?**

——At the time I was going to Vista Bonita a lot . . . and so, on the day I was supposed to go to work, I didn't go. Marcos hid my handbag so I couldn't go. So the next time I went there the woman was all angry and stressed out because one of her children was sick and she said, "You are very irresponsible. I don't want you here anymore." So, I left and lost my job. I still went there occasionally to do day work. Sometimes, when there was a party, she'd ask me to help out, you know, to serve food . . . and it paid well. She'd pay me 50 *Reais*. On Sundays, sometimes she needed someone to help out on Sundays. I'd go over and stay until five o'clock in the afternoon. She paid me 100 for this because Sundays count double.

——**And so, by the end, you worked every now and then but you didn't have a fixed schedule.**

——She asked me to go work at her office but by that time I was involved with Marcos.

——**So, by then, Marcos was giving you money.**

——He gave me money each week . . . but it was very little compared to what I was making there.

——**But there was little to keep you here . . . and, as a result, you spent more of your time in Vista Bonita.**

——Yes.

——**How long did you spend there once you left here?**

——I went back and forth. I came back here almost every week . . . but I stayed about two years.

——**So, after Rogério, how long did you stay here in Jakeira?**

——Not very long. At most . . . a year.

——**So, looking back, would you say that your experience at work had anything to do with your involvement in drugs? Was there a particularly bad experience that you had or were you just tired of working in shops?**

——I've seen a lot of discrimination . . .

——**How so?**

——I've seen lots people with lots of money, and others with nothing. I always owed more than I earned because I wanted to buy perfume or shoes or something for my daughter. So I'd receive my salary, and by the fifteenth, I'd have to ask for an advance to pay last month's bills. So, by the end of the month my salary was already reduced and good for almost nothing. And I worked hard . . . because I figured out that people with little education work hard and people with education sit there at a little desk watching people work for them. It's always like this. People without education are always discriminated against because people work for a person who earns without working. I always see it like this.

———When you were involved with *traficantes*, did they always give you a certain amount of money, like a salary? And how much did they give you?

———Marcos gave me a minimum salary each week. There was another one from around here who gave me lots of money to spend on whatever I wanted. So I could go to all those stores that I couldn't go to with my old salary . . . I was treated well. Because when they see you have lots of money you are treated well. There were times when I went to these stores with other girls from the favela. Some of them were very dark skinned. We weren't well attended to when we went to these stores . . . but the people who took care of us earned a lot because we bought a lot, and we paid with cash. So we tested the salespeople to see who would attend to us well . . . because whenever we went back to these stores we always bought from them.

———So do you think it was an issue of class?

———Without a doubt . . . because sometimes they wouldn't even attend to us. I had to wrap the stuff up myself. I sold the stuff to myself and they got the profit. One time I went with my two sisters and a cousin to a store because we really wanted a certain dress . . . we loved that dress! They wouldn't attend to us so we stood there holding on to the dress. Only after a while did they write up a receipt and hand it over. So my cousin said that we didn't have to humiliate ourselves in front of these *piranhas*. She said, if they aren't willing to work, why don't they give their job to someone who wants to work? But in the end, I bought it . . . because I really wanted it. There's one shoe store I've been to many times, but every time I go there they treat me badly. People always get involved to have money . . . and to be treated well.

———Does this form of discrimination take place in other places, such as restaurants?

———It happens everywhere. But to me it's like this, we have to look for our own space. Because if you know you will not be well received somewhere, what are you doing there? I won't go to fancy restaurants if I can go to a luncheonette because I know that the people who work there are from the favelas or the *subúrbios* and will treat us well. I won't go to restaurants because they think that I won't be able to pay. I won't go to

shows because there are always these *loiraças* who stare at us. I go to a
pagode.

——So you know the places you will be well received.

——Of course. Because I think that everyone should know where they
can go. For example, down below there are what we call *mauricinhos*.
Why would I want to hang out with them? I might hang out with them for
one night. But what for? So that the next day they can tell everyone what
they did and didn't do with you? I don't like it. There are a lot of girls here
who try this. But it's absurd. I reckon that everyone should be in a certain
place. It's divided . . . everyone knows that. I only feel comfortable in
certain places, so I will go to places where I feel comfortable.[4]

——So, favelados don't like the world outside.

——No, they don't like it much. We are discriminated against in that
environment.

——And is it the same at work?

——It's the same. Even the lunch hour is different. Everything's
different. Even the food's different. I had to take food from home.
They got luncheon vouchers . . . they went to a restaurant or a
luncheonette.

——So when you became involved, you had money and you didn't
have to suffer this discrimination. But what about your sisters? Didn't
they have the same experience?

——I believe so . . . but everyone has their own way of thinking. I have
a certain way of doing things and my sisters another.

——So it's not that you don't like to work, it's just that the
opportunities are few and the work is badly paid.

——If I went looking for work now I wouldn't find good work . . .
because I didn't finish secondary school. I don't know computers and I
don't speak another language. So what am I going to do? The best I can
do is to get a cleaning job . . . and I'm not going to leave my house to go to
some shopping center to be a cleaner. For example, to sell things you
need a good education . . . to treat customers well. There are lots of
people who work in stores who don't know how to sell, who don't know
how to treat people well and have finished secondary school. A lot of
them are university students who just do it to pass the time. People like
me who live in a favela and who really need the work could take far
greater advantage of this . . . but they don't understand this.

——And they earn a lot more, right?

——They earn a salary and commission.

——So why did you leave school?

——I didn't want to continue. I didn't have the will.

——Not even to finish secondary school.

——Now that I'm with Bruno, he keeps pushing me to study, study. He gave me the incentive to go back to school, to learn to drive, and to learn computers. He asks a lot of me. So now I am thinking of going back . . . because of him . . . because the others weren't bothered with this. Even this is different about him.

——How old were you when you left school?

——Sixteen. I just stopped going. I was already involved. They gave me my money so I didn't care about anything else. I already had the things I wanted. So I never bothered with work.

——So, at the time, you never believed that education would open doors for you.

——I never believed this.

——But you have friends who finished secondary school.

——There are many.

——And where do these friends work?

——They work in stores. They get better jobs. It's difficult to get work in offices here. Around Christmas they have extra positions and those who do well earn a contract. But now they are beginning to ask a lot of people. But I always thought that as long as I was pretty, one would die and be replaced by another. I would always have my money and wouldn't have to work. But on the other hand, I was risking my life . . . my liberty . . . everything. It's very difficult . . . it's not easy at all.

——So it's not an easy road to take.

——Not at all. You have to stay out of sight and you can't go where you want to. Our lives are confined to the favela. This is especially true when someone from the favela is arrested. Then you are really visible and it's really difficult to leave.

——Because you are known as a *bandido*'s woman?

——Yes . . . and they'll kidnap you to get money.

——Has this happened to you?

——After Marcos died two police assassins came to my house looking for me, saying they were Marcos' cousins. They came with Maria and her sister to kidnap me. They took two of my *comadre*'s children hostage in Vista Bonita. But on the two days that they came I wasn't here . . . because I moved around a lot. They asked for a photograph of me, but my sister couldn't find one.

——Were they policemen from Vista Bonita?

——Yes. They wanted to know if I had kept any money. They wanted to kidnap me and extort it from me. As if I'd kept anything all these years! They wanted to know if I'd kept anything after all these years with Marcos. But I didn't keep anything . . . but they wanted to make sure if I had anything.

——Had you saved any money?

——No. I didn't save any money. Marcos gave me a lot of money once, which I kept. But, after that, selling drugs got . . . they got squeezed. So there were times when there weren't any drugs to sell . . . and at one time they didn't have any money. The only person who had any money was me. So I felt sorry for them and Marcos told me that if I gave him back the money he'd return it double. So I took all the money he had given me and gave it back to him. But then we fought and he told me he wasn't going to give it back to me. So I didn't even bother . . . I left it at that. So then he only gave me small amounts to spend.

——Did Rogério also give you money?

——At the time, Rogério and I were very young. So we never thought of saving anything. We went out a lot. We went to a lot of restaurants. I had lots of fun with him. When we traveled, we stayed in hotels every night . . . in suites. I only went to the market to buy junk food . . . to buy clothes . . . everything that I wanted to buy. I never saved any money. I didn't even think about it.

——So how much money did Marcos make a month?

——He made a lot. He made a lot because he had two *bocas*. He didn't have just one favela . . . he had various.

——So, do you have any idea how much he made? One thousand *Reais* per month, or more?

——No. A lot more.

——Ten thousand?

——I don't know. I know that from one kilo they'd make 23,000 *Reais*. But then there were various expenses . . . and he bought a lot of property.

We didn't really know. He never talked about it . . . but it was always held jointly. And when he died the other *dono* got to keep everything.

——**Did you know how much cocaine they sold each week or month?**

——At a place where they did well, they would sell a kilo of cocaine every two weeks. From a kilo they bought from a *matuto* they would make two kilos . . . because they'd mix it with something else. So, if they bought a kilo, in reality, they'd have two kilos.

——**And how much did a kilo cost?**

——Around 7,000 *Reais*.

——**That means a profit of around 16,000 *Reais*.[5] What did they invest the money in?**

——Cars, jewelry, guns . . . anything they could buy.

——**Did they travel a lot?**

——A lot.

——**By car or by plane?**

——By car. They thought the same way I did in that they had almost nothing and they kept seeing these rich people on TV and they wanted the same things . . . and with the money they could have the same things. They could stay in hotels. They could travel. They could go to good restaurants. They could do all this . . . and with the money they could show that they could do this.

——**Did they talk about the possibility of dying? Were they afraid of death?**

——No, they said that they'd already killed a lot, so it didn't matter if they died. Marcos had already bought his own coffin. He said that when he died we wouldn't have to do anything. He was buried in a cemetery in Vista Bonita.

——**Did you go?**

——No, I was in Fortaleza. But my comadre sent me the newspaper clipping.

——**Did a lot of people go to the funeral?**

——A lot of people went. They killed him and took him to the hospital because they had to show that they had tried to help him. They were still talking to him, asking him if he had any more money. The policeman who killed him really hated him. There was an agreement between them ... but this one policeman said that if he came across Marcos, only one of them would survive.

——But why?

——Because they were enemies.

——**But if the police make money from drugs, why would they want to kill the dono?**

——They kill them because the agreement between them has somehow been broken. Sometimes they demand such a large sum of money that the dono says he will get it and can't. So when they get a hold of him, they don't give him another chance.

ECONOMY

W HEN LUCIA'S MOTHER Conceição first came to Rio, Brazil was a predominantly rural country with a population of somewhere between 70 and 80 million. Almost 40 percent of the population over the age of five was illiterate, and the average Brazilian could not expect to live long past his or her fiftieth birthday. Forty years later, 80 percent of Brazilians live in cities or urban areas, and the population is fast approaching 180 million. Furthermore, illiteracy is on the decline and is now a condition that afflicts primarily the elderly and those living in the more isolated areas of the country. And finally, Brazilians can now expect to live well into their mid to late sixties.

The other big change between then and now has to do with the way most Brazilians earn a living. In 1960, more than half the economically active population of the country worked on the land in agriculture. By 1990, however, this figure had fallen to a little over 20 percent. This dramatic shift reflects both a decline in the importance of traditional agricultural products such as coffee, cotton, and sugar and the emergence of a modern and technologically sophisticated industrial economy in and around the cities of the South and Southeast.[1]

Over the past forty years, Brazil has become one of the world's largest industrial producers.[2] However, despite consistently high rates of economic growth throughout the 1960s and 1970s, the industrial economy has failed to absorb a labor force surplus created by agricultural restructuring and decline, internal migration, and high fertility rates.[3] Consequently, more than half of the economically active population in Brazil is now employed in the service sector. A job in the service sector can mean anything from a highly trained doctor or career civil servant to a shoeshine or street vendor. Severe economic recession throughout much of the 1980s and 1990s has meant that the vast majority of jobs that have been created in the service sector are of the latter variety. Most of these jobs are extremely low paid, intermittent, and precarious. More importantly, the majority lack legal status and the formal protections that, in theory, are provided by a *carteira assinada*. This means that an increasing number of workers in Brazil are not covered by labor laws and are excluded from the benefits of social security, unemployment, and pensions.[4]

There is considerable controversy as to the composition and broader significance of what is often referred to as the informal sector.[5] Some argue that the informal sector is entrepreneurial and dynamic and supplies much needed goods and services that the formal sector is unwilling or unable to provide.[6] Then there are those who argue that the informal sector plays no effective economic role and that it is a sector of survival and of last resort. Finally, there are those who argue that the informal sector represents an industrial reserve army that exerts downward pressure on wages and therefore cheapens the cost of the reproduction of labor. Either way, the rapid expansion of the informal sector over the past two decades has increased the divide between the haves and have-nots in Brazil and has stripped millions of their citizenship.[7]

The recessions of the 1980s and 1990s hit Rio de Janeiro particularly hard and accelerated a long period of decline from the city's former position as the country's commercial and political capital.[8] Between 1976 and 1988, for example, real earnings in Rio fell by 29 percent. And between 1982 and 1988, the percentage of the economically active population employed by the service sector increased from 67.5 to 75 percent, leaving a third of Rio's estimated 3.5 million workers without a formal contract. In fact, the situation in Rio has deteriorated faster than in any other metropolitan area of Brazil.[9] Of course, the processes of "informalization" and impoverishment affect some groups more than others. And, in Brazil, despite protestations to the contrary, the more visible injuries of class are compounded by those of race and gender.

Many, if not most, Brazilians believe that, despite the existence of extreme poverty and inequality, they live in a racial democracy. Brazil is different from other postslave societies, they insist, because of its history of widespread miscegenation, a dynamic and imprecise system of racial classification, and an almost total lack of racial prejudice and discrimination.[10] Since the late 1970s, however, the racial democracy "myth" has been challenged—at least intellectually—on the basis of national-level census data that reveal that Brazilians of African descent lag far behind their white counterparts in terms of a whole range of social, economic, and quality-of-life indices.[11] A recent study based on census data, for example, found that while Brazil ranks seventy-ninth in the world in terms of the United Nation's Human Development Index, the situation is very different for blacks than for whites. When the Human Development Index is calculated just for whites in Brazil, the country ranks forty-ninth. When it is calculated just for blacks, Brazil ranks 108th.[12]

The other major group to lose out in this process is women. Brazilian women have been moving into the workforce at a steady pace since the 1960s.[13] This transformation in the relationship between gender and employment has been due in part to rapid rates of urban to rural migration, increased opportunities for women's education, declining fertility, and delayed marriage. Over the course of the past two decades, however, the increase in the proportion of women who work has also been due to declining wages and household incomes, increased unemployment among men, and the rapid rise of female-headed households.[14] The majority of women who work in Brazil do so in clerical, domestic, and service occupations. As such, they are paid less than men and are less likely to find work involving a carteira assinada.[15] Brazilian women of color are at an even greater disadvantage and remain heavily concentrated in the realm of domestic service.[16]

Lucia's family has always had one foot in the formal sector and the other in the informal sector. By pooling their resources and living under one roof, however, they have thus far managed to survive.[17] By the time I finished interviewing, only Lucia's youngest sister Camilla held a regular, formal sector job. Camilla worked long hours from Monday to Saturday as a waitress in a local restaurant. She had been working there for three years and earned 380 Reais, which, at the time, was equivalent to two minimum salaries. Lucia's mother had only recently been fired from her last job as a maid. The job paid extremely well until the woman who employed her realized she could hire four people for the amount she was paying Conceição. The money Lucia's mother made while working there pretty much supported the family and paid for the improvements that were made to the house. Now she had to make do with a modest pension, which she was having trouble collecting because of all the time she spent working off the books.

Lucia did not work at all while I was there. During the day, she stayed at home and looked after her daughter, her sister's two daughters, and various other children that ended up at her house. Because she wasn't working, she felt obliged to help out around the house, do the shopping, and prepare and cook lunch and dinner for the rest of the family. Her other sister, Andrea, also did not work and stayed at home the whole day. It was difficult for Lucia and her sister to work because day care in Jakeira was either inadequate or prohibitively expensive. There was one low-cost day-care center in Jakeira that was funded by the municipal government. It was affordable but chronically understaffed and overcrowded.[18] The other day-care centers were privately owned and charged what Lucia considered a lot of money. The alternative was to leave the children with friends and pay them to look after them or, failing all else, to leave them with Lucia's mother. Friends proved unreliable, however, and Lucia found it increasingly difficult to impose on her mother who, in her mother's own words, had "done enough."

The four men living in the house were Lucia's father, Lucia's brother-in-law, Bruno, and Diago. Lucia's father was retired and disabled and spent his entire pension on medications.[19] Lucia's brother-in-law, Sérgio, held numerous jobs while I was there, none of which lasted very long or generated much in the way of income. When I first arrived, he was operating a makeshift car wash with a friend around the corner. Then, when that business failed, he worked for one of the many van operators that charged 1 *Real* to take people to and from the shopping center. Finally, by the time I left, he was helping a friend at a stall along the main road.

Bruno had been unable to find a steady job since his release from prison. Part of the problem had to do with his past. He was, after all, an ex-convict. Part of the problem also had to do with Bruno. He was not used to going without and was not about to take any old dead-end minimum salary job. So he spent his days chasing down leads in the city—anything to keep him occupied and out of the *favela*. Then of course, there was Diago. Diago participated in the most lucrative informal sector business of them all. Anything Diago earned, however, went straight up his nose. Occasionally, he actually cost the family money when he ran up debts, debts that Lucia and her family could no longer afford.

CHAPTER 7

Born Again

——Let's talk about the religious beliefs of your family . . . starting with your grandmother.

——In the beginning, my grandmother worked with these dark spirits in *Candomblé*.

——**Where . . . in the Northeast?**

——No, my grandmother started here. So she already had experience with both sides—you know, the good and the evil. She began with Candomblé and all that other stuff . . . the clothes and everything. Then there was a time, when she was around forty years old, when she would pass by my grandfather's church . . . and he would always ask her to come inside. He would ask her to come inside but she never accepted. Then, one time, she went in on her own.

——**Where was this church?**

——Near the bus station. So anyway, she went inside hearing all those words . . . and then at the end they always ask, "Who wants to accept Jesus as their savior?" So my grandmother went and raised her hand. From this day on . . . my grandmother says that after a person accepts Christ she accepts the truth.

——**How old is she now?**

——Eighty-two. She is one of the founders of the Assembly of God[1] in Santa Clara. And from there she came here to this church in Jakeira . . . close to the neighborhood association.

——**When did these churches first appear in Jakeira?**

——They were always here.

——**But there are a lot more now, right?**

——Yes, because now they have different names. They're all *cristão.* There's the Universal Church, the God Is Love, and the Baptist Church.[2] There's also another new one over there (gesturing).

——**And are they all different?**

——They're not all the same . . . because some have strict doctrines. Others don't. The Baptist Church doesn't. The Universal Church doesn't. The Assembly of God does . . . the God Is Love as well.

——**And your mother and grandmother are members of the Church of God Is Love?**

——Yes. So anyway, my grandmother moved to the church here in Jakeira. And then one time my grandmother asked for an opportunity, because the pastor at the church here was giving opportunities mainly to young people.

——**Opportunity to do what?**

——To sing. He gives people opportunities and they do whatever their heart tells them. They sing, they cite verses of the Bible, or they deliver, as they say . . . because they have received a vision from God. But that night she'd received a vision from God that he told her to deliver. Because it's like this . . . cristões say that when God orders you to deliver . . .

——**Deliver?**

——To deliver a vision to someone . . . to advise. Advice that has to be delivered to a certain person. Because if that person doesn't deliver the advice, God will send them to bed. They'll get sick. Because if God tells

us to deliver something, we cannot disobey him. It's like a command. So
she told me that she had to deliver this message. So she asked permission.
So the pastor who was there made fun of her ignorance . . . and began
to shout at her. But she's one of the founders of the church . . . and people
say that these old people are the pillars of the church. So right then my
grandmother left and went home. And the brothers of the church, who
had known my grandmother for many years, came after her. But among
the pastors there is always a head. Because all these churches are
branches. What happened among the churches . . . it's like a store. There's
the original store that's the main office. And the branches are the other
stores that are affiliated with the main store but are scattered about the
neighborhood. So the main office is in Santa Clara. Everything that goes
on in the branches has to be cleared with the pastor there. So the pastor
asked my grandmother to go there and tell him what happened. But my
grandmother refused. My grandmother said that he might be the head of
all the churches, but that the real head was God. My grandmother said
that she had a message from God. And so God would punish them
because what my grandmother was saying was not from her. My
grandmother wanted to pass on a message that God had told her to
deliver. So my grandmother asked to give up her membership. My
grandmother wanted to leave the church. But no one can leave the
church on their own. You have to pray for the church where you used to
go and God will send someone to talk to you . . . even if you don't know
them. But he will talk to you. So, no matter where my grandmother went
to church, in her prayers God used someone to tell her that her time at
this church was done . . . that she had to take on other work in another
place. My grandmother was like a missionary. In the Gospel there's . . . in a
store there's a manager, a salesperson and an assistant, right? It's the same
with the church. My grandmother is like a missionary because a
missionary is someone who travels and holds meetings in other churches.
My grandmother has the gift of a missionary. In the church, people are
baptized with the Holy Spirit⌊God gives a gift to each person . . . a power.
God always sends her to other places . . . always.⌉So she's always invited.
She has already traveled as far as Corumbá.[3] So at the prayer meetings
she goes to people tell her that her time in this place, her work here, has
finished. So what did my grandmother do? She returned to the place
where she accepted Jesus in the first place . . . in Santa Clara. And there

God put her on the altar. Because here they didn't respect her for her age or for who she was. And there in Santa Clara they put her on the highest platform of the church. She was among those people way up there. Like the ones during Carnaval they call the *Guarda Velha*. Do you see the difference? Here she was nothing, but there she was a very important person.

——**Who is the pastor here?**

——I don't know his name.

——**Is he still there?**

——He got sick. God made him pay . . . because there are churches where they want to become pastors quickly. You see, they all have their eyes on the money. Each member has to give the *dízimo*, which is 10 percent of their salary. Others, who don't understand, say that we are being taken advantage of. But they don't know . . . because a person gives because of her faith. Because it's written in the Bible. And each member follows the Bible. If they use the money for something else . . . it's between them and God, you understand? Whenever they do this kind of thing, just like in a robbery, something happens to them. God sorts out the good from the evil.

——**In how many churches around here do they give money?**

——There must be eight of them.

——**And are most of them Assembly of God?**

——They are mostly Evangelical.[4]

——**Okay. Continuing with your story. Your grandmother was one of the founders.**

——For many years prayer meetings were held in her house. One day each week people would go there to pray.

——**Did your whole family go, including your mother? Didn't your mother go to Catholic mass at the time?**

——No, our family never went to Catholic Church.

——**But aren't you Catholic?**

——I'm Catholic because I'm not a member of the Assembly of God. But we're not even Catholic. We don't have a fixed religion like that. I don't feel I am a Catholic because . . . but I'm not a cristão. I am more cristão than anything because of my family and the way I was raised. I always go to prayer meetings . . . because I believe that when someone really accepts the church they have to live a certain way. Because the church that my grandmother goes to has a doctrine . . . the clothes, you know? You have to change everything. So, if a person isn't prepared to change, I think that . . .

——Your mother changed, right?

——My mother changed. It's already been two . . . almost three years. But she really changed. Because accepting Jesus isn't easy. It's difficult. I mean it's easy to accept Jesus. But to follow him is difficult. Because there are really difficult things . . . there are many doctrines. There's a doctrine for clothes. You have to totally change . . . totally . . . the way you think . . . the way you act.

——And what about your brother-in-law Sérgio? Didn't he want to become a pastor?

——To become a pastor is not easy. Now there are many different levels in the church. You begin with nothing and, like in a store, a pastor in a church goes to a higher and higher position. A person has to have studied the Bible. They have to know all the doctrines . . . all the words. Because the pastor has to preach to many flocks . . . and if you don't know how to speak . . . if you don't know the words of the Bible . . . because a pastor cannot keep opening the Bible the whole time. A pastor has to have everything inside his head so that he can communicate with people. He is like a father. He has to make sure that no one loses their way. Because it's written in the Bible that everyone has seven spirits. And then there are the bad spirits that tempt us. You see, sometimes people kill or rape and, afterwards, they don't know why they did it. I don't know . . . there's no logical explanation. So a person always has to be firm and focused to feel the power of God.

——So when did this new pastor appear? And what is his name?

——His name is Albinate . . . and it was like this. The brothers of the church visit each other a lot. So he also made lots of visits . . . because he didn't have his own church. So he held prayer meetings in peoples houses. He held prayer meetings in churches. He came whenever he was invited . . . and there was this little church by the bus stop.

——Next to the key cutter's?

——No, it was near to where there used to be a fish stall. They opened a little Assembly of God church there. The pastor always invited the deacon and members of other churches to start a prayer meeting. So then the pastor of this church knew Albinate and invited him . . . and in his past life he had been a *traficante*.

——Where was he from?

——Zona Oeste. He used to be a traficante.

——And was he, you know, a killer?

——He'd done a lot of bad things.

——Did he tell you what he'd done?

——When a person accepts Jesus he tells all the things he's done in the past. He repented. And God gives a great gift to these people who kill and then repent. And God gave it to him. He has the gift of revelation. So he was invited and he brought many people to this little church. The church filled up because of his words. In his prayers, God reveals things to him about other people. He came every Thursday. The place was always full. There were people who didn't believe . . . who still weren't cristão. There were always revelations of sickness for some people . . . and then there were people who where possessed by evil spirits. So then he'd ask, why were these spirits in a person's body? Sometimes, these spirits were in a person's body to use them as prostitutes. So then, my mother, who was a founder of that church, asked him if he could hold a prayer meeting here.

——When was this, a year ago?

——Yes, about a year ago. So then she got to know him . . . and they became friends. So my mother wanted to have a regular prayer meeting here. So people came each week . . . lots of people accepted Jesus here.

——How many people came each week? Twenty? Thirty?

——No, there weren't that many. Maybe fifteen. It depends. There were times when more people came . . . and there were times when fewer people came. People came from other places. Now he's with the God Is Love Church. The pastor of his church told him that it would be a while before he could take over. So he's working there and earning money.

——How far away is this new church?

——It's about two . . . two and a half hours by bus. So there are times when he is working far away. When he is at a church that is far away he can't come here every Sunday.

——Who in your family is the most involved? Your mother? Your grandmother? Your brother-in-law?

My mother and my grandmother. Sérgio has almost given up.

——Why?

——God baptized Sérgio with the Holy Spirit and gave him the gift of speech . . . of revelation. Because each person that God baptizes . . . my mother has been going all these years. She attends services in hospital.

She goes to prayer meetings in various places. She goes to early morning vigils. But my mother hasn't been baptized yet, you understand? God baptized Sérgio real soon . . . and when God baptizes you, he gives you a power. Each person has a different power. There are those who have the power to cure. There are those who have the power of words. There are others who have the power of revelation. Not all of them are equal. There are others who have the power that comes to them in their sleep. Each one has a power. Sérgio was baptized and had a power.[5]

——And your sister?

——No.

——But she goes to prayer meetings . . . she believes in all this, right?

——She goes now and then . . . and, yes, she believes.

——And your brother?

——He believes. Everyone believes because everyone knows it exists because of all the things that have happened to us . . . because of the confidence we have in God . . . because worse things haven't happened. Even my brother . . . he's afraid. He fears God, you know?

——Really?

——He fears him a lot. He asks like this . . . well no, he doesn't go to prayer meetings. But he's afraid. After all that he's done. All those things I told you about. The things he's owed . . . and all those other things. It's more powerful, you understand? It's more powerful than him. Because a normal person . . . a person with a normal mind wouldn't do such things. What he did . . . we've seen so much happen. He's seen a lot of things happen. So how can a person do bad things knowing that those same bad things could happen to him? Is this a normal person? No it's not.

——You mean Diago.

——You know that something's going to happen to that person. You're right there. You're part of it.

——What do you mean?

——These deaths. All these bad things that happen. He's part of all of it. So why does someone do this when they know it could happen to them? Why does someone, when they love their family, put their family at risk?

——For the money?

——They lose control . . . because a person can remain in control. There are many that do, you understand? But there are those who lose all control . . . they can't control themselves.[6]

——Tell me a little more about his life . . . about how he became involved.

——It was many years ago. He wasn't involved directly.

——What do you mean?

——He wasn't directly involved with drug trafficking. He used drugs . . . he was an addict.

——How long ago was this?

——About eleven years ago.

——How old is he now?

——Thirty.

——So is he the oldest?

——Yes. He didn't have . . . he was always difficult. That's how it is in the beginning. They are friends . . . and when a person is an addict they have to steal and sell. So a person steals and enters the drug trade . . . they have to find a way to get drugs.

——And what did he do for a living at that time?

——He worked. He worked as an office boy.

——Was this a long time ago?

——Many years ago.

——And he had already left school.

——My mother went to work . . . and we stayed home all alone because we were all little . . . you know? So he got himself ready and when he left home he would change his clothes and not go to school and skip class. He would change his clothes and fly kites. That was his addiction. His thing was kites and marbles. He wasn't interested in studying . . . just in messing about. So then the school principal expelled him because it wasn't working out. He could no longer study because he'd missed so many classes. So then he grew up and began to get involved with friends who were addicts. They must have offered him some . . . they must have offered him some to try . . . and he must have accepted.

——But unlike most of them, he's survived.

——He's always survived . . . even though different people have been in command.

——Did he ever fall out of favor?

——There was one time . . . I think it was last year or the year before. There was a guy who was here a short time. It was just after Diago was released from prison. He told Diago that he couldn't come back here.

——Who was it?

——They called him Duquinho. Duquinho's a *bandido* who's in prison. He's very dangerous. He invaded Jakeira and stayed here for about three months. Then he was caught again.

——So what's going to happen when he gets out?

——He'll come back here . . . there'll be another war.

——Why is he so dangerous?

——He's extremely violent . . . he never trusted anyone. And this time, when he was sent to prison, he went after everyone who was involved. Even if they were involved only a little . . . a lot of people died. So anyway, after he was caught, my brother could come back here again . . . because it was controlled by different people. People say that worse things haven't happened to him because of God . . . and because of the respect they have for my family. They've known us for a long time . . . because he's done a lot of shit.

——How so?

——He's wasted their money. He's messed with drugs. In any other place that means death, you understand?

——And it was just last year that he was kidnapped by the police, right? How much did the *dono* have to pay. Do you know? I heard it was 3,000 *Reais*.

——They asked for this amount but then they only sent 300. So they didn't really pay. So then my brother was pursued by the police. So, if one day, they catch him and remember him, they could take him away and kill him. They could do anything because of this debt that he owed . . . and even if he didn't have anything on him, they could plant something to incriminate him. All because they were mad that that they never received their money.

——Did the police ask your family for money?

——No. They asked the dono directly because the traficantes have a lawyer and the lawyer works out everything . . . the amount to be paid . . . everything.

——So the lawyer negotiated a price with the police and paid them the money . . . and then Diago was released?

——Yes . . . and the dono was really mad because he lost a lot of stuff. You see they sleep all day and work at night. But on this day my brother didn't come home. He must have done a lot of drugs . . . he must have been drinking. . . mixing drinks and drugs and wandering about. Then he fell asleep on a ledge with all his stuff next to him. Then a ton of policemen appeared out of nowhere and starting asking questions around the *favela*. They found my brother asleep on the steps . . . and when they searched him they found his bag of stuff. Because it's a business, it costs them when they lose things. So, to lose a bag of stuff, of guns or drugs, is to lose money.

———Is this why the dono was mad?

———Yes. He was real mad. He beat Diago up and threw him out.

———But he didn't kill him.

———No, he didn't kill him.[7]

———And then, after a few days.

———He stayed at home calling the dono to ask him if he could come back . . . because he had no money . . . and they let him. They knew he couldn't go without drugs so they made him work for them. So they gave him the job of dividing up the drugs between the various *vapores*. It was worse . . . because now he was in charge of the entire stock. I mean, if a person's already addicted and they see drugs in front of them, there's going to be a time when they lose control. And once a person starts, they never stop. As long as there are drugs, they'll keep going. So the whole thing was out of control . . . and we just sat and waited for the worst to happen.

———So then what happened?

———My mother told them they we couldn't pay off any more of his debts.

———Were there a lot?

———We'd already paid many debts. One of 80 . . . another of 40. The last one was for 500.

———500! Money that your mother didn't have.

———She didn't have the money. So my mother had to go to her employer and tell her that she had a debt that she had to pay . . . and her employer gave her the money. She gave her 700!

———Did her employer know what it was for?

———No.

———So then your family decided that it was time for your brother to go away.

———Because we couldn't pay anymore. I was in no condition to pay and neither was Bruno. We couldn't do it any more. I had to use my money to buy things for myself to help out . . . Bruno too.

——So you chipped in.

——We had to buy the bus tickets. My mother had no money. So Bruno used the money he earned driving a van.

——**Where did he get this money?**

——Every now and then he works for a friend.

——**So he hasn't messed with drugs.**

——He got involved once in the beginning ... I know that one time he left to sell drugs or something. But now that I am pregnant, you know? Before I'd travel to far off places ... but now everything's more difficult. But now his friend tells him when he has work ... and off he goes. There's also this other guy who calls him now and then to work. He met him through a friend at church. And then there's another guy who works at the docks. Every now and then they need someone at night. They pay 40 *Reais* per night. So, when he's needed, he goes.

——**Let me see. What else. Does Diago have children?**

——No.

——**And what about your sisters. Have they ever been involved?**

——Never. Their experiences have been completely different. But even so my brother got involved because of me ... because he used to run messages for me.

——**Where?**

——Here in Jakeira. He used to run messages to Fábio for me. He'd run messages and they'd give him drugs in return ... that's how it all started.

——**And do you think that he'll stay out once he gets back?**

——He'll only not go back if the dono doesn't want him back. Because for him ... I think they like this life ... because they are respected and feared in the favela. Everything they ask for is taken as an order.

——**But your brother's not like this.**

——No. He's more simple. I don't really understand what it is with him. These days, its not making as much money as it used to ... because there's less around. No one trusts anyone ... a lot has changed. So, the person who brings the drugs here runs a big risk ... the risk of bringing them and losing them. In the old days, they worked with large quantities ... so they never went without. Now they can't get enough. There are more people involved and less money. Nowadays they earn practically nothing ... because what they earn they spend on drugs and fall further into debt. And then they stay out each night and get home in the morning and sleep the whole day and don't want to go back to work. And then if they're caught their families have to visit them each week. I quit my job because of this.

——**Did you visit on weekends?**

——The most common days for visiting were Wednesdays and Saturdays. It cost a lot of money. I had to take a bus from here to Trés Rios because there wasn't one that went to the city. You had to get off in São Isabel and take another one from there to the bus station. From there I'd take a van . . . which is a lot faster but a lot more expensive. And then, when I got there, I'd take another bus or a *kombi* to the entrance to the prison. You had to walk from there in the hot sun carrying all these heavy things. Then you had to get in line at seven and at around one they'd begin to call you. Then you had to rent a floor pad for 1 *Real*. I used to spend more than 5 Reais on bus fares, a floor pad, and taking a shower . . . and the earlier you got there, the lower the number of the ticket that got you in.

——**You mean you had to get there at seven in the morning to join the queue?**

——Everything you brought with you had to be in a plastic bag . . . sugar . . . biscuits. All the food had to be in a plastic container that they stuck their hands in like it was pig's swill. Then, after they had been through your things you had to go into a separate room . . . there they went through everything. You had to crouch naked with your legs apart I don't know how many times.

——**Why?**

——Because there are women who hide drugs inside their body. There are a lot of women . . . a lot of people who bring drugs in.

——**And you have to do this every time you go?**

——Every single time . . . and it doesn't matter how old you are. Young . . . old . . . everyone has to do it. You go in three by three and then they look you over. There are some that are really abusive . . . you know, ignorant. They mess around with your hair and then, soon after, they call the prisoners.

——**So you go into a room . . . you and Diago on your own.**

——No. There was a large field. You could walk around . . . they put down mats.

———And did Diago appreciate your visits?

———Yes, because if you didn't get visits you didn't go out. He'd stay locked up all week . . . but we visited him a lot.

———And how long did it take you to get there?

———Two hours. It was really difficult. Sometimes I'd stay at a friend's house the day before because it was easier to get a bus . . . from there I'd leave at dawn with my things so I'd get there early.

I T IS OFTEN SAID that Brazil is the largest Catholic country in the world. When it comes to Catholicism, however, Brazilians are not particularly orthodox or devout, and the Catholic Church's hold over the vast majority of its flock is tenuous at best. Few Brazilians attend Mass on a regular basis, are familiar with the Gospels or the Bible, or have contact with ordained bishops or priests.[1] Also, in many of the poorer and more rural areas of the country, Catholic rituals and dogma coexist with a strong devotion to the saints and a belief in miracles, exorcism, and witchcraft. Indeed, it could be argued that Catholicism became the dominant religion in Brazil only because it turned a blind eye to and incorporated various African and indigenous elements.[2]

Beginning in the 1960s, however, attempts were made to transform and modernize the Catholic Church in Brazil. There was less tolerance of magic and saintly devotions and an increased commitment to the poor and secular struggles for social justice and, in particular, human rights.[3] By the mid-1970s, the Catholic Church in Brazil was arguably the most progressive in the world and was at the forefront of efforts to denounce and bring an end to military rule. The Catholic Church in Brazil also played an important role in promoting agrarian reform, an independent labor movement, and Christian Base Communities. Christian Base Communities brought together small groups of poor lay Catholics to pray and to discuss a broad range of social and political issues. There is still no agreement as to the number of Christian Base Communities that existed in Brazil. In the late 1970s and early 1980s, however, they were widely considered key players in the process of democratization.[4]

By the late 1980s, popular participation in Christian Base Communities had fallen off precipitously. There were a number of reasons for this. First, the return to democracy shifted everyone's attention from new social movements and resistance to the military to political parties and competition over elections. Second, during the 1990s, priests and bishops who were associated with "liberation theology" found themselves increasingly isolated in what was fast becoming a more conservative Catholic Church.[5] And finally, while Christian Base Communities offered a radical critique of society, they failed to provide solutions or ways of dealing with poverty and, increasingly, violence at a personal and individual level.

The decline in the influence of the Catholic Church in the *favelas* was as sudden as it was dramatic. In the 1980s, the Catholic Church, via the Pastoral de Favelas, spearheaded attempts to organize and revitalize neighborhood associations in Rio and provided individual favelas with much needed political and legal assistance. By the mid-1990s, however, the Pastoral de Favelas was no longer a force. First, it lost important sources of international financial aid.[6] Second, it lost the support and backing of the Catholic Church hierarchy, who accused Pastoral agents of pursuing a political as opposed to religious agenda. Third, the Pastoral de Favelas lost its once secure grip on neighborhood associations as more and more drug gangs interfered with public life and eventually took over. And finally, the Catholic Church's position was increasingly challenged by other denominations. Thus, somewhat ironically, while the Catholic Church had, at long last, opted for the poor, the poor were opting in increasing numbers for religious alternatives and, in particular, Pentecostalism.

The first Pentecostal churches in Brazil, the Assembly of God and the Christian Congregation of Brazil, were founded at the beginning of the twentieth century by Swedish and Italian missionaries who came to the country via the United States. In both cases, the missionaries were expelled from protestant churches because of their belief in faith healing, miracles, and baptism in the Holy Spirit.[7] The third Pentecostal Church to be established in Brazil was the American Church of the Four-Square Gospel, in 1955. All three churches subsequently gave rise to various other denominations. The most important of these were the Church of Brazil for Christ, the Church of God Is Love, the Pentecostal Assembly of God Church, and the Church of the Universal Kingdom of God.[8]

All of the various Pentecostal churches in Brazil recruit heavily from among the poor and the disenfranchised.[9] The Pentecostal churches require absolute devotion and loyalty, even though they draw extensively from Catholic, Afro-Brazilian, and indigenous traditions. They also require that, in accordance with the Bible, the faithful donate one-tenth of their salary, or what is known as the *dízimo*. And finally, many Pentecostal churches, such as the Assembly of God and the Church of God Is Love, impose strict moral and aesthetic codes of conduct that govern speech, behavior, and dress.[10]

In return, all of the various Pentecostal churches in Brazil offer the possibility of faith healing, baptism in the Holy Spirit, and personal assistance with the problems of everyday life. This may mean coping with hunger and poverty, or reigning in a philandering husband, or curing someone of a sickness or a disease, such as cancer or, more likely, alcoholism. It may also mean getting someone to leave a life of violence and crime that, in Pentecostal circles, is seen as the work of evil spirits and the devil.[11]

The pastor at Lucia's house had various techniques at his disposal. On occasion, he would ask people to bring photographs of the ill and the afflicted to the front of the congregation to be blessed. On other occasions, he would reveal that someone in the audience was about to come into some money or was about to get a new job. Then he would wait until the person he had in mind raised his or her hand before the beneficiary of the prophecy was revealed. On still other occasions, he would produce a bottle of holy oil that he would use to bless people's foreheads and, if they had them, credit cards. And finally, he would banish evil spirits that occasionally possessed the members of his congregation.

At the end of each prayer meeting, the pastor would hand around small white envelopes on which were written the words "All or Nothing." There were no half measures when it came to Jesus, he explained. You had to give of yourself freely, without question. At first, I considered it madness that Lucia's mother and other members of her family gave 20 or 30 *Reais* when they struggled to put food on the table. But then, as Lucia's mother Conceição pointed out, "Who else am I to turn to? The authorities? The police!" And then there was the fact that the weekly prayer meetings gave Conceição and her predominately female friends the opportunity to speak out about personal issues and strengthen their resolve to resist temptation and to carry on their battle against all the evil in the world.[12]

Soon after her conversion, a few years back, Lucia's mother got rid of her lover, who would often stay over despite the presence of her disabled and estranged husband. By the time I left, however, he was back in her arms. Apparently, some sacrifices were harder to make than others.

CHAPTER 8

Getting Out

——After all the things I've seen. After all the things I've experienced these ten years in this world of *bandidos* . . . shoot-outs and drugs. I've seen a lot of things happen. Nowadays, I don't know and I don't want to know what's happening . . . but I've seen a lot. I've been really sad. I've seen many people I like die. So I wanted to change. Amanda was growing up and I was afraid of dying and leaving her without a father and a mother. That's when I began to go out and have fun and stay away from bandidos. I did everything I could not to get involved. I tried to get work. I was willing to do whatever, because I liked to buy new clothes. I've always liked to buy clothes . . . and shoes, and to have a little money,

you know? So, one day, I got down on my knees. I got down on my knees
on the ground and I asked God to send me someone who was not like the
others . . . to send me someone who would live with me . . . who would put
a stop to all this and live with me. And, I don't know why, but God sent
me this guy. So then I said to God, "Why didn't you send me someone
who had money, a house, and everything else?" But then, as it says in the
Bible, God knows everything . . . and he sent me this young man. But even
so, I wanted to leave, to let go of him . . . because I felt nothing for him.
He wasn't someone who, you know, attracted my attention. Because I've
always like *morenos* . . . you know, dark-skinned guys. I was used to a
certain kind of guy . . . but I didn't want any more bandidos. And then, he
gradually won me over because he's a person with a good heart. I felt
sorry for him and couldn't let him go because he had no one to visit him.
He didn't have any family. So then, little by little, I began to like him . . .
and the plans that he had all changed. When he was released . . . just
before he was released, he said to me that he wasn't going to live
here . . . in Jakeira. That he was going to go away and take me with him.
But I never wanted to leave my family . . . to be separated from my family.
Because I was afraid. Because so much had already happened. And that
was when he came here to visit me and my family. Because when he got
out he came straight here. But he never intended to stay here. But then
he stayed and stayed and he's still here today. But I've changed the way he
thinks a lot. Because he used to think completely differently. He used to
want to go out. When he was released from prison he told me that·he
wanted to go out, to have fun, and to take advantage of everything he
missed when he spent all those years in prison . . . because he lost
everything. But then, things happened real fast. Before we could even
think, I got pregnant. And then everything about his life changed . . .
unfortunately. Before, there were just us two and Amanda . . . who was
already grown up. Then came our daughter. And she made things really
difficult. Because we didn't have a house. We didn't have any money. And
we didn't have a job. Everything happened all at once.

———But Bruno tried to find work, right?

———He tried, but even so he's paying a price. In fact, he's paid more
than he ever owed. He spent his whole sentence in jail. He never got
parole.

———Why?

———Because they wouldn't give him parole.

——Because he was in the Army?

——I think so. I think that's why ... because all the other *traficantes* got it. They all got parole. But him? No. He was in there the whole time. He served seven years and a few extra days. And if it weren't for me and his lawyer I don't know what would have happened to him. Because when we went to court they said that his paperwork had already been sent to the prison ... you know, his release papers. But they didn't get there. So we went to the judge and we were treated very badly. And so Bruno's lawyer kept on insisting ... because if she hadn't kept on insisting, he might still be there today. Because there are a lot of people there who are just forgotten. People who have already served their sentences and are still there ... forgotten. I also think that they were trying to extort money from us, because he was jailed as a traficante ... a traficante. And because he was in the Army they thought he must have a lot of money hidden away. Because his papers were hidden underneath everything else. And, in another office in the same building, they told us that he'd been free for a week! And yet he was still there in prison! The whole situation was very difficult. Bruno was really nervous the whole time. He wanted to, you know, do whatever it took to get out. Because in there, they look for any excuse to keep you in longer. So I went there many times ... to tell Bruno to calm down so he could get out. And then, pretty soon after that, he was released.

——Is it still difficult for him to find work?

——It's really difficult because they always check his record. His records at the police station say that he's been in prison. And so, no one trusts him. And it's not written anywhere but the number on his identity card means that he's been inside. But he's still looking ... because the only way he can get a job is through someone who knows him, or if someone who is known recommends him. Then the person won't go and check up on him. Because when someone is recommended by someone else they don't check up on them.

——So what happened to the job at the motel that José found for him?

——They found out that he'd had a problem with the authorities ... and that his case had not been cleared. But I don't think they knew what it was. Because the boss there only asked if he'd had a problem with the authorities. So he lied and said yes ... that when he was in the Army he had run over a guy, you know, in his car ... but that the case hadn't gone anywhere. So he said that he'd run a guy over a long time ago but that the case had come to nothing but hadn't been cleared. He lied and told him this instead. He didn't tell him the truth ... to see if he could still get the job.

——So, even though José recommended him, he still had problems.

——Bruno's lawyer says that his case has already been cleared. But now he has to pay money to see if that's true. I told him to go there and see. But he's embarrassed to go back there. Because the guy said that if he resolved this problem he could go back. But after all this he felt embarrassed. He didn't want anything to do with it ... because in a hotel they check everything. His lawyer says that it's against the law ... that they can't do this. But they deal with money and jewelry there. They have to check things out. It's the same around here. A friend of mine told me that her husband works in the personnel department at a local hotel. And that if a guy from Jakeira looks for work there, they check him out as well. She says that they get together in the personnel department and decide whether they will give him a chance or not. And a lot of them are against it. They believe that if a person makes a mistake, they'll make a mistake again ... they don't trust them any more.

——So, it's a mark against them.

——Yes ... and it's forever.

——And, at the same time, he must know that there's money to be made on the other side.

——It seems like half the population's in prison ... because there are lots of overcrowded jails. And when these people get out, they are completely lost. They have no idea what goes on the outside ... because they are in prison you understand? All this time ... sure, they get to watch the news on TV. But when they get out ... on the street ... everything's different ... everything ... everything that they left behind. When they get out here, everything's different.

——How so?

——People ... places. They don't know where to start. They don't know how to look for work. They don't even know what to do in a store. It takes a person a while to stop and figure out what's going on ... to begin all over again. It's really difficult. People become afraid ... it's horrible. And then there are some that have no family and don't care about anything. They get out and become involved all over again. They get involved and do drugs all day and night. They don't even care. They take someone ... they kill them ... they cut them up ... they burn them ... as if it were nothing ... it's horrible. So he always gives advice to young guys around here. Bruno helped two guys who didn't have papers ... who didn't care about anything. Bruno always advises them, puts the idea in their heads that they should look for work ... or at least do something. But there are some that say, "Ah no. Why look for work if it pays minimum salary. That's not what I want. That's not what I want at all."

———But Bruno has been in trouble with the police, right?

———He was held by them for a few hours ... they wanted 100,000 *Reais*.

———Why? What happened?

———Because he was with this other guy who was involved. This other guy who was involved wasn't from Rio.

———So why was Bruno with him?

———Because ... he didn't know the guy. He met him through a friend of his in the Army who gave this guy his telephone number and told him to contact Bruno in Rio. He said, "There's a friend of mine in Rio. You should look him up." So that's what the guy did. And Bruno, not knowing him, tried to help him out. This guy was waiting for another guy who came with him. The friend of this guy had gone off to find the money to pay a guy for transporting the stuff he'd brought with him. So Bruno met him and told him, "Look, all I'm going to do is put you in contact with some people I know from there ... you know, from prison. Then you can go about your business." But then, when Bruno and this guy were waiting for the courier ... while they were waiting for the courier to bring the drugs, he'd already blown their cover. He got drunk ... the police caught him ... he told them everything. And so Bruno was with the other guy in a bar ... and then the police showed up and sat down next to them and told them to come outside, and to act as if they were friends, as if nothing had happened ... so people in the bar wouldn't notice. And then they drove around with them all over the place.

———What were they after?

———Money ... and Bruno didn't have any. The guy didn't have any money either. He wasn't even from here.

———Did Bruno call you?

———No, I called him. And I could tell that he was different ... that something was going on. Because he said he'd be home by seven ... and it was already ten and he hadn't come home. And he didn't usually come home late. So I began to worry and, unfortunately, I heard him say, "I'll be home in a little while." And then someone laughed. So I said to myself, "Something's happened." You know, because someone behind him was laughing. I thought, he's not coming home. Then he said, "Tell my children I love them." He never says that . . . because when he says that he says it to them in person. So why was he saying it over the telephone? So I thought, something's happening. So I said to him, "Is something going on?" And he said, "Yes." But he couldn't say anything because they were right there next to him.

——Couldn't they tell from the telephone where you were calling from?

——No. Because Bruno had set up the phone so the number of the person who called didn't appear. They wanted to find out the telephone number . . . but it didn't appear . . . not even Bruno's number. Listen, God did something. My grandmother got all my cousins and sisters together and we prayed all night. It was God's doing that they didn't find out the telephone number here . . . that they didn't find out our address. They didn't even find out Bruno's name. And the other guy didn't know anything either. He only knew that Bruno was from Rio. But he didn't know anything else. He didn't know where he lived. He didn't know his name. He called him *pretinho*. And Bruno didn't give them his name . . . and the telephone number that Bruno had given the guy was this one . . . it was a new number. But when the police started calling it, because they wanted more money, the number disappeared . . . it vanished! God does everything right. The number passed to another person. And so, when the police called, they didn't call Bruno . . . they called someone else because the number had been transferred to someone else . . . honest! When they started to call me I was desperate. I thought I was losing my mind. I was afraid they'd come here and kill everyone . . . that they'd keep after us . . . it was horrible.

——How did Bruno get away?

——They told him he could go.

——Without getting anything?

——What do you mean, without getting anything. They got the drugs. The truck was full. They don't take them back to the station. They keep them for themselves. They resell them in the *favelas*. They came away with a lot! Bruno got back here at four in the morning. He told me to call this person and that person . . . but I didn't manage to speak to anyone. So I said to Bruno that if they wanted to take him to the police station, he had to go. He was going to go to jail. I don't know for how long . . . but we'd figure something out. I would just have to visit him. And he was saying, "Lucia, don't tell me that I have to go!" I had no choice . . . there was no choice! We had no money . . . he would have to go! So me and his lawyer tried to figure out what to do. We didn't know if we should go to the authorities. Because if we reported it to the authorities he would go to jail. They would arrest all of them. The police would be arrested . . . they would be arrested . . . they'd all be arrested. And the guy who was with him was an officer in the military police. His wife didn't even imagine he was doing such things. It was horrible. I don't know if it was a weakness on his part . . . that he brought this stuff. I don't know if it was because he was experiencing certain difficulties. But you see how it is. I got to know him a little through Bruno. He was a very calm person. But he was really scared . . . he was terrified. All he wanted was to get out of here. All he talked about was his wife and kids. He was really upset about the whole thing. He couldn't even look at a police car . . . he was terrified. Bruno didn't hear from him after this. He only knew him for the few days he was here . . . during this whole mess. The police also knew nothing about Bruno. They didn't know his address . . . they didn't know anything . . . thank God. If not, we'd be persecuted until today . . . God help us . . . horrible.

———So, tell me about your decision to go back to work again . . . at the hair salon.

———I was looking to return to the job market. I'd been doing nothing for a long time . . . and I was having my own difficulties as well. Bruno was having trouble making money . . . to buy things for the kids. There were days when we didn't have any. So I wanted to find work so that at the end of the month I could buy things . . . so that Bruno wouldn't be so worried.

———Did you give anything to your mother?

———Every month. Every month . . . we had to give her something. But there are months when we don't have any. So we don't give her anything. But when Bruno . . . Bruno always manages to put together 50, 100 *Reais*. So he gives that to my mother to help with the shopping. But there really are months when we don't have anything . . . and we don't give anything. So then my brother-in-law helps out. My sister as well. Everyone gives a little for the shopping. So then I said to myself . . . I left my children with my mother so that I could help out with the house as well, you know? So I took on this new job. But it was the same old discrimination.

——What do you mean?

——Anyone who has more than one child right now has a difficult time finding a job with a *carteira assinada* . . . because they blame the family wage . . . which is 15 *Reais* . . . 15 *Reais* for each child. A family wage. The family wage is a wage, it's a percentage of a payment that they have to give for each employee's child. When an employee has more than one child, it gets to be more difficult. They claim that they can't afford the family wage.

——How much do they give you per month?

——15 *Reais*.

——In addition to your salary.

——That's right.

——So, if you earn a minimum salary, which is 180 *Reais* . . .

——You get 30. Fifteen more for each child.

——So they don't like employing women with children because it costs more.

——First of all, they claim "Ah, your children will get sick." You can't miss a day you see. They don't want to employ you because if a child gets sick the woman has to stay at home. That's the way they think. So I explained to her that my children stayed with my mother and that there would be no problem . . . and that they were very healthy . . . that they were covered by a health plan.[1] So, she said, "Ah, so there really isn't a problem. And you really won't miss work." And I said, "No, no. I won't miss work." I talked to the owner about it. I went down there to talk to her . . . you know, the owner of the salon.

——So, did she pay the 30 *Reais*?

——No.

——But it's compulsory. It's the law. You have to pay, right?

——Well, she didn't pay. The first thing she said to me was . . . I told her that I really needed the job, that I had these kids. So then she claimed that she didn't have the money to pay the family wage.

——You mean, either you work without benefits or you don't work at all.

——I really needed the work . . . I couldn't. So I forgot about the extra payment. I told her that I had no problem if she didn't pay me . . . because I didn't need it . . . because I would lose . . . I would lose the chance to work. I would lose the family wage, which was 30 Reais, or I would lose the job.

——**How many days did you work?**

——From Tuesday to Saturday.

——**From nine to five?**

——From eight until seven.

——**How much were you paid?**

——My salary was 180 *Reais*. I earned 200 *Reais* because I cleaned for her on Mondays. I told her that I wouldn't do it for free because Monday was my day off . . . it was my day to stay at home. And most salons hire a cleaner from the outside. They have nothing to do with the salon, you understand? So she gave me 20 *Reais*. So I earned 200 *Reais*. But she claimed she couldn't afford the family wage, which was this other 30 *Reais*.

——**So then you only had one day off . . . which was Sunday.**

——Yes, just Sunday . . . and it goes by real fast. I worked a lot. I didn't stop. Only at lunch. I had to bring my lunch from home, you know. There was a little oven there. We used to heat up our lunch . . . rice . . . beans . . . meat. I put it in a plastic bag and took it with me. And after this . . . we had one hour for lunch. Afterwards I had to go downstairs to clean up. The hairdressers there were really lazy. Many times . . . there were these basins for washing hair and they would spill over or something. They let water run all over the floor. So I had to run around with a cloth cleaning everything up. I asked them not to fill the basins but they did and, after a while, I'd have to come down and clean up all over again. I had to keep my eye on the bathroom. I had to clean it and fold the towels . . . take out the dirty towels to be sent for cleaning . . . fold things up and separate them . . . hang them out to dry.

——**So what was your job?**

——Everything!

——**Whatever there was to do.**

——Serve coffee, water, run errands for the clients . . . do everything. It was really tiring because the coffee was made upstairs. And, when I finished serving someone, another one wanted it. I asked everyone and no

one wanted any. Then one would ask for one, and I would go and make a
cafezinho and put it on a tray with sugar and everything . . . and sweetener.
I would serve it and come downstairs and another person would want it.
So I'd climb up the stairs all over again. Then I'd come down and someone
else would want it. I spent my time going up and down all day . . .
and I had to keep my eye on the bathroom the whole time because the
bucket for the toilet paper would fill up, and I'd have to deal with it. It
was a very small bucket you see . . . and I'd have to change it the whole
time.[2] Or I'd have to check to see if the bathroom was wet . . . if
something was dirty, if there was no paper, if there was no soap. And I had
to keep checking the towels. Or I'd have to call the owner's husband to
bring more towels. Because we couldn't go without. If we went without it
would be my fault. The whole thing was crazy . . . crazy. And so I felt really
tired the whole time. And that's when the girls there started to say, "For
the love of God Lucia." Because there were people there who did
nothing. There were some ugly black hairdressers' assistants who, I
suspect, earned lots of money. And then there was me, working really
hard and earning nothing . . . earning nothing. Because they were friends,
you know? They became friends with one of the hairdressers who made
them their assistants. And me, who had the good looks . . . who had the
ability . . . who had worked in a salon . . . serving coffee! Not for me. So
then the girls said, "Lucia, why don't you take a course . . . you are such a
nice person . . . educated and all that. If not, you'll waste your time making
nothing." Because they all earned well. A manicurist only does nails . . .
only does nails and earns between 500 and 600 *Reais*. And then there's
the owner of the salon making all this money and complaining that she
doesn't have any. I couldn't do it any more. It's always like this . . . and she
still claimed she had no money. That woman was blind. But it opened my
eyes! And I got even more upset when the girls said to me, "Ah Lucia,
don't worry about it." Then the owner of the salon saw that they liked
me . . . because we were all talking upstairs. So then the girls said, "Lucia,
we have to go down now." Because they were also employees . . . she
signed their carteiras too. They had to work too. They weren't as
pressured as me . . . because they made money for the salon. I cost money,
because I was a simple employee. So they could sit down. They could sit
around and chat. No problem. But I couldn't. So they said, "Lucia, you
know how it is. In most salons the hairdressers and people like that don't

talk to the help." That got me really mad. Because in the salon I worked in there was never this kind of discrimination ... and it was a really chic salon ... and I earned a lot more money ... and the hairdressers were great with me. They gave me presents. I went out to buy things for them for lunch and they paid for things for me. I didn't feel inferior ... I felt normal. But in this other, very small salon, it was very different. There was less of everything. The quality wasn't as good. It was like this ... so they told me that in most salons the hairdressers and other people, and not even the owners spoke to the help. I was really mad. I never imagined that such a thing could happen. And so I looked around and said to the owner, "No thanks. I won't put up with this." I said, "I won't put up with this kind of humiliation ever again." I've done everything I can to sign on for this course. And when I come back to the salon, everything's going to be different (sobbing). It was because I was so desperate that I did everything. I had to do all these things. She knew that I needed the work. She thought that I wouldn't leave, that I wouldn't give up the job. And so she made me do everything. So then I talked to her straight. I told her that I was going to do this course ... to see if she would change my hours so that I could leave. But not even that. She got annoyed. She was mad ... because she had paid a 7 *Reais* fee when I started work ... to, you know, check out my health. So then, when I spoke with her about doing this course, I said, "Dona Maria, I'm going to take this course so I can improve myself. So I can make a little bit more. The money that I'm making here doesn't do." And she said, "But you told me that you really needed the work. How could you do this? After I had agreed to sign your carteira. How could you do a thing like this?" So then I said, "No Dona Maria, I'm going to have to do this course because the money's not enough for me." And so she got mad.

——So, she wanted you to stay for the same money.

——She wouldn't give me a raise. She paid me a base salary of 200 or 210 *Reais* and she wouldn't give me the family wage. I discussed it with her and she said, "If you're not satisfied, then stay at home." So I said to her, "Making the worthless amount of money you're giving me, I'd prefer to stay at home. I'd make more at home ... because I wouldn't spend money on bus fares ... I wouldn't go out ... I wouldn't spend money on food. I'd look after my children." So she said, "Okay then, go." I spoke to her that way because I had to. I was one day away from working for a month. So I said to her, "So, Dona Maria, I'll be here tomorrow," so she wouldn't deduct it. So then she got mad and said, "You don't need to come tomorrow. I'll deduct a day's pay." So I said, "Very well. Go ahead and deduct it." I know that in the end she deducted it. So then I went over my account again with the manager and said to her, "No. She has to give me this much." And the manager said, "Ah, but Lucia, she has only left you this much." And so I said, "Look, I'm going to get my 20 *Reais* because it's worth a packet of diapers for my daughter. I'm not going to leave it for her. I worked for it. I want my money." So the manager said, "Okay, then we'll wait for her." So I said, "Okay, we'll wait for her." So then they went over the account again and again and again. And, in the end, my calculations didn't come out right . . . but neither did hers. But, in spite of all this, I was still going to make some money. She calculated that she had to give me 12 *Reais*. I calculated that she had to give me 20 *Reais*. So then she said, "Look my child, I may be bad at some things but I'm excellent with numbers." So I said, "Of course your excellent with numbers because you are going to give me less." You see, she was still trying to make money off of me. "You are excellent with numbers but I still won't let you have my 20 *Reais*. Because 20 *Reais* will buy diapers for my daughter." So I took the money and the girls said to me, "Ah Lucia, don't argue with her. Don't argue with her. Leave it alone." So I said, "No. No I won't leave it alone." And then I said to her, "Dona Maria, God's watching you. God's watching everything" (crying).

———So then you went and did the course and really liked it, right?

———I liked it. I liked the course a lot . . . and I intend to do another. And now when I work in a salon it will be totally different. I will be able to do everything. Like the other girls. You know . . . like normal. Because I will be making money. I won't be costing anyone money. And I will be treated the same way as all the others . . . like all the others who were there. They all told me what it was like at first. But they put up with it, you understand. Me no. Me no. My temperament is very different. I wouldn't accept it.

———It's important for you to be treated as an equal, isn't it?

———Everybody's the same. Dona Maria used to live in a public housing project. She used to work around there too. She was just a manicurist . . . and today she is the owner of a salon. But she doesn't look back. She doesn't like to remember how things were before . . . the difficulties she had . . . the humiliations. She's forgotten everything . . .

everything. She used to work in a very well-known salon around here. And, after that, she put together some money . . . after a lot of difficulty. She opened a salon and the salon has done well. Because she's the owner. So she's getting on well. But in compensation . . . she's done well in her life as an entrepreneur. But with her children, she hasn't had the same luck. She pays for her daughter to go to a very expensive college. I know because I went there to take her daughter some clothes . . . a really expensive college. She had already taken her daughter out from another college because she was involved with drugs. Her daughter doesn't respect her. She doesn't respect her at all. She hates her. She calls her names behind her back. I've heard her daughter many times say bad things about her to the other hairdressers . . . saying that she's going to do the opposite of what her mother tells her. You know, that she's going to serve the devil because her mother goes to church. And she says that she's against everything, you understand. She doesn't have a happy household. Her son is already rebellious. He doesn't want to go to school anymore. And he must be, you know, fourteen or fifteen . . . and he has everything. His mother had nothing, you understand? But her children already have everything . . . and they're like, rebelling against her. The youngest doesn't go to school anymore. He also studies at an expensive school that his mother pays for. He doesn't want to go to school . . . and she's getting thinner and thinner. She doesn't eat . . . she can't eat. She's a super stressed-out person. And so, she takes her anger out on her employees. It's true. So she pays for it in this way. Her children are terrible. They don't help or anything. The man who lives with her isn't her children's father. He came here one day crying because her son had robbed him of everything. But he said he couldn't say anything because the mother didn't like it. It's all very odd. Remember that store you went to . . . that store owner was super chic. She owned the store and lived in an apartment in town. And she's a very unassuming person. She invited me to spend Christmas at her house. She bought things for Amanda. She was very different. She could have been . . . she could have been, you know. But she wasn't. She was very different.

———So it depends on the person.

———She brought me home. Every day, after work, she brought me back here in her imported car. She was a wonderful person. Very different. And these people who come from nothing forget the past (crying).

——And then?

——So this was my experience. I tried taking the course so I could specialize . . . and by the end of the year I hope to be working.

——**And, looking back on this period of . . .**

——Ten years.

——**What do you make of the whole experience?**

——I lost a lot of time . . . back then. But I've learned a lot in this life . . . I've learned a lot . . . a lot of things that I can pass on to someone. And I'm not sorry that I've done all this. I'm not sorry about anything. Now I am . . . I have a different perspective now. Because before I wasn't scared of anything. Now I'm scared of getting involved.

——**And of Bruno getting involved.**

——Especially Bruno. There's no way I'll let him . . . I'm always with him. If he goes out and stays away for twenty minutes, I go after him. I bring him back to the house. I won't let him . . . there's no way. And he too . . . his mind. He never meant to, you know, become involved . . . you know, as a traficante . . . to be a bandido and all that. He was never like that. So he sees that this life is not for him. Because he's a guy who likes to go out . . . to travel and everything. Because it's not easy for those who are part of this life. So I know he won't . . . even if he needs the money. Because many get involved because of the money, you understand?

——**So it's better to be without than to go down that path again.**

——It's much better . . . a thousand times better. And now that I have another child, I don't want it. I always want to show her good things so she doesn't have that perspective on life. It's the same for Amanda. There are many girls her age who are already involved. But Amanda has few friends. I don't let her hang out on the street . . . I don't let her. She doesn't wander about. She doesn't do any of these things. Only when it's with family . . . with my sister . . . or with her cousin, you understand. But she already knows about the world. She always says . . . she sees what goes on. She grew up seeing almost everything. So I always say to her . . . she sees these young girls getting involved. I always say, "In a little while, they'll have large bellies. They'll be out on the street. You have to study, study a lot if you want to be someone." Because you see . . . I didn't study and I'm here . . . unemployed (crying). I can't buy anything. But I know that all is not lost . . . all is not lost. Because now I have the will to learn everything . . . I will do better.

——Start all over again, right?

——Yes . . . start all over again . . . all is not lost. But I always say to her, "Look, if you don't study you'll be like me. Do you understand? You'll be nobody. You'll be nobody. So you have to study . . . as hard as you can . . . learn about computers . . . learn English . . . everything." Because as time passes things only get worse. They ask more and more of you . . . more and more. And whoever doesn't have it, stays behind . . . always behind. And she never, you know . . . she's a child. She plays. She doesn't have that . . . she doesn't ask for designer clothes . . . none of those things. Whatever I buy for her . . . there's never a problem, thank God. She doesn't have that greed for things that I had . . . she really doesn't. And I try not to talk about her father. I never talk about him.

——So, for her, he doesn't exist.

——He exists . . . but my father is her father. She knows that she had a father who died. But I never remind her of this, you understand. And she forgets . . . she forgets. I don't put such things in her head.

——And because of what you've been through, do you put more faith in God?

——Not really . . . but I have a certain perspective. After all the things that have happened to me . . . after all the things that have happened. I believe in God more because I am alive today. I saw all those who were by my side die. There are few people left who can tell this story . . . very few. So, if I was there with them and I am here today to tell this story, I believe that it was God. And I believe that I had to go through all this. I somehow had to go through all this. Because when your destiny is written, it has to happen. And I think that this was mine . . . it was written.

LAST CALL

I CALLED LUCIA two weeks before my last research trip to the field in March 2002. Things were not good, she told me. Bruno was in jail, again, in Brasília. I asked her what had happened. In tears, she told me that he had been arrested because the car he was driving was stolen. "What was he doing driving a stolen car?" I asked. She said that he did not know it was stolen. There were other surprises. As I reached Lucia's front gate, I could not help noticing that an addition had been made to the house. Rising above me was a three-room apartment that Bruno and Lucia had had built. It was not finished. But the walls and roof were in place and you could already imagine where things went. "How did you pay for all this?" I inquired. "Oh, we put together some money," responded Lucia, casually. "How much did it cost?" "Oh, about 3,000 *Reais*." "And when will it be finished?" "Bruno was driving a Jeep from Rio to a dealership in Brasília, for 2,000 *Reais*. We were going to use the money to pay someone to finish it. But the car he was driving was stolen. He didn't realize it, honest! I told him not to go but he said that his friend had shown him the papers and that everything checked out okay." "Have you called Bruno's friend?" I asked. "Yes, but he claims he didn't know either ... but of course he knew," she complained disconsolately.[1]

Bruno was being held at a police station on the outskirts of Brasília for handling stolen goods. He had told the police he was innocent. He claimed he would not have taken the main road if he had known the car was stolen. He was going to be released once Lucia came up with the 2,000 *Reais* fee.[2] This was the exact amount that he was going to make by doing the job in the first place. Lucia had already visited him at the police station. She had finished her training courses but had not gotten a job. Instead, she was working off the books as a maid in an elderly woman's apartment three days a week. She earned as much money there as she would in a hairdressing salon and got to spend more time with her kids. It also meant that when she had the money she could take the bus Friday night and spend Saturday

day and Saturday night with Bruno. She returned home early the next day. According to Lucia, Bruno was beside himself.

I could not help thinking that Bruno had been dealing again. There was no other explanation for the addition to the house. I became angry and upset. I had so much wanted to believe that Bruno and Lucia were going straight. But then, sitting in the comfort of my air-conditioned hotel room, I thought, Who am I to judge? How could I possibly know what it was they were going through? And how could I possibly know who was wrong and who was right in this situation? There are no certainties, no guarantees in the world in which they live. It is far more complicated than that. What would I do if I were in their shoes? I can honestly say that I do not know. How could I know?

Apart from this, things in general were much the same. The house was full of unattended and screaming kids. Diago, who was now back from Fortaleza, continued to do drugs and run up debts that taxed the family's already meager budget. And young men continued to die. In September, I was inspecting the work that had been done on Camilla's apartment since my last visit when a window opened behind me and a ball of spit landed at my feet. I was about to say something but thought better of it. I was told later that it was a *bandido*, a boy of fourteen years of age who had recently joined up. We were making too much noise and disturbing his morning sleep, so it was his way of telling us to shut up. By March he was already dead. At the hands of the police, of course.

Oh yes, there was one other piece of news. Amanda had failed her grade and was being told to repeat. Apparently, the school she attended, which was not in Jakeira, took education seriously and refused to pass along those who were not ready. I sat there on my last day watching Amanda watching her mother remove hair from a friend's legs. I wondered what would become of her, and I was overcome by an overwhelming sense of sadness.

EPILOGUE

O N APRIL 9, 2004, an army of about sixty heavily armed *traficantes* launched an attack on Rocinha, the largest *favela* in Rio, which is located in the heart of a wealthy residential district in Zona Sul. The attack marked an attempt by the Comando Vermelho to regain control of the favela on behalf of its former *dono*. The dono had been serving time for nine years for homicide and drug trafficking. On January 12, however, he was granted permission by a judge to spend his daytime hours with family. So, five days later, he walked out of the prison and never came back. According to practice, donos who are released, or who manage to escape from prison, are entitled to reassume control of their favelas. In this case, the dono who had taken his place in Rocinha refused. Everyone knew that an attack was imminent.[1] The authorities, however, were powerless to do anything about it, demonstrating once again that they had lost control of whole areas of the city, and once again prompting calls for the occupation of Rio's favelas by Brazil's armed forces.[2]

The decision by the dono of Rocinha to disobey orders, and the subsequent attempt by the Comando Vermelho to reassert its authority, are symptomatic of a more generalized crisis facing prison-based criminal organizations. Over the past two years, the state government in Rio has made a concerted effort to break the power of such organizations by placing their leaders in strict isolation, cutting back on visitation rights and other privileges, and acting to prevent messages from getting in and orders from reaching the outside.[3] These measures have made it far more difficult for inmates to manage the drug trade. Consequently, the measures themselves have met with fierce resistance in the form of prison riots and waves of coordinated attacks on public buses, government buildings, and the police, and the assassination of prison officials and employees.[4] More significantly, perhaps, the crackdown on prison-based criminal organizations has sparked a new round of territorial disputes for control of Rio's favelas and has led to the emergence of a new generation of drug dealers who are younger, less disciplined, less accountable, and far more violent, both in their dealings with the police and with members of their own communities.

The change in the situation in Jakeira has been dramatic. My friends no longer go out after dark unless they absolutely have to. They know that once the sun goes down the streets are patrolled by traficantes who flaunt their authority, who make no effort to hide their sophisticated and high-powered weaponry, and who are increasingly from other favelas. They also know that at any point, during the day or night, their houses can be commandeered as positions from which to shoot at the police or as places for traficantes to sleep.[5] And, while they also know from experience that periods of violence and relative calm are cyclical, my friends are talking seriously, for the first time, about selling up and moving out to one of a handful of communities that have the reputation of being drug free because of the presence of locally organized vigilante groups, often involving retired policemen, known as *polícia mineira*.

The authorities in Rio have reacted to this situation by calling in the military, recruiting more police, and attempting to suffocate and shut down the drug trade by surrounding and occasionally occupying favelas.[6] The problem remains, however, that the police are not to be trusted. In May 2003, former governor and presidential hopeful Antonio Garotinho assumed the position of state secretary for public security in Rio and pledged to reduce violent crime that, in his own words, was "out of control."[7] A few months later, however, he was forced to admit publicly that his efforts were being undermined by widespread police involvement in crime and corruption.[8] Unfortunately, despite the large number of legal proceedings that have subsequently been brought against the police, it has proven extremely difficult to purge criminal and corrupt elements.[9]

The other problem remains police violence. While homicide rates for Rio, in general, have been on the decline for the past four years, the number of civilians killed by the police in so-called acts of self-defense has almost tripled.[10] In 2000, for example, the police in Rio killed 427 civilians. In 2003, however, the police killed a staggering 1,195 civilians.[11] Of course, the police claim that they are only killing drug dealers and those who "deserve to die."[12] In reality, however, attempts to wage urban warfare and to root out insurgents have come at a high cost to a civilian population that has turned more and more against the police. The only good sign, once again, is the changing attitude of the state authorities in Rio who now recognize that police violence and homicide are serious issues. The problem is still one of impunity, however, and the fact that, despite recent changes to the criminal justice system, it is difficult to convict the police for human rights violations.[13]

Of course, let us not forget that the reason for the assault on Rocinha was the millions of dollars in potential drug revenues. The federal police in Brazil intercept a larger volume of drugs each year.[14] This includes not only cocaine and marijuana, which have been staples of the drug trade in the favelas for decades, but also LSD, ecstasy, and, more recently, heroin.[15] Not all of these drugs are distributed to and sold from the favelas. In fact, there is evidence that because of violence, more and more *bocas de fumo* are being established in wealthy residential areas in Rio where the price that can be charged for drugs is higher. Rocinha was a target precisely because it was known as a relatively peaceful favela where consumers could come and go at their pleasure. In other favelas, like Jakeira, violence—or the fear of violence—has driven consumers away and has prompted the drug gang to become involved in other moneymaking activities.[16]

Finally, let us also not forget the issues of unemployment and poverty. On January 1, 2003, President Luiz Inácio Lula da Silva took office amidst much fanfare and hope that, finally, the day of the common man and woman on the street had come. To the dismay and deep disappointment of most of my friends, however, the Partido dos Trabalhadores has failed to deliver on its promise to embrace a new economic model that creates jobs that pay decent wages and provide social protection. Until that happens, I am afraid, there will be a long line of increasingly alienated and angry young men and women who refuse to endure conditions of slave labor and who will be seduced by the—albeit short-lived—power and status associated with drug gang life.

Perhaps the only bright spot in all this are the stirrings of various civic groups and NGOs in favor of peace. Over the course of the past few years, organizations such as Viva Rio, for example, have been developing programs that provide alternatives for underprivileged youth, and, among other things, human rights training for the police.[17] Under certain circumstances, the combined action of civic groups and NGOs can create public spaces that are safe and are not dominated by drug gang elements, just as they did in the late 1970s and early 1980s.[18] The problem is that they have little impact on or control over the broader social and economic factors that really need to change.

A few days after the assault on Rocinha, Viva Rio led a group of volunteers, including a few celebrities, on a visit to express love and affection for the residents of the embattled favela. Wearing t-shirts emblazoned with the logo "People make peace," the group of 200 or so made their way around the community for two hours handing out flowers and plastic clown noses and vampire teeth for children. They were met with the sound of gunfire from a shoot-out that took the life of a traficante and wounded two policemen. They were also met by a group of local residents carrying signs asking for education, jobs, and an income. It was as the president of the neighborhood association in Rocinha said: "What good is love and affection? Without work and an income, the violence will continue."[19]

Notes

Foreword

1. Kathleen Logan, "Personal Testimony: Latin American Women Telling Their Lives," *Latin American Research Review* 32, no. 1 (1997): 200.
2. For example, see the novel by Richard Price, *Clockers* (New York: Houghton Mifflin, 1992) and the sociological study of Douglas S. Massey and Nancy A. Denton, *American Apartheid. Segregation and the Making of the Underclass* (Cambridge: Harvard University Press, 1993).
3. See Arturo Arias, editor, *The Rigoberta Menchú Controversy* (Minneapolis: University of Minnesota Press, 2001).
4. Daphne Patai, "Introduction," p. 6 in Daphne Patai, editor and translator, *Brazilian Women Speak. Contemporary Life Stories* (New Brunswick: Rutgers University Press, 1988).
5. Ibid., 8, 18.
6. Robert M. Levine, "The Cautionary Tale of Carolina Maria de Jesus," *Latin American Research Review* 29, no. 1 (1994): 55.
7. Ibid., 60. For the English-language edition, see Carolina Maria de Jesus, *Child of the Dark: The Diary of Carolina Maria de Jesus*, trans. David St. Clair (New York: New American Library, 1962).
8. Publications associated with Robert M. Levine can provide English-language readers ample exposure to Carolina's life and works. In addition to "The Cautionary Tale of Carolina Maria de Jesus" cited above, see Robert M. Levine and

José Carlos Sebe Bom Meihy, *The Life and Death of Carolina Maria de Jesus* (Albuquerque: University of New Mexico Press, 1995); Carolina Maria de Jesus, *I'm Going to Have a Little House: The Second Diary of Carolina Maria de Jesus*, trans. Melvin S. Arrington, Jr. and Robert M. Levine (Lincoln: University of Nebraska Press, 1997); Carolina Maria de Jesus, *Bitita's Diary: The Childhood Memoirs of Carolina Maria de Jesus*, ed. Robert M. Levine; trans. Emanuelle Oliveira and Beth Joan Vinkler (Armonk, NY: M. E. Sharpe, 1998); and Carolina Maria de Jesus, *The Unedited Diaries of Carolina Maria de Jesus*, eds. Robert M. Levine and José Carlos Sebe Bom Meihy, trans. Nancy P. S. Naro and Cristina Mehrtens (New Brunswick: Rutgers University Press, 1999).

9. Levine, "The Cautionary Tale of Carolina Maria de Jesus," 80.

10. Bill D. Moyers, "An Interview with Chinua Achebe," p. 336 in Betty S. Flowers, editor, *A World of Ideas* (New York: Doubleday, 1989).

11. José Luis Romero, *Latin America. Its Cities and Ideas* (Washington: Organization of American States, 1999), pp. 3, 255.

12. Jorge Balán, "Introduction," p. 2 in Susana Rotker ed. in collaboration with Katherine Goldman, *Citizens of Fear. Urban Violence in Latin America* (New Brunswick: Rutgers University Press, 2002).

13. James W. Wilkie, *Statistical Abstract of Latin America*, vol. 20 (Los Angeles: UCLA Latin American Center, 1980), p. 77; United Nations, Economic Commission for Latin America and the Caribbean, *Statistical Yearbook for Latin America and the Caribbean, 2003* (New York, 2004), 12, http://www.cepal.org (June 2004).

14. Population estimates of metropolitan areas and their world rankings vary. These figures come from http://www.mongabay.com/igapo/Brazil.htm (June 2004).

15. Thomas H. Holloway, *Policing Rio de Janeiro: Repression and Resistance in a Nineteenth-Century City* (Stanford: Stanford University Press, 1993), p. 6.

16. Jeffrey D. Needell, *A Tropical Belle Epoque: Elite Culture and Society in Turn-of-the-Century Rio de Janeiro* (New York: Cambridge University Press, 1988), pp. 49–50. See also Sandra Lauderdale Graham, *House and Street: The Domestic World of Servants and Masters in Nineteenth-Century Rio de Janeiro* (New York: Cambridge University Press, 1988), and Mary C. Karasch, *Slave Life in Rio de Janeiro, 1808–1850* (Princeton: University Press, 1987).

17. Julio César Pino, *Family and Favela. The Reproduction of Poverty in Rio de Janeiro* (Westport, CT: Greenwood Press, 1997), p. 338.

18. Alan Gilbert, *The Latin American City* (London: Latin America Bureau, 1994), p. 28.

19. Cathy A. Rakowski, "Introduction: What Debate?" p. 4 in Cathy A. Rakowski, editor, *Contrapunto. The Informal Sector Debate in Latin America* (Albany: State University Press of New York, 1994).

20. Janice E. Perlman, *The Myth of Marginality. Urban Poverty and Politics in Rio de Janeiro* (Berkeley: University of California Press, 1976), pp. 242–43. See also Pino, 47–57.

21. See Chapter 2 and also Robert Gay, *Popular Organization and Democracy in Rio de Janeiro. A Tale of Two Favelas* (Philadelphia: Temple University Press, 1994).

22. Inter-American Dialogue, *Against the Odds. Democracy in Latin America* (Washington, DC: 2004), 1, http://www.thedialogue.org (June 2004).

23. Inter-American Dialogue, *The Troubled Americas* (Washington, DC: 2003), 17, http://www.thedialogue.org (June 2004).

24. United States Government, Department of Health and Human Services, Centers for Disease Control and Prevention, *Morbidity and Mortality Weekly Report* 53, no. 8 (5 March 2004): 169.

25. Donna M. Goldstein, *Laughter Out of Place. Race, Class, Violence, and Sexuality in a Rio Shantytown* (Berkeley: University of California Press, 2003), p. 2.

26. See Robert N. Gwen and Cristóbal Kay, "Latin America Transformed: Changing Paradigms, Debates, and Alternatives," pp. 12–13 in Robert N. Gwynne and Cristóbal Kay, editors, *Latin America Transformed. Globalization and Modernity* (London: Arnold, 1999).

27. Alejandro Portes and Kelly Hoffman, "Latin American Class Structures: Their Composition and Change During the Neoliberal Era," *Latin American Research Review* 38, no. 1 (2003): 75.

28. See Paul B. Stares, *Global Habit. The Drug Problem in a Borderless World* (Washington, DC: Brookings Institution, 1996).

29. Frank O. Mora, "Victims of the Balloon Effect: Drug Trafficking and US Policy in Brazil and the Southern Cone of Latin America," *The Journal of Social, Political, and Economic Studies* 21, no. 2 (1996): 121, 140.

30. See Alba Zaluar, "Perverse Integration: Drug Trafficking and Youth in the Favelas of Rio de Janeiro," *Journal of International Affairs* 53, no. 2 (2000): 653–71.

31. Goldstein, 217.

32. See Jere R. Behrman, Alejandro Gaviria, and Miguel Székely, editors, *Who's In and Who's Out. Social Exclusion in Latin America* (Washington, DC: Inter-American Development Bank, 2003) and the World Bank Urban Poverty page, http://www.worldbank.org/urban/poverty/ (June 2004).

33. Sylvia Chant with Nikki Craske, *Gender in Latin America* (New Brunswick: Rutgers University Press, 2003), pp. 204–8.

34. Enrique Desmond Arias, "Faith in Our Neighbors: Networks and Social Order in Three Brazilian Favelas," *Latin American Politics and Society* 46, vol. 1 (Spring 2004): 2, 8.

35. On Viva Rio's computer program, see Inter-American Foundation, "Capitalizing on Communications and Technology in the Favelas of Rio de Janeiro," http://www.iaf.gov/grants/downloads/vivari_oeng.pdf.pdf (June 2004). See also Maria Helena Moreira Alves, "The Socio-Political Dimension of Human Security: A Latin American Perspective," The World Bank Seminar on Viva Rio, 26 February 2004, http://www.nd.edu/~kellogg/calendar/pdfs/malves.pdf (June 2004).

Introduction

1. Igreja Pentecostal Deus É Amor.
2. Of course, I realize that in light of recent critiques of the ethnographic tradition there will be those who consider this project problematic. I agree with Donna Goldstein, however, in that I would "hate to see us abandon our work with less privileged groups and, in the spurious hope of avoiding the pitfalls of writing about those groups, devote ourselves only to the study of elites, or cosmopolitan intellectuals, or transnational social movements." Donna Goldstein, *Laughter out of Place: Race, Class, Violence, and Sexuality in a Rio Shantytown* (Berkeley: University of California Press, 2003), p. 43.
3. There is no standard definition of violent crime in Brazil. The legal definition, however, includes homicide, attempted homicide, robbery, harmful bodily injury, rape, and attempted rape.
4. The homicide rate in Brazil increased 130 percent, from 11.7 per 100,000 inhabitants in 1980 to 27 per 100,000 in 2000. This increase is greater than for any other country in Latin America. For comparative statistics see, Alberto Conchman-Eastman, "Urban Violence in Latin America and the Caribbean: Dimensions, Explanations, Actions," pp. 37–54 in Susana Rotker, editor, *Citizens of Fear: Urban Violence in Latin America* (New Brunswick: Rutgers University Press, 2002).
5. The highest homicide rates in 2000 were recorded in the states of Pernambuco (54 per 100,000), Rio de Janeiro (51), Espírito Santo (46), and São Paulo (42). And from 1991 to 2000, the mortality rate for homicides committed with firearms for men between the ages of fifteen and twenty-four in Brazil increased 95 percent. Instituto Brasileiro de Geografia e Estatística (IBGE), "Síntese de Indicadores Sociais 2003."
6. According to the Instituto de Pesquisa Econômico Aplicada (IPEA), 53 million Brazilians lived below the poverty line in 2002. This means that they could not cover the basic costs of food, housing, clothing, and transportation. IPEA also estimates that 23 million Brazilians survive what can only be described as miserable conditions, in that they cannot afford a basic diet of 2,000 calories per day. *Veja*, January 23, 2002: 84.
7. For trends in poverty and inequality in Latin America in the 1980s and 1990s, see Roberto Korzeniewicz and William Smith, "Poverty, Inequality, and Growth in Latin America: Searching for the High Road to Globalization," *Latin American Research Review* 35(3)(2000): 7–54; and Alejandro Portes and Kelly Hoffman, "Latin American Class Structures: Their Composition and Change During the Neoliberal Era," *Latin American Research Review* 38(1)(2003): 9–40.
8. Having said this, marijuana is grown fairly extensively in the Northeast and the country has become an important exporter of precursor chemicals for illegal drug manufacture.
9. According to some estimates, the "Atlantic route" through Brazil, Venezuela, and Guyana now accounts for half of the cocaine leaving Colombia. *Financial Times*, October 31, 2003. For the origins of the drug trade in Brazil, see Christian

Geffray, "Social, Economic and Political Impacts of Drug Trafficking in the State of Rondônia, in the Brazilian Amazon," pp. 90–109 in *Globalisation, Drugs and Criminalisation* (MOST/UNESCO, 2002).

10. The Federal Police estimates that 20 percent of the cocaine that passes through the city of Rio is sold locally. NEPAD and CLAVES (UERJ/FIOCRUZ), "Estudo Global Sobre O Mercado Ilegal de Drogas no Rio de Janeiro," October 2000.

11. It is often claimed that the drug problem in Brazil is confined to what is referred to as the "White Republic" of Rio. There is evidence, however, that, in terms of sheer volume, São Paulo is the larger market. There are significant differences between the two. The market in Rio is dominated by cocaine, as opposed to crack cocaine, and is far more organized and violent. For the case of São Paulo, see Guaracy Mingardi and Sandra Goulart, "Drug Trafficking in an Urban Area: The Case of São Paulo," pp. 92–118 in *Globalisation, Drugs and Criminalisation* (MOST/UNESCO, 2002).

12. In its annual report on international narcotics, the U.S. Department of State recognizes that "There is currently no widely available, easily renewable commodity more lucrative than illegal drugs. In most cases, they are relatively cheap to produce and offer enormous profit margins that allow the drug trade to generate criminal revenues on a scale without historical precedent. For example, assuming an average U.S. retail street price of $100 dollars a gram, a metric ton of pure cocaine is worth $100 million on the streets of the United States; twice as much if the drug is cut with additives. By this measure, the 100 or so metric tons of cocaine that the USG (U.S. Government) typically seizes each year could theoretically be worth as much as $10 billion to the drug trade—more than the gross domestic product of some countries." U.S. Department of State, *International Narcotics Control Strategy Report—2002*, p. 4.

13. A study of police inquiries and court cases in Rio de Janeiro in 1991, for example, revealed that 57 percent of the homicides in the city that year were linked in some way to drug trafficking.

14. Jorge Balán argues that in cities of Latin America, "Fear is now as much a threat to democracy as violence itself, since it may justify repression, emergency policies that circumvent the constitutional rule, and, more broadly, alienation from the democratic political process." Jorge Balán, "Introduction," pp. 1–6 in Rotker, editor, *Citizens of Fear.*

15. It is difficult to date the arrival of drugs and, in particular, cocaine, in Rio. I have heard many people say, however, that 1986 was their first "White" Christmas.

16. In terms of my own research, the most influential works have been Alba Zaluar, *A Máquina e a Revolta: As Organizações Populares e o Significado da Pobreza* (São Paulo: Brasiliense, 1985); Alba Zaluar, *Condomínio do Diablo* (Rio de Janeiro: Editora Revan, 1994); Marcos Alvito, *As Cores de Acari: Uma Favela Carioca* (Rio de Janeiro: Getulio Vargas, 2001); Teresa Pires do Rio Caldeira, *A Política Dos Outros: O Coitidiano dos Moradores da Periferia e o que Pensam do Poder e dos Poderosos* (São Paulo: Brasiliense, 1984); Robin Sheriff, *Dreaming Inequality:*

Color, Race, and Racism in Urban Brazil (New Brunswick: Rutgers University Press, 2001); and Goldstein, *Laughter out of Place*.

17. Tobias Hecht claims that similar problems plague studies of street children that are "like a snapshot, a portrait at a particular moment in time, with no effort to discover what happens over the long run." Tobias Hecht, *At Home in the Street: Street Children of Northeast Brazil* (Cambridge: Cambridge University Press, 1998), p. 202.

18. Antonius Robben and Carolyn Nordstrom argue that violence "is not outside the realm of human society, or that which defines it as human." Antonius Robben and Carolyn Nordstrom, "The Anthropology and Ethnography of Violence and Sociopolitical Conflict," pp. 1–23 in Antonius Robben and Carolyn Nordstrom, editors, *Fieldwork Under Fire: Contemporary Studies of Violence and Survival* (Berkeley: University of California Press, 1995). See also, Michael Taussig, "Terror as Usual: Walter Benjamin's Theory of History as a State of Siege," *Social Text* 23(1989): 3–20; and, of course, Nancy Scheper-Hughes, *Death Without Weeping: The Violence of Everyday Life in Brazil* (Berkeley: University of California Press, 1992).

19. For a more traditional, male-centered perspective, see Caco Barcellos, *Abusado: O Dono do Morro Dona Marta* (Rio de Janeiro: Editora Record, 2003).

20. For the rare exception, see Alba Zaluar, "Mulher do Bandido: Crônica de uma Cidade Menos Musical," *Estudos Feministas* 135(1993): 135–42.

21. Claudia Salazar observes that "In the 'Third World,' women's autobiographical texts have become an integral part of the intellectual, ideological, political, and even armed struggle waged by oppressed and silenced people against the power of repressive states and hegemonic groups." She goes on to say, however, that "In Western intellectual circles . . . there is a tendency to romanticize these voices and to conceive of the subjects of the testimonials unproblematically." Claudia Salazar, "A Third World Woman's Text: Between the Politics of Criticism and Cultural Politics," pp. 93–106 in Sherna Berger Gluck and Daphne Patai, editors, *Women's Words: The Feminist Practice of Oral History* (London: Routledge, 1991).

22. Guillermo O'Donnell refers to this as "low-intensity citizenship." James Holston and Teresa Pires do Rio Caldeira refer to it as "disjunctive democracy." Guillermo O'Donnell, "On the State, Democratization and Some Conceptual Problems: A Latin American View with Glances at Some Postcommunist Countries," *World Development* 21(8): 1355–69; and James Holston and Teresa Pires do Rio Caldeira, "Democracy, Law, and Violence: Disjunctions of Brazilian Citizenship," pp. 263–296 in Felipe Aguero and Jeffrey Stark, editors, *Fault Lines of Democracy in Post-Transition Latin America* (Coral Gables: University of Miami, 1998).

23. Another friend asked me why I didn't rent a room from her while I was in Rio. I told her that, given the sensitive nature of what I was doing, I would worry that they would come and get me during the night. To which she said, "If they wanted to get you, it wouldn't matter what time of day it was."

24. For a similar experience, see Sheriff, *Dreaming Inequality*, pp. 225–33.

25. For the dangers of this kind of fieldwork, see also Leigh Payne, *Uncivil Movements: The Armed Right Wing and Democracy in Latin America* (Baltimore: Johns Hopkins University Press, 2000), p. xxix.

26. The police accused Lopes of self-promotion and implied that he got what he deserved. *Jornal do Brasil*, August 8, 2002. See also the report in the *New York Times*, June 28, 2002.

27. A recent study by the Centro de Estudos de Segurança e Cidadania da Universidade Candido Mendes (Cesec-Ucam) found that the number of missing persons in Rio almost doubled from 2,473 in 1993 to 4,800 in 2003. Most of these missing persons are males between the ages of eighteen and twenty-six years of age and 70 percent are drug related. *O Globo* May 1, 2004.

28. It also does not mean that I leveled the vast difference in status between the interviewer and interviewee. For a discussion of this and related issues, see Daniel James, *Doña María's Story: Life History, Memory and Political Identity* (Durham: Duke University Press, 2000), pp. 133–42; and Daphne Patai, "U.S. Academics and Third World Women: Is Ethical Research Possible?" pp. 137–53 in Gluck and Patai, editors, *Women's Words*.

29. See, Martha Huggins, Mika Haritos-Fatouros, and Philip Zimbardo, *Violence Workers: Police Torturers and Murderers Reconstruct Brazilian Atrocities* (Berkeley: University of California Press, 2002); and Antonius Robben, "The Politics of Truth and Emotion Among Victims and Perpetrators of Violence," pp. 81–103 in Robben and Nordstrom, editors, *Fieldwork Under Fire*.

30. It annoyed my other friends intensely that I had chosen Lucia for the study when they had endured the exact same circumstances without becoming involved.

31. At first, I was troubled by this aspect of our relationship, in the sense that I feared it might unduly raise her expectations. As the years passed, however, and I became more and more apologetic about how long the process was taking, Lucia assured me that she had learned from experience not to concern her self with things in life that might never happen.

32. The observation that interviewing individuals from sectors of society that are usually ignored or invisible bestows respect is a common one. See for example, Phillipe Bourgois, *In Search of Respect: Selling Crack in El Barrio* (New York: Cambridge University Press, 1996).

33. Lucia's responses to this second set of questions were then inserted into the original interview text where appropriate.

34. This contrasts with the more standard approach of ethnographies of using dialogue to illustrate themes. See Bourgois, *In Search of Respect*.

35. Michael Herzfeld characterizes this approach as "ethnographic biography" in that unlike most ethnographies it is focused on a single person and that "unlike most biographies, it is less concerned with the personality of the central character than with the significance of his life and times for a tangle of intersecting worlds." Michael Herzfeld, *Portrait of a Greek Imagination: An Ethnographic Biography of Andreas Nenedakis* (Chicago: University of Chicago Press, 1997), p. 1.

36. In the text, ellipses represent pauses in the conversation.

37. For a useful description of the depth interviewing process, see William Miller and Benjamin Crabtree, "Depth Interviewing," pp. 185–202 in Sharlene Nagy Hess-Biber and Patricia Leavy, editors, *Approaches to Qualitative Research: A Reader on Theory and Practice* (Oxford: Oxford University Press, 2004).

38. This approach to interviews contrasts, for example, with that of Daphne Patai. See Daphne Patai, *Brazilian Women Speak: Contemporary Life Stories* (New Brunswick: Rutgers University Press, 1988).

39. For the war on drugs, see Ted Galen Carpenter, *Bad Neighbor Policy: Washington's Futile War on Drugs in Latin America* (New York: Palgrave, 2003); Robin Kirk, *More Terrible than Death: Massacres, Drugs, and America's War in Colombia* (Cambridge: Public Affairs, 2003); and Frank Mora, "Victims of the Balloon Effect: Drug trafficking and U.S. Policy in Brazil and the Southern Cone of Latin America," *Journal of Social, Political and Economic Studies* 21(2)(1996): 115–40.

40. In April 1986, President Ronald Reagan signed National Security Decision Directive (NSDD) 221, declaring drug trafficking a threat to national security. This has enabled successive administrations to ignore human rights abuses and has meant that the lion's share of the billions of dollars spent on the war on drugs has been in the form of military hardware and weapon systems.

41. For the idea of a parallel state, see Elizabeth Leeds, "Cocaine and Parallel Polities in the Brazilian Urban Periphery: Constraints on Local-Level Democratization," *Latin American Research Review* 31(3)(1996): 47–83. For a critique of this idea, see Enrique Desmond Arias, "Faith in Our Neighbors: Networks and Social Order in Three Brazilian Favelas," *Latin American Politics and Society* 46(1)(2004): 1–38.

Chapter 1: Getting In

1. For the vulnerability of poor female youth, see Donna Goldstein, *Laughter Out of Place: Race, Class, Violence, and Sexuality in a Rio Shantytown* (Berkeley: University of California Press, 2003), pp. 246–58.

2. *Bailes* are funk dance parties that bring together rival groups of youths who engage in stylized sparring and fighting. For the different types of baile and their social significance, see Fátima Regina Cecchetto, "Galeras Funk Cariocas: os Bailes e a Constituição do Ethos Guerreiro," pp. 145–66 in Alba Zaluar and Marcos Alvito, editors, *Um Século de Favela* (Rio de Janeiro: Getulio Vargas, 1998); and Hermano Vianna, *O Mundo Funk Carioca* (Rio de Janeiro: Zahar, 1988).

3. Lucia is referring to public housing projects built for residents of favelas removed in the 1960s and 1970s by the military.

4. The minimum salary was introduced by President Getúlio Vargas in 1940 to meet the basic needs of workers. In 1999, 14,790,205 workers, or 24.4 percent, of the economically active population in Brazil earned less than or equal to one minimum salary. That a quarter of the economically active population in Brazil earns less than or equal to one minimum salary has less to do with gains in wages, however, than with the steady loss in the real value of the minimum salary itself. When I

began my fieldwork in the summer of 1999, the minimum salary was 136 *Reais* per month. By the time I had finished, in spring 2002, it was 180 *Reais*. Because of the devaluation of the *Real* in recent years, however, the value of the minimum wage in both instances was approximately 77US$. And, according to the Departamento Intersindical de Estatística e Estudos Sócio-Econômicos (DIEESE), as of February 2000, the minimum salary in Brazil should be 930 *Reais*.

5. Because cocaine is a relatively expensive drug, in comparison with, say, marijuana, it has led to an increase in assaults, robberies, and break-ins and in the size of the stolen goods market. See, for example, *Jornal do Brasil*, September 8, 2003.

6. See, for example, *Jornal do Brasil*, October 10, 2002.

7. I never brought this up with her, but when I first got to know Lucia, she occasionally smoked marijuana.

8. For an analysis of childhood among the poor in Brazil, see Tobias Hecht, *At Home in the Street: Street Children in the Northeast of Brazil* (Cambridge: Cambridge University Press, 1998).

9. For the historical origins of the drug trade and criminality in Rio in general, see Michel Misse, "Malandros, Marginais e Vagabundos: a Acumulação Social da Violência no Rio de Janeiro," Ph.D. Thesis, IUPERJ, 1999.

Lucia's House

1. A few years back, the drug gang-appointed president of the neighborhood association issued a warning that residents who failed to clean up after their dogs would be punished—apparently to no avail.

2. For conditions in the contemporary Northeast, see Nancy Scheper-Hughes, *Death Without Weeping: The Violence of Everyday Life in Brazil* (Berkeley: University of California Press, 1992).

3. For the circulation of poor children in Brazil, see Claudia Fonseca, "Orphanages, Foundlings and Foster Mothers: The System of Child Circulation in a Brazilian Squatter Settlement." *Anthropological Quarterly* 59(1)(1986): 15–27.

4. There are various definitions as to what constitutes a favela, from an illegal settlement on private or public land to a "disordered nuclei of impoverished persons." When most people think of favelas they think of the self-built shantytowns in all of their irregular and haphazard forms. The term is also used, however, to describe clandestine subdivisions and public housing projects. For a discussion of this issue, see Julio César Pino, *Family and Favela: The Reproduction of Poverty in Rio de Janeiro* (Westport: Greenwood Press, 1997), pp. 38–46.

5. See Anthony Leeds and Elizabeth Leeds, *A Sociologia do Brasil Urbano* (Rio de Janeiro: Zahar, 1978); and Lucien Parisse, *Favelas do Rio de Janeiro: Evolução e Sentido* (Rio de Janeiro: Centro Nacional de Pesquisas Habitacionais, 1969).

6. See Victor Valla, *Educação e Favela: Política para as Favelas do Rio de Janeiro* (Rio de Janeiro: Zahar, 1986), pp. 44–55.

7. Rio de Janeiro, "À Margem, Cresce a Grande Cidade: Favela." *Revista do Tribunal de Contas do Município do Rio de Janeiro* I (1981): 53–60.

8. For the removal process, see Sérgio Azevedo and Luis Andrade, *Habitação e Poder: Da Fundação da Casa Popular ao Banco Nacional de Habitação* (Rio de Janeiro: Zahar, 1981); Robert M. Levine, *Brazilian Legacies* (London: Sharpe, 1997), pp. 172–75; Janice Perlman, *The Myth of Marginality: Urban Poverty and Politics in Rio de Janeiro* (Berkeley: University of California Press, 1976); and Lícia Valladares, *Passe-Se uma Casa: Análise do Programa de Remoção de Favelas de Rio de Janeiro* (Rio de Janeiro: Zahar, 1978).

9. The population of the favelas in Rio de Janeiro has increased from an estimated 169,305 in 1950, to 335,063 in 1960, to 565,135 in 1970, to 722,424 in 1980, to 962,793 in 1991. In 1991 there were also 944,200 people living in public housing projects and 381,345 in illegal subdivisions. Together, the population residing in favelas, public housing projects, and illegal subdivisions in 1991 represented 40 percent of the city's population. Iplanrio, *Anuário Estatístico* (1993).

10. For a discussion of recent government programs toward the favelas and, in particular, the program Favela-Bairro, which received massive funding from the Interamerican Development Bank, see Marcelo Baumann Burgos, "Dos Parques Proletários ao Favela-Bairro: as Políticas Públicas nas Favelas do Rio de Janeiro," pp. 25–60 in Alba Zaluar and Marcos Alvito, editors, *Um Século de Favela* (Rio de Janeiro: Fundação Getulio Vargas, 1998).

11. The other problem associated with the regularization of property rights is, of course, that it fuels real estate speculation and an increase in house prices, precisely the conditions that led to the establishment of favelas and other forms of irregular housing in the first place.

12. See Perlman, *The Myth of Marginality*, p. 28.

13. According to a survey recently conducted by the Centro de Informações e Dados do Rio de Janeiro (CIDE), the provision of electricity and water has shown the most improvement over the past few years. According to the survey, approximately 97 percent of households in the state of Rio have access to water (including from wells) and 98 percent have access to electricity. *Jornal do Brasil*, February 12, 2001.

14. According to the Caixa Econômica Federal, 55 percent of Rio's households are connected to the public sewage system. The percentage of favela households that are connected is far less. See, for example, P. L. da Silva Moura, "Um movimento em Busca de Poder: as Associações de Moradores do Rio de Janeiro e a sua Relação com o Estado - 1970–1990." Masters Thesis. UFF, 1993.

15. Of course, this is where other problems begin. Rio's sewage collection and treatment system is woefully inadequate to deal with the output of the metropolitan area's 11 million or so people. Despite highly publicized programs by successive governments, investment in sewage collection and treatment has lagged behind other services. The outcome is the discharge of an estimated 1.73 billion gallons of sewage per day into Guanabara Bay and the pollution of Rio's greatest resource: its beaches. *Jornal do Brasil*, September 24, 2000.

16. Voting is compulsory in Brazil, so, unlike the United States, political parties have to pay at least some attention to the poor.

17. This alludes to the fact that most of the early favelas were built on the steep hills, or *morros*, surrounding the city center.

Chapter 2: Rogério

1. Cocaine is usually mixed with bicarbonate of soda or cornstarch. It can also, however, be mixed with synthetic cocaine substitutes like xylocaine, lidocaine, and procaine. In October 2003, the federal police in Rio uncovered two businesses involved with the production of cocaine substitutes that were mixed with pure cocaine at a ratio of eight to one. *Jornal do Brasil*, October 8, 2003.

2. The *Real* has been Brazil's currency since July 1994. Since then it has progressively lost value against the US dollar. As of the beginning of January 1995, one US dollar was worth 0.844 *Reais*; January 1996, 0.9723 *Reais*; January 1997, 1.0394 *Reais*; January 1998, 1.1164 *Reais*; January 1999, 1.2074 *Reais*; January 2000, 1.805 *Reais*; January 2001, 1.938 *Reais*; January 2002, 2.31 *Reais*; and January 2003, 3.5425 *Reais*.

3. For years, drug gangs have run delivery services to clients in surrounding neighborhoods, often disguised as pizza deliverymen.

4. In recent years, firecrackers have been replaced as early warning systems by cell phones and walkie-talkies.

5. For a description of the many different positions in drug gangs, see Luke Dowdney, *Children of the Drug Trade* (Rio de Janeiro: 7Letras, 2003), pp. 46–51.

6. Since the 1980s, drug gangs have replaced handguns with more sophisticated, higher-caliber weapons such as automatic rifles, submachine guns, and grenades.

7. See also, *Jornal do Brasil*, August 6, 2002 and March 9, 2003.

8. Earlier on, Lucia claimed that she hadn't done any of the mixing. This contradiction is partly because the interviews for this chapter were conducted at different times. Rather than call her on it, however, I felt it best to let her memories speak.

9. The Comando Vermelho is one of three powerful criminal organizations that were established in Rio's prisons in the early 1980s. The other two are the Terceiro Comando and the Amigos dos Amigos. The relationship between prison-based criminal organizations and local drug gangs is detailed in the section that follows. The drug gang in Jakeira has always been affiliated with the Comando Vermelho. The terms mean Red Command (Comando Vermelho), Third Command (Terceiro Comando), and Friends of Friends (Amigos dos Amigos).

10. Rock concerts that brought major international artists to the city each year.

11. According to one study, the increased use of military-grade weapons by drug gangs means that emergency room doctors rarely encounter bullets lodged inside a victim. Instead, high-velocity projectiles enter and leave the body, inflicting massive amounts of damage. Dowdney, *Children of the Drug Trade*, p. 99.

12. The Instituto Brasileiro de Inovações em Saúde Social (IBISS) reports that in 2002, 27 percent of children living in the streets in Rio were there because they were expelled from their communities by drug gangs. This percentage is up from 4 percent in 1998. *Jornal do Brasil*, June 1, 2003.

13. Means crazy or mad.

Drug Gangs

1. For new social movements in Brazil see Jean Cohen, "Strategy or Identity: New Theoretical Paradigms and Contemporary Social Movements," *Social Research* 52(4) (1985): 663–716; Arturo Escobar and Sonia Alvarez, editors, *The Making of Social Movements in Latin America* (Boulder: Westview Press, 1992); and Tilman Evers, "'Identity': The Hidden Side of New Social Movements in Latin America," pp. 43–72 in David Slater, editor, *New Social Movements and the State in Latin America* (Amsterdam: CEDLA, 1985).

2. Unlike other countries in Latin America, albeit restricted elections were held in Brazil throughout the military dictatorship.

3. See Robert Gay, *Popular Organization and Democracy in Rio de Janeiro: A Tale of Two Favelas* (Philadelphia: Temple University Press, 1994), pp. 25–34.

4. See, for example, Alba Zaluar, "Crime, Medo e Política," pp. 209–32 in Alba Zaluar and Marcos Alvito, editors, *Um Século de Favela* (Rio de Janeiro: Getulio Vargas, 1998).

5. For an account of this process, see Carlos Amorim, *Comando Vermelho: A História Secreta do Crime Organizado* (Rio de Janeiro: Record, 1993), pp. 61–102. For an alternative explanation, see Michel Misse, "Malandros, Marginais e Vagabundos: a Acumulação Social da Violência no Rio de Janeiro," Ph.D. Thesis, IUPERJ, 1999.

6. The most famous of these was the escape by "Escadinha" from the Ilha Grande prison by helicopter in 1985.

7. Amorim, *Comando Vermelho*, p. 142.

8. In 2000, 227 kilos of cocaine were found on passengers attempting to leave Rio's international airport. The cocaine was concealed in the false bottoms of suitcases, in the soles of tennis shoes, and in bottles of hair gel. More recently, it has been found hidden in passengers' stomachs.

9. On April 21, 2001, the Colombian army kidnapped Luiz Fernando da Costa, otherwise known as Fernandinho Beira-Mar. Beira-Mar was, and still is, considered the most powerful drug dealer in Brazil. After he escaped from jail in the state of Minas Gerais in 1996, Beira-Mar established relations with drug suppliers in Paraguay and Colombia that accounted for what some estimate was 70 percent of the drugs that entered the country. Beira-Mar was captured during an operation against the Revolutionary Armed Forces of Colombia (FARC). In recent years, Beira-Mar had supplied FARC with weapons in exchange for drugs. There is also the suspicion that FARC operatives are active in Rio. *Jornal do Brasil*, September 12, 2002, and February 28 and April 14, 2003.

10. The domain of the Comando Vermelho stretched beyond the city to other areas of the state such as the tourist resorts of Cabo Frio, Búzios, and Angra dos Reis and the industrial city of Volta Redonda.

11. In recent years, the Comando Vermelho has been losing ground to its rivals. It is this struggle for territorial control that has increased the level of violence in Rio.

12. For the relationship between drug gangs and the surrounding community, see Marcos Alvito, *As Cores de Acari: Uma Favela Carioca* (Rio de Janeiro: Getulio

Vargas, 2001), p. 152; Elizabeth Leeds, "Cocaine and Parallel Polities in the Brazilian Urban Periphery: Constraints on Local-Level Democratization," *Latin American Research Review* 31(3)(1996): 47–83; Zuenir Ventura, *Cidade Partida* (São Paulo: Schwartz, 1994), pp. 103–4; and Alba Zaluar, *Condomínio do Diablo* (Rio de Janeiro: Editora Revan, 1994).

13. There is a tendency to exaggerate the degree to which local residents support as opposed to fear drug gangs. Marcos Alvito makes what I think is a useful distinction between drug gang leaders in the old days who were cruel but fair and a new generation who are not respected because they torture and kill for the sake of it. Alvito, *As Cores de Acari*, p. 152.

14. It is estimated that ten thousand men dominate the lives of 1 million people in 800 communities in Rio. *Jornal de Brasil*, June 16, 2002. See also, Josinaldo Aleixo de Souza, "Sociabilidades Emergentes—Implicações da Dominação de Matadores na Periferie e Traficantes nas Favelas," Ph.D. Thesis, UFRJ, 2002.

15. In November 1994, the military was sent into dozens of the more violence-plagued favelas in what was dubbed Operation Rio. Soldiers set up checkpoints at the entrance to the favelas and required all those entering or leaving to present identification. They also conducted extensive house-to-house searches. Most of the occupations lasted one or two days. For a discussion, see Juliana Resende, *Operação Rio* (Rio de Janeiro: Editora Página Aberta, 1995).

16. A similar situation is described by Alvito, *As Cores de Acari*, p. 152. See also, Leeds, "Cocaine and Parallel Polities."

17. According to one source, 100 community leaders were assassinated and a further 100 expelled by drug gangs in Rio between 1992 and 2001. Commissão Contra a Violência e a Impunidade/ALERJ. Published in *O Globo*, July 20, 2001.

18. This is not to say that civil society is under threat in all of Brazil. For signs of life, see Rebecca Abers, *Inventing Local Democracy: Grassroots Politics in Brazil* (Boulder: Lynne Reinner, 2000); and William Nylen, "The Making of a Loyal Opposition: The Workers' Party (PT) and the Consolidation of Democracy in Brazil," pp. 126–43 in Peter R. Kingstone and Timothy J. Power, editors, *Democratic Brazil: Actors, Institutions, and Processes* (Pittsburgh: Pittsburgh University Press, 2000).

Chapter 3: Marcos

1. The state of Minas Gerais borders Rio de Janeiro to the northwest.

2. A more common punishment for women who fight is shaving their heads.

3. Public hospitals in Rio are severely underfunded and suffer regularly from shortages of supplies and equipment. See, for example, *Jornal do Brasil*, November 12, 2003.

4. Politicians are widely acknowledged to be associated either directly or indirectly with the drug trade. For the impact of drug money on elections, see Christian Geffray, "Social, Economic and Political Impacts of Drug Trafficking in the State of Rondônia, in the Brazilian Amazon," pp. 90–109 in *Globalisation, Drugs and Criminalisation* (MOST/UNESCO, 2002).

5. In many favelas in Rio, the authorities know exactly who is in charge and have to obtain the dono's permission to come in and work. See, for example, *Jornal do Brasil*, August 15, 2002, and September 10, 2002.

6. The Cooperativa de Habitação Popular do Estado de Guanabara (COHAB) was established in 1962 to urbanize selected favelas in Rio and to construct low-income housing units for the urban poor. As it turned out, however, COHAB was almost solely responsible for the first wave of favela removals between 1962 and 1965.

7. According to the Campanha por uma Convenção Interamericana de Direitos Sexuais e Direitos Reprodutivos, it is estimated that 1 million illegal abortions are performed in Brazil each year and abortion is ranked fifth in terms of the leading causes for the hospitalization of women in Brazil. *Jornal do Brasil*, September 28, 2003.

Police

1. For a discussion of the Plan, see Human Rights Watch/Americas, *Police Brutality in Urban Brazil* (Human Rights Watch, 1997). For an evaluation of the Plan's progress, see Human Rights Watch/Americas, *Brazil Slow on Human Rights Reform* (Human Rights Watch, 1999).

2. During the dictatorship, the military police were placed under the direct control of the Army, and specialized units were established to hunt down so-called terrorists. Many of the police that were involved remained on the force following the transition to democracy. See Caco Barcellos, *Rota 66. A História da Polícia que Mata* (Rio de Janeiro: Editora Globo, 1987).

3. Paul Chevigny, *The Edge of the Knife: Police Violence in the Americas* (New York: New Press, 1995), p. 145.

4. The civil and military police in Rio killed 397 civilians in 1998, 453 civilians in 1999, 483 civilians in 2000, 514 civilians in 2001, and 834 civilians in 2002. The greatest increase occurred after the death of Tim Lopes. *Jornal do Brasil*, September 17 and December 3, 2002.

5. A study of police killings between 1993 and 1996 found that half of the victims had four or more bullet wounds and more than half had at least one gunshot wound from behind or to the head. Ignacio Cano, "The Use of Lethal Force by Police in Rio de Janeiro," ISER, Rio de Janeiro, 1997.

6. Human Rights Watch, *Police Brutality*, p. 13.

7. See Jorge Zaverucha, "Military Justice in the State of Pernambuco After the Brazilian Military Regime: An Authoritarian Legacy," *Latin American Research Review* 34(2)(1999): 43–74.

8. For problems associated with the Brazilian judiciary, see Paulo Sérgio Pinheiro, "Democratic Governance, Violence, and the (Un)Rule of Law," *Daedalus* 129(2) (2000):119–44; and Daniel Brinks, "Informal Institutions and the Rule of Law: The Judicial Response to State Killings in Buenos Aires and São Paulo in the 1990s."

Paper presented at the Conference on Informal Institutions and Politics in the Developing World. Harvard University, April 2002.

9. See Dulce Pandolfi, "Percepção dos Direitos e Participação Social," pp. 45–58 in Dulce Pandolfi, José Murilo de Carvalho, Leandro Carneiro, and Mario Grynszpan, editors, *Cidadania, Justiça e Violência* (Rio de Janeiro: Getulio Vargas, 1999).

10. See Human Rights Watch/Americas, *Final Justice: Police and Death Squad Homicides of Adolescents in Brazil* (Human Rights Watch, 1994); and Martha Huggins, *Political Policing: The United States and Latin America* (Durham: Duke University Press, 1998).

11. Anthony Pereira argues that the "assumption that citizens will protest the abuse of others' rights for fear they might be victimized themselves has not held in Brazil." Anthony W. Pereira, "An Ugly Democracy? State Violence and the Rule of Law in Postauthoritarian Brazil," pp. 217–35 in Peter R. Kingstone and Timothy J. Power, editors, *Democratic Brazil: Actors, Institutions, and Processes* (Pittsburgh: Pittsburgh University Press, 2000).

12. See, for example, Paulo Mesquita Neto, "Violência Policial no Brasil: Abordagens Teóricas e Práticas de Controle," pp. 130–48 in Dulce Pandolfi, José Murilo de Carvalho, Leandro Carneiro, and Mario Grynszpan, editors, *Cidadania, Justiça e Violência* (Rio de Janeiro: Getulio Vargas), 1999.

13. In September 2002 and February 2003, whole areas of the city were closed for days by order of drug gangs. See *Jornal do Brasil*, September 12, 2002 and March 3, 2003.

14. The contradictions associated with the situation in Rio are well illustrated by an event that occurred on June 12, 2000. In mid afternoon, Sandro de Nascimento, age 21, held up a bus at gunpoint. For the next four and a half hours, Sandro negotiated with the police that had surrounded the bus for the release of the eleven passengers he had taken hostage. On giving himself up, however, a police marksman opened fire and, in the confusion, the woman Sandro was using as cover was killed. Sandro never made it to the police station alive. He was strangled to death in the back of a police van. As implausible as it may seem, Sandro was one of the survivors of the massacre of eight street children outside Candelária Cathedral in 1993. A few of my friends expressed sympathy for the victim. The vast majority, however, said that the police should have done the job right the first time. The public apparently agreed, because a public jury subsequently acquitted the police who were involved.

15. In 2001, the police apprehended 16,796 firearms in Rio. Only 1,149 were manufactured abroad. And between 1998 and 2001 there were eighty-one reported incidences of firearms going missing from military establishments in Brazil. *Jornal do Brasil*, April 26, 2004. See also, Luke Dowdney, *Children of the Drug Trade* (Rio de Janeiro: 7Letras, 2003), p. 100.

16. Press reports have claimed that drug gangs in Rio possess an arsenal of 1,500 rifles and machine guns. *O Globo*, June 16, 2002.

17. Despite a 1997 antitorture law, a recent report by the United Nations states that "police routinely beat and torture criminal suspects to extract information, confessions or money," and that "the problem of police brutality, at the time of arrest or during interrogation, was reportedly endemic." United Nations Commission on Human Rights. "Report of the Special Rapporteur on Civil and Political Rights, Regarding the Questions of Torture and Detention," Nigel Rodley (August 20–September 12, 2000).

18. An estimated 30 percent of the police who are admitted to the military police hospital in Rio are injured by their own weapons. *Jornal do Brasil*, November 29, 2000.

19. The police force has provided rare and significant opportunities for Afro-Brazilians.

20. See, for example, *Jornal do Brasil*, March 23, 2003.

21. For police involvement with the drug trade, see Elizabeth Leeds, "Cocaine and Parallel Polities in the Brazilian Urban Periphery: Constraints on Local-Level Democratization." *Latin American Research Review* 31(3)(1996): 47–83. For police corruption in general, see José Carlos Blat and Sérgio Saraiva, *O Caso da Favela Natal: Polícia Contra o Povo* (São Paulo: Editora Contexto, 2000).

22. It took months for the police to capture Tim Lopes' killer, Elias Maluco. The secretary for public security in Rio attributed the delay to the fact that the police were being paid to protect him and that they had already been paid 600,000 *Reais* on one occasion to let the drug dealer go. There have even been reports in the press that military police recruits are trained in the art of extortion, or what is known as *mineiração*. *Jornal do Brasil*, March 13, 2002.

23. For a discussion of the different kinds of relationship between drug gangs and the police, see Marcos Alvito, *As Cores de Acari: Uma Favela Carioca* (Rio de Janeiro: Getulio Vargas, 2001), p. 105; and Zuenir Ventura, *Cidade Partida* (São Paulo: Scwartz, 1994), p. 67.

24. The phone line Disque-Denúncia receives on average ten thousand calls per month, of which 30 to 35 percent have to do with information about drug trafficking. *Jornal do Brasil*, September 25, 2004. The phone line is supposed to be secure and anonymous. My friends told me, however, that they never use it, for fear of being overheard and turned in. In fact, most of my friends refuse to talk about anything concerning drug gang activities when I call them from the United States because they suspect, rightly or wrongly, that drug gangs are in possession of sophisticated listening devices. Furthermore, since the police ombudsman was first established in 1999, very few of the thousands of complaints that have been lodged against the police have resulted in punishment, dismissal, or prosecution. And the vast majority of those who have been punished have not been officers but regular recruits. *Jornal do Brasil*, November 26, 2002.

25. Alba Zaluar makes the useful distinction between extermination and extortion groups. The former are more akin to death squads that seek to eliminate a certain type of person. The latter only kill in the process of demanding their share of the

profits from drug trafficking. Alba Zaluar, "The Drug Trade, Crime and Policies of Repression in Brazil," *Dialectical Anthropology* 20(1995): 95–108.

Chapter 4: Bruno

1. For the illegal economy in border states, see Christian Geffray, "Social, Economic and Political Impacts of Drug Trafficking in the State of Rondônia, in the Brazilian Amazon," pp. 90–109 in *Globalisation, Drugs, and Criminalization* (MOST/UNESCO, 2002); and Roberto Araújo, "The Drug trade, the Black Economy and Society in Western Amazônia in Brazil," pp. 134–40 in *Globalisation, Drugs, and Criminalization* (MOST/UNESCO, 2002).
2. Brazil's remote and porous nine-thousand-mile-long border makes the control of drug trafficking extremely difficult, if not impossible.
3. Suriname is one of the more important transshipment points of cocaine on the Atlantic route from Latin America to the United States and Europe.
4. A wealthy seaside district of Rio.
5. As of January 2001, there were 20,766 prisoners in thirty-three different establishments in Rio.
6. A couple of years back, I showed up at a favela I used to work in in Zona Sul to be greeted by a convoy of representatives from international development banks and NGOs who were celebrating the inauguration of a public works they had invested in. They were treated to a demonstration of Brazilian culture by children from the favela and then driven up the hill to admire the view from the top. In the newspaper the next day, many of them were quoted as saying how lucky people were to live there and how wonderful it was to see community participation in action. What they didn't know was that they were there by permission of the drug gang leader who had ordered everyone to clean up the streets and remove all cars and who had viciously tortured, dismembered, and murdered the previous neighborhood association president just weeks before. The neighborhood association president had been suspected of organizing an invasion by a rival gang. Unfortunately, the neighborhood association president's body parts washed ashore on the beach at Ipanema.

Prison

1. In July 1990, Congress passed the Law of Heinous Crimes (Lei de Crimes Hediondos) that lengthened sentences for kidnapping and drug trafficking and made suspects of either crime ineligible for pretrial release. Consequently, the number of prisoners involved in the drug trade and in drug-related crime has increased dramatically. *Jornal do Brasil*, September 1, 2001. For a discussion of the justice system and drug-related crimes, see Alba Zaluar, "Violence Related to Illegal Drugs, Easy Money and Justice in Brazil: 1980–1995," pp. 142–63 in *Globalisation, Drugs and Criminalisation* (MOST/UNESCO, 2002).

2. In 1996, there were 80,000 spaces for 117,000 inmates in Brazil. As of November 2001, there were 160,000 spaces for 231,463 inmates.
3. By law, prisoners in Brazil are required to work and be paid. And in theory, one day of a prisoner's sentence is to be deducted for each three days of work.
4. Legal aid in Brazil's prisons is so deficient that it is not uncommon for prisoners to serve more than their sentence.
5. As of April 2001, 63,499 prisoners were being held in Brazil outside of the prison system. Of these, 25,878 already had been convicted.
6. See Hosmany Ramos, *Pavilhão 9: Paixão e Morte no Carandiru* (São Paulo: Geração, 2001).
7. The colonel, Ubiratan Guimarães, insisted that his men acted in self-defense. He remains something of a hero among the military police and even served briefly in the São Paulo state congress.
8. See Márcio Christino, *Por Dentro de Crime: Corrupção, Tráfico, PCC* (São Paulo: Fiuza, 2001).
9. The prison authorities in São Paulo made the initial mistake of farming out the leaders of the Primeiro Comando do Capital to other cities in Brazil. Now the organization has a foothold in the states of Rio de Janeiro, Paraná, Mato Grosso, Mato Grosso do Sul, and Rio Grande do Sul. And there is evidence of a working relationship between the Primeiro Comando do Capital and the Comando Vermelho.
10. The prison authorities in Rio separated rival factions as far back as 1983. Consequently, there were no major prison rebellions in Rio between 1979 and 2002. It is also the case that, relatively speaking, more prisons have been built in Rio and improvements made in prisoner care.
11. It is common for drug gang leaders in prison to accompany torture sessions and executions by phone. See, for example, *Jornal do Brasil*, September 6, 2002.
12. In 2000, the Department for State Prisons in Rio (DESIPE) sent the Brazilian Lawyers Association a list of 130 lawyers who were suspected of being involved with drug trafficking. It turns out that only fifteen of them were actual lawyers. The other 115 had all obtained false documents. *Jornal do Brasil*, April 16, 2001. For an interview with the attorney of Fernandinho Beira-Mar, see *Jornal do Brasil*, March 28, 2003.
13. The police have discovered digital and satellite-operated phone banks that can transfer calls to and from prison without revealing the identity of the caller, and software that can clone privately owned cell phones and change their numbers up to twenty times per day. The equipment for this type of operation is extremely sophisticated and expensive, costing up to US$40,000, and is similar to technology that is used by guerilla outfits in Colombia. *Jornal do Brasil*, August 9, 2002.
14. On August 5, 2002, the prison authorities confiscated 114 cell phones and 135 cell phone chargers in the Bangu prison complex in Rio. The prison authorities in Rio are now looking into technology that will block cell phone signals, such is their inability to stamp out corruption. *Jornal do Brasil*, August 6, 2002.

15. Most prisons in Brazil have generous visitation policies, including conjugal visits for male inmates and their wives and partners. Visitation rights are often used as a disciplinary tool, however, and the visitors themselves must stand for hours in line and be subjected to humiliating and intrusive searches by prison guards.

16. In 1998, the *traficante* known as Celso de Vintém paid 90,000 *Reais* to escape through the front door of a prison hospital. Inmates also escape on a regular basis through tunnels that are dug by inmates on the inside or, alternatively, by teams of paid workmen on the outside. On September 11, 2002, Fernandinho Beira-Mar led a rebellion of inmates associated with the Comando Vermelho in one of the prisons in the Bangu complex. With the obvious assistance of someone on the inside, Beira-Mar and his associates overcame two guards, passed through three steel doors, crossed a corridor, opened three other doors, and took out four traficantes from a rival faction. The traficantes had guns and keys to all the doors in the prison, even though a thorough search had been conducted only twenty-four hours earlier. Apparently, a prison guard had been paid 400,000 *Reais* to smuggle in the guns and make copies of the keys.

17. See, for example, *Jornal do Brasil*, March 20, 2003.

18. The Ministry of Justice calculates that 25 percent out of every million dollars generated by the drug trade is invested in the corruption of the authorities. *Veja*, September 18, 2002.

Chapter 5: School

Education

1. Between 1985 and 1999, enrollment in primary school in Brazil increased from 24,770,000 to 36,170,000. During the same period, enrollment in secondary school increased from 3,016,000 to 7,770,000. The proportion of the population that is considered illiterate has declined from 39.5 percent in 1960 to 14.7 percent in 1996. *Veja*, June 25, 2000, p. 20.

2. Fundef stands for Fundo de Manutenção e Desenvolvimento do Ensino Funda-mental e de Valorização do Magistério. Fundef was first introduced in September 1996 and implemented nationally on January 1, 1998.

3. The Programa Nacional de Renda Mínima -"Bolsa Escola" was introduced by President Fernando Henrique Cardoso on April 11, 2001. It was modeled on experimental programs run by individual states in Brazil since the mid-1990s.

4. *Jornal do Brasil*, December 1, 2001. See also, *New York Times*, January 3, 2004.

5. Brazilian public spending on higher education as a percentage of GNP is the highest in the world. Claudio de Moura Castro, "Education: Way Behind but Trying to Catch Up," *Daedalus* 129(2)(2000): 291–314.

6. The quality of education in Brazil also varies by race. The 2000 Census revealed that whereas 8.3 percent of the white population is illiterate, illiteracy rates for Brazilians of Indian and African ancestry are 26.1 percent and 21.5 percent, respectively. *Jornal do Brasil*, December 21, 2002.

7. Between 1950 and 1980, the percentage of the population in Brazil with a primary school education increased from 33.8 percent to 62.2 percent. At the same time, the completion rate in Brazil dropped from 60.1 percent to 19.0 percent. Nancy Birdsall, Barbara Bruns, and Richard Sabot, "Education in Brazil: Playing a Bad Hand Badly," pp. 7–47 in Nancy Birdsall and Richard Sabot, editors, *Opportunity Foregone: Education in Brazil* (Washington DC: Interamerican Development Bank, 1996).

8. *Jornal do Brasil*, September 21, 2000.

9. Students in Rio spend, on average, 8.2 years in school. The national average is 5.5 years. *Jornal do Brasil*, May 12, 2001.

10. The Instituto Brasileiro de Geografia e Estatística (IBGE) calculates that 30 percent of the population in Brazil over fifteen years of age can recognize letters and words but cannot understand a simple text and are, therefore, functionally illiterate. *Jornal do Brasil*, December 16, 2001.

11. A study by the Instituto de Estudos do Trabalho e Sociedade (IETS) found that when residents of Rio's favelas complete their elementary and secondary education and college, they earn, on average, half as much as residents of other areas of the city. *Jornal do Brasil*, August 13, 2002.

12. Secondary schools in Brazil have become predominately night schools to accommodate the working schedules of overage students.

13. One of the teachers at the public school in Jakeira told me that she was becoming a *baba de luxo,* or high-priced baby-sitter.

14. The other problem is that many poor children of school age work to support their families. A study by the IBGE in 2001 revealed that 5,482,515 children work in Brazil. The study also revealed that a third of these children work forty-hour weeks, more than 1 million of them are out of school, and 2.2 million are between the ages of five and fourteen, which means that they are working illegally. *Jornal do Brasil*, April 17, 2003.

15. According to a study conducted by the Instituto Pereira Passos (IPP) 53 percent of the 1,029 municipal schools in Rio are affected by drug gang-related violence. *Jornal do Brasil*, August 13, 2002.

16. *Jornal do Brasil*, March 8, 2002.

Chapter 6: Work

1. Mobral (Movimento Brasileiro de Alfabetização) was established by the military at the beginning of the 1970s. The goal was to eradicate illiteracy within ten years by turning churches, prisons, and private houses into schools for those who had already been through school but still could not read or write. Studies have shown that somewhere in the region of 90 percent of the people who participated in the program remained functionally illiterate, and in November 1985, President José Sarney, the first civilian president after the military rule, signed Mobral out of existence.

2. A large supermarket chain in Rio.
3. A carteira assinada is a signed work card that defines an employee's function and guarantees him or her rights to a minimum wage, a month's extra salary (known as the thirteenth), paid holidays, sick leave, unemployment benefits, and, in the case of women, maternity leave and other such benefits. When an employer signs a work card he or she has to pay approximately 8 percent of the employee's salary into the federal social security system. It also costs the employee a portion of his or her salary.
4. For similar observations, see Robin Sheriff, *Dreaming Equality: Color, Race, and Racism in Urban Brazil* (New Brunswick: Rutgers University Press, 2001), p. 92.
5. It is estimated that in Rocinha, the largest favela in Rio, the drug trade takes in 50 million *Reais* per month. *Jornal do Brasil*, March 29, 2003.

Economy

1. The most important of these cities, by far, is São Paulo. The state of São Paulo accounts for 45 percent of the country's industrial production, 35 percent of its exports, and 35 percent of its wealth.
2. Brazil is now the fifth largest steel producer and the seventh largest automobile manufacturer in the world.
3. Fertility rates were high in Brazil until the late 1980s. They are now at a level equivalent to the United States, and the population is expected to stabilize at about 230 million by the year 2030. Having said this, the proportion of babies born to women of twenty years of age or less has been on the increase since 1991. *Jornal do Brasil*, December 18, 2003.
4. Surveys in the early 1990s discovered that more than half of Brazilian workers did not have a carteira assinada, and a 1995 survey revealed that 57 percent did not contribute toward social security. Timothy Power and J. Timmons Roberts, "A New Brazil? The Changing Sociodemographic Context of Brazilian Democracy," pp. 236–62 in Peter R. Kingstone and Timothy J. Powers, editors, *Democratic Brazil: Actors, Institutions, and Processes* (Pittsburgh: University of Pittsburgh Press, 2000).
5. See Alejandro Portes, Manuel Castells, and Lauren Benton, editors, *The Informal Economy: Studies in Advanced and Less Developed Countries* (Baltimore: Johns Hopkins University Press, 1989); Alan Gilbert, *The Latin American City* (London: Latin American Bureau, 1994), pp. 65–78; and John Cross, *Informal Politics: Street Vendors and the State in Mexico City* (Stanford: Stanford University Press, 1998).
6. The classic example, of course, is the informal housing sector that provides low-cost housing for a significant proportion of the city's population.
7. It could be argued that the only right that truly exists in Brazil is the right to vote. And even then, subhuman and deteriorating social conditions have meant that the vote is often used as a means of procuring goods and services that should be provided by the state. See, for example, Robert Gay, "The Broker and the Thief: A

Parable (Reflections on Popular Politics in Contemporary Brazil)," *Luso Brazilian Review* 36(1)(1999): 49–70.

8. Two events, in particular, accelerated this process. The first was the establishment of the port of Santos, which provided a coastal outlet for São Paulo. The second was the transferal of the nation's capital from Rio to the purpose-built city of Brasília in the interior in 1960.

9. See Hamilton Tolosa, "Rio de Janeiro: Urban Expansion and Structural Change," pp. 203–23 in Alan Gilbert, editor, *The Megacity in Latin America* (New York: United Nations University Press, 1996).

10. For the "myth" of racial democracy in Brazil and, in particular, the complex relationship between race and class, see Robin Sheriff, *Dreaming Equality: Color, Race, and Racism in Urban Brazil* (New Brunswick: Rutgers University Press, 2001).

11. Carlos Hasenbalg, "Race and Socioeconomic Inequalities in Brazil," pp. 25–41 in Pierre Michel Fontaine, editor, *Race, Class and Power in Brazil* (Berkeley: University of California Press, 1985).

12. *Jornal do Brasil*, May 13, 2001.

13. Women's labor force participation increased from 17 to 39 percent between 1960 and 1990.

14. The Instituto Brasileiro de Geographia e Estatística (IBGE) reports that between 1991 and 2002 there was a 30 percent increase in the number of separations and a 56 percent increase in divorce. *Jornal do Brasil*, April 24, 2004. For the relationship between female-headed households and poverty, see Rosa Ribeiro and Ana Lúcia Sabóa, "Crianças e Adolecentes na Década de 80: Condições de Vida e Perspectivas para o Terceiro Milênio," pp. 16–39 in I. Rizzini, editor, *A Criança no Brasil Hoje* (Rio de Janeiro: Santa Úrsula, 1993).

15. See Peggy Lovell, "Gender, Race and the Struggle for Social Justice in Brazil," *Latin American Perspectives* 27(6)(2000): 85–102.

16. A 1999 survey found that 7.3 percent of white women, 12.3 percent of dark-skinned women, and 19.4 percent of black women in Brazil work as domestic servants. *Jornal do Brasil*, April 6, 2001. For the world of domestic work in Rio, see Donna Goldstein, *Laughter out of Place: Race, Class, Violence, and Sexuality in a Rio Shantytown* (Berkeley: University of California Press, 2003).

17. For trends in household diversity, see Sylvia Chant with Nikki Craske, *Gender in Latin America* (New Brunswick: Rutgers University Press, 2003), pp. 206–16.

18. It was also full of the children of *bandidos*.

19. Lucia's father spent the entire day on a chair outside the kitchen door. In this sense, Lucia's household was not so much female-headed as female-led. For the relationship between household structure and income, see Sylvia Chant, "Female Household Headship, Privation and Power: Challenging the 'Feminisation of Poverty' Thesis." Paper presented at the conference, "Out of the Shadows: Political Action and the Informal Economy, Latin America and Beyond." Center for Migration and Development, Princeton University, November 15–17, 2001.

Chapter 7: Born Again

1. The Church of the Assembly of God (Assembléia de Deus).
2. These are the Universal Church of the Kingdom of God (Igreja Universal do Reino de Deus), the God Is Love Pentecostal Church (Igreja Pentecostal Deus É Amor), and the Baptist Church (Igreja Batista).
3. On the border between Brazil and Bolivia.
4. The term *Evangelical* means protestant and includes Pentecostal and more traditional denominations.
5. For a discussion of the frequency and distribution of different "gifts of power," see R. Andrew Chesnut, *Born Again in Brazil: The Pentecostal Boom and the Pathogens of Poverty* (New Brunswick: Rutgers University Press, 1997), pp. 97–98.
6. For attitudes toward addicts in the favelas, see also Marco Alvito, *As Cores de Acari: Uma Favela Carioca* (Rio de Janeiro: Fundação Getulio Vargas, 2001), pp. 246–52.
7. In fact, the dono fractured Diago's skull with the butt of a pistol.

Religion

1. About one in five Catholics attend Mass on a weekly basis in Brazil and, as of 1995, there was only one priest for every ten thousand inhabitants, which is well below the regional average. On the other hand, between 1972 and 2001, there was a 774 percent increase in the number of seminarians in Brazil (retrieved December 18, 2004 from www.providence.edu/las/Statistics.htm#Increase%20in%20Seminarians. http://www.providence.edu/las/Statistics.htm.
2. For religious diversity and syncretism in Brazil, see Robert M. Levine, *Brazilian Legacies* (New York: M. E. Sharpe, 1997), pp. 119–40.
3. See Edward Cleary, "Brazilian Catholic Church and Church-State Relations: Nation Building," *Journal of Church and State* 3(2) (1997): p. 253, 20p.
4. For a discussion of the literature vis-à-vis Christian Base Communities, see Cecília Loreto Mariz, *Coping with Poverty: Pentecostals and Christian Base Communities* (Philadelphia: Temple University Press, 1994), pp. 15–18.
5. This is not to say that the gains of the "Popular Church" in Brazil were completely erased. See, for example, Kenneth Serbin, "The Catholic Church, Religious Pluralism, and Democracy in Brazil," pp. 144–61 in Peter R. Kingstone and Timothy J. Power, editors, *Democratic Brazil: Actors, Institutions, and Processes* (Pittsburgh: Pittsburgh University Press, 2000).
6. From the Ford Foundation in particular.
7. Unlike more mainstream protestants, Pentecostals believe that the outpouring of the Holy Spirit described in Acts is not a historically specific event.
8. The number of practicing Protestants in Brazil increased from 4 percent of the population in 1960 to 20 percent in 1999. The overwhelming majority of these Protestants are Pentecostal.

9. For the significance of gender and race in the rise of Pentecostalism, see John Burdick, *Looking for God in Brazil: The Progressive Catholic Church in Urban Brazil's Religious Arena* (Berkeley: University of California Press, 1993).

10. See, for example, R. Andrew Chesnut, *Born Again in Brazil: The Pentecostal Boom and the Pathogens of Poverty* (New Brunswick: Rutgers University Press, 1997).

11. Possession cults such as Umbanda and Candomblé do not define good and evil in absolute terms. In fact, many Pentecostal leaders accuse Afro-Brazilian spiritualists of complicity with leaders of the drug trade. Patrícia Birman and Márcia Pereira Leite, "Whatever Happened to the Largest Catholic Country in the World?" *Daedalus* 129(2)(2000): 271–90.

12. Cecília Loreto Mariz and María Das Dores Campos Machado argue "the conversion experience does lead to a revaluing of the self in relation to God and others that increases women's autonomy and undermines traditional machismo." Cecília Loreto Mariz and María Das Dores Campos Machado, "Pentecostalism and Women in Brazil," pp. 41–54 in Edward L. Cleary and Hannah W. Stewart-Gambino, editors, *Power, Politics, and Pentecostals in Latin America* (Boulder: Westview Press, 1997).

Chapter 8: Getting Out

1. When Lucia was pregnant I bought her and Bruno a bed and dresser for the new baby. Then I found out that she had run out of money to pay for her private health plan. After much persuasion, I convinced her and Bruno to spend the money on the health plan instead, so they would be covered until a couple of months after the birth.

2. Because of plumbing deficiencies, used toilet paper is usually not flushed away but disposed of in a pail.

Last Call

1. It is common practice for stolen foreign cars in Brazil to be exchanged for drugs at the Bolivian border. See, for example, *Jornal do Brasil*, August 23, 2002.

2. Initially, the police asked for 5,000 *Reais* for Bruno's release. Because he did not have that kind of money, they arrested him and took him to the police station.

Epilogue

1. I was told, before it happened, that all the donos associated with the Comando Vermelho in Rio had signed a document approving the attack.

2. There were also calls to build a wall around the favela.

3. For a description of the new prison regulations, see *Jornal do Brasil*, November 19, 2003.

4. Since 2000, sixty-three prison workers have been assassinated in Rio. Some of these individuals were executed because they were responsible for imposing harsh

measures. Others were executed because they refused to take bribes or because they backed out of agreements to facilitate escapes. See, for example, *Jornal do Brasil*, March 5, 9, and 10, 2004.

5. This is a particular danger for large households, such as Lucia's, which provide drug gangs with the best cover. See also, Marcos Alvito, *As Cores de Acari: Uma Favela Carioca* (Editora Fundação Getulio Vargas, 2001), p. 258.

6. The military deployed three thousand troops in twenty-five different locations to keep the city safe for tourists during Carnival in 2003.

7. *Jornal do Brasil*, May 8, 2003.

8. There have been many instances of the police occupying favelas and finding nothing because the drug gang in question has been tipped off beforehand. There have also been instances of police involvement with schemes to exchange cars they have stolen for drugs and to service and maintain firearms on behalf of traficantes. *Jornal do Brasil*, October 17, and November 25 and 30, 2003.

9. In 2003, the military police initiated 1,032 investigative proceedings against its own workforce. Only sixty-four resulted in dismissal. *Jornal do Brasil*, January 13, 2004. See also Julita Lembruger, Leonardo Musemeci, and Ignacio Cano, *Quem Vigia os Vigias? Um Estudo Sobre Controle Externo da Polícia no Brasil* (Rio de Janeiro: Record, 2003); and Paul E. Amar, "Reform in Rio: Reconsidering the Myths of Crime and Violence," NACLA 37(2)(2003): 37–42.

10. Homicide rates in the municipality of Rio have fallen 8.7 percent between July 1999 and June 2001. However, much of this decline is attributable to policing efforts in the wealthy districts of Zona Sul and the city center. Instituto de Estudos da Religião (ISER), "Epidemiologia das Causas Externas—Dados para Tomada de Decisão: Indicadores de Violência e Acidentes no Rio de Janeiro" (retrieved February 14, 2005 from www.iser.org.br/portug/indicador_intro.html).

11. *Jornal do Brasil*, March 11, 2004.

12. See, for example, the comments made by then state secretary Josias Quintal and the mayor of Rio, Cesar Maia. *Jornal do Brasil*, February 28, 2003.

13. For a critical evaluation of the criminal justice system in Brazil, including recent changes introduced by President Lula and the Partido dos Trabalhadores (PT), see "Report of the Special Rapporteur on Extrajudicial, Summary or Arbitrary Executions," Asma Jahangir, (September 16–October 8, 2003) United Nations Commission on Human Rights.

14. Which it claims, of course, to be due to improved surveillance.

15. The federal police seized 27.4 kilos of heroin in 2001, 56.6 kilos in 2002, and 66.2 kilos in 2003. *Jornal do Brasil*, January 15, 2003 and January 18, 2004. The shift toward heroin production in Latin America is attributed to the fact that it is easy to cultivate and can be grown at high altitudes and on scattered plots that are more difficult to detect and eradicate than lowland crops such as cocaine. *New York Times*, June 8, 2003.

16. In Jakeira, the drug gang makes money by taxing storeowners and operators of vans and motorcycles that ferry residents in and around the favela and by charging

fees for administering public utilities and amenities. It also makes money from the monthly dues that residents have to pay to neighborhood association, which it also controls.

17. For more information on Viva Rio, visit http://www.vivario.org.br.

18. For an analysis of the role of civic groups, see Enrique Desmond Arias, "Faith in Our Neighbors: Networks and Social order in Three Brazilian Favelas," *Latin American Politics and Society* 46(1)(2004): 1–38.

19. *Jornal do Brasil*, April 22, 2004.

Glossary

alemães: enemies, drug gang rivals; literally "Germans"
baile: funk dance party
bandido: drug gang member
boca de fumo: selling point for drugs; literally "mouth of smoke"
cafezinho: small cup of coffee
cagoete: spy or informer
caldo de feijão con angu: black bean broth mixed with a kind of polenta
Candomblé: one of many Afro-Brazilian religions
carteira assinada: signed work card
cativeiro: safe house where kidnapping victims are held
comadre: godmother of one's child
Comando Vermelho: prison-based gang faction
compadre: godfather of one's child
cristão: member of new protestant religious group; literally "Christian"
culto: prayer group
delegacia: police station, precinct
diarista: day laborer
dízimo: tithe of 10 percent of a believer's income required by many new Pentecostal
    denominations
dono: drug gang leader
favela: shantytown
favelada(o): pejorative term for someone who lives in a favela

gerente: manager of a drug gang who looks after drugs, guns, or money

gerente geral: general manager of a drug gang

Guarda Velha: senior members of a samba school; literally "the old guard"

kombi: Volkswagen van

lei de silêncio: code of silence

loiraça: good-looking blond woman

matuto: drug distributor

mauricinho: spoiled rich kid

menor: someone under the age of eighteen; literally "minor"

moreno: mixed racial category meaning not white but not black

mutirão: collective, self-help events

negão: large black guy

olheiro: lookout for a drug gang

pagode: show featuring a popularized and commercialized form of samba

piranha: loose woman, tart

polícia mineira: vigilante groups, often involving off-duty or retired policemen

pretinho: little black guy

Primeiro Comando Do Capital: prison-based gang faction; literally "First Command of the Capital"

Real: Brazilian currency since 1994

sítio: house, plot of land, or farm outside of the city or town

subúrbios: predominantly poor, violence-plagued areas of Rio beyond the wealthy neighborhoods of Zona Sul; literally "suburbs"

Terceiro Comando: prison-based gang faction

trabalhador: working person

tráfego de formigas: small-scale drug trafficking; literally "ant-trafficking"

traficante: drug gang member

triagem: house of detention, holding cell for those awaiting trial; literally "triage"

Umbanda: one of many Afro-Brazilian religions

vagabundos: vagabonds, scoundrels, tricksters; often associated with people of Rio

vala negra: sewage channel; literally "black ditch"

vapor: gang member who sells drugs to users; literally "vapor" or "steam"

Bibliography

Abers, Rebecca. *Inventing Local Democracy: Grassroots Politics in Brazil* (Boulder: Lynne Rienner, 2000).

Alvito, Marcos. *As Cores de Acari: Uma Favela Carioca* (Rio de Janeiro: Getulio Vargas, 2001).

Amar, Paul E. "Reform in Rio: Reconsidering the Myths of Crime and Violence," *NACLA* 37(2)(2003): 37–42.

Amorim, Carlos. *Comando Vermelho: A História Secreta do Crime Organizado* (Rio de Janeiro: Record, 1993).

Araújo, Roberto. "The Drug Trade, the Black Economy and Society in Western Amazônia in Brazil," pp. 134–40 in *Globalisation, Drugs and Criminalization* (MOST/UNESCO, 2002).

Arias, Enrique Desmond. "Faith in Our Neighbors: Networks and Social Order in Three Brazilian Favelas," *Latin American Politics and Society* 46(1)(2004): 1–38.

Azevedo, Sérgio and Luis Andrade, *Habitação e Poder: Da Fundação da Casa Popular ao Banco Nacional de Habitação* (Rio de Janeiro: Zahar, 1981).

Balán, Jorge. "Introduction," pp. 1–6 in Susana Rotker, editor, *Citizens of Fear: Urban Violence in Latin America* (New Brunswick: Rutgers University Press, 2002).

Barcellos, Caco. *Rota 66. A História da Polícia que Mata* (Rio de Janeiro: Editora Globo, 1987).

Barcellos, Caco. *Abusado: O Dono do Morro Dona Marta* (Rio de Janeiro: Editora Record, 2003).

Birdsall, Nancy, Barbara Bruns, and Richard Sabot, "Education in Brazil: Playing a Bad Hand Badly," pp. 7–47 in Nancy Birdsall and Richard Sabot, editors, *Opportunity Foregone: Education in Brazil* (Washington DC: Interamerican Development Bank, 1996).

Birman, Patrícia and Márcia Pereira Leite, "Whatever Happened to the Largest Catholic Country in the World?" *Daedalus* 129(2)(2000): 271–90.

Blat, José Carlos and Sérgio Saraiva, *O Caso da Favela Natal: Polícia Contra o Povo* (São Paulo: Editora Contexto, 2000).

Bourgois, Phillipe. *In Search of Respect: Selling Crack in El Barrio* (New York: Cambridge University Press, 1996).

Brinks, Daniel. "Informal Institutions and the Rule of Law: The Judicial response to State Killings in Buenos Aires and São Paulo in the 1990s." Paper presented at the Conference on Informal Institutions and Politics in the Developing World. Harvard University, April 2002.

Burdick, John. *Looking for God in Brazil: The Progressive Catholic Church in Urban Brazil's Religious Arena* (Berkeley: University of California Press, 1993).

Burgos, Marcelo Baumann. "Dos Parques Proletários ao Favela-Bairro: as Políticas Públicas nas Favelas do Rio de Janeiro," pp. 25–60 in Alba Zaluar and Marcos Alvito, editors, *Um Século de Favela* (Rio de Janeiro: Fundação Getulio Vargas, 1998).

Caldeira, Teresa Pires do Rio. *A Política Dos Outros: O Coitidiano dos Moradores da Periferia e o que Pensam do Poder e dos Poderosos* (São Paulo: Brasiliense, 1984).

Cano, Ignacio. "The Use of Lethal Force by Police in Rio de Janeiro," ISER, Rio de Janeiro, 1997.

Carpenter, Ted Galen. *Bad Neighbor Policy: Washington's Futile War on Drugs in Latin America* (New York: Palgrave, 2003).

Castro, Claudio de Moura. "Education: Way Behind but Trying to Catch Up," *Daedalus* 129(2)(2000): 291–314.

Cecchetto, Fátima Regina. "Galeras Funk Cariocas: os Bailes e a Constituição do Ethos Guerreiro," pp. 145–66 in Alba Zaluar and Marcos Alvito, editors, *Um Século de Favela* (Rio de Janeiro: Getulio Vargas, 1998).

Chant, Sylvia. "Female Household Headship, Privation and Power: Challenging the 'Feminisation of Poverty' Thesis." Paper presented at the conference, "Out of the Shadows: Political Action and the Informal Economy, Latin America and Beyond." Center for Migration and Development, Princeton University, November 15–17, 2001.

Chant, Sylvia with Nikki Craske, *Gender in Latin America* (New Brunswick: Rutgers University Press, 2003).

Chesnut, R. Andrew. *Born Again in Brazil: The Pentecostal Boom and the Pathogens of Poverty* (New Brunswick: Rutgers University Press, 1997).

Chevigny, Paul. *The Edge of the Knife: Police Violence in the Americas* (New York: New Press, 1995).

Christino, Márcio. *Por Dentro de Crime: Corrupção, Tráfico, PCC* (São Paulo: Fiuza, 2001).

Cleary, Edward. "Brazilian Catholic Church and Church-State Relations: Nation Building," *Journal of Church and State* 3(2)(1997): 253, 20p.

Cohen, Jean. "Strategy or Identity: New Theoretical Paradigms and Contemporary Social Movements," *Social Research* 52(4)(1985): 663–716.

Conchman-Eastman, Alberto. "Urban Violence in Latin America and the Caribbean: Dimensions, Explanations, Actions," pp. 37–54 in Susana Rotker, editor, *Citizens of Fear: Urban Violence in Latin America* (New Brunswick: Rutgers University Press, 2002).

Cross, John. *Informal Politics: Street Vendors and the State in Mexico City* (Stanford: Stanford University Press, 1998).

Dowdney, Luke. *Children of the Drug Trade* (Rio de Janeiro: 7Letras, 2003).

Escobar, Arturo and Sonia Alvarez, editors, *The Making of Social Movements in Latin America* (Boulder: Westview Press, 1992).

Evers, Tilman. "'Identity': The Hidden Side of New Social Movements in Latin America," pp. 43–72 in David Slater, editor, *New Social Movements and the State in Latin America* (Amsterdam: CEDLA, 1985).

Fonseca, Claudia. "Orphanages, Foundlings and Foster Mothers: The System of Child Circulation in a Brazilian Squatter Settlement," *Anthropological Quarterly* 59(1)(1986): 15–27.

Gay, Robert. *Popular Organization and Democracy in Rio de Janeiro: A Tale of Two Favelas* (Philadelphia: Temple University Press, 1994).

Gay, Robert. "The Broker and the Thief: A Parable (Reflections on Popular Politics in Contemporary Brazil)," *Luso Brazilian Review* 36(1)(1999): 49–70.

Geffray, Christian. "Social, Economic and Political Impacts of Drug Trafficking in the State of Rondônia, in the Brazilian Amazon," pp. 90–109 in *Globalisation, Drugs and Criminalisation* (MOST/UNESCO, 2002).

Gilbert, Alan. *The Latin American City* (London: Latin American Bureau, 1994).

Goldstein, Donna. *Laughter out of Place: Race, Class, Violence, and Sexuality in a Rio Shantytown* (Berkeley: University of California Press, 2003).

Hasenbalg, Carlos. "Race and Socioeconomic Inequalities in Brazil," pp. 25–41 in Pierre Michel Fontaine, editor, *Race, Class and Power in Brazil* (Berkeley: University of California Press, 1985).

Hecht, Tobias. *At Home in the Street: Street Children of Northeast Brazil* (Cambridge: Cambridge University Press, 1998).

Herzfeld, Michael. *Portrait of a Greek Imagination: An Ethnographic Biography of Andreas Nenedakis* (Chicago: University of Chicago Press, 1997).

Holston, James and Teresa Pires do Rio Caldeira, "Democracy, Law, and Violence: Disjunctions of Brazilian Citizenship," pp. 263–96 in Felipe Aguero and Jeffrey Stark, editors, *Fault Lines of Democracy in Post-Transition Latin America* (Coral Gables: University of Miami, 1998).

Huggins, Martha. *Political Policing: The United States and Latin America* (Durham: Duke University Press, 1998).

Huggins, Martha, Mika Haritos-Fatouros, and Philip Zimbardo, *Violence Workers: Police Torturers and Murderers Reconstruct Brazilian Atrocities* (Berkeley: University of California Press, 2002).

Human Rights Watch/Americas. *Final Justice: Police and Death Squad Homicides of Adolescents in Brazil* (Human Rights Watch, 1994).

Human Rights Watch/Americas. *Police Brutality in Urban Brazil* (Human Rights Watch, 1997).

Human Rights Watch/Americas. *Brazil Slow on Human Rights Reform* (Human Rights Watch, 1999).

Instituto Brasileiro de Geografia e Estatística. "Síntese de Indicadores Sociais 2003."

Iplanrio, *Anuário Estatístico* (1993).

ISER. "Epidemiologia das Causas Externas—Dados para Tomada de Decisão: Indicadores de Violência e Acidentes no Rio de Janeiro," Instituto de Estudos da Religião.

James, Daniel. *Doña María's Story: Life History, Memory and Political Identity* (Durham: Duke University Press, 2000).

Kirk, Robin. *More Terrible than Death: Massacres, Drugs, and America's War in Colombia* (Cambridge: Public Affairs, 2003).

Korzeniewicz, Roberto and William Smith, "Poverty, Inequality, and Growth in Latin America: Searching for the High Road to Globalization," *Latin American Research Review* 35(3)(2000): 7–54.

Leeds, Anthony and Elizabeth Leeds, *A Sociologia do Brasil Urbano* (Rio de Janeiro: Zahar, 1978).

Leeds, Elizabeth. "Cocaine and Parallel Polities in the Brazilian Urban Periphery: Constraints on Local-Level Democratization," *Latin American Research Review* 31(3)(1996): 47–83.

Lembruger, Julita, Leonardo Musemeci, and Ignacio Cano, *Quem Vigia os Vigias? Um Estudo Sobre Controle Externo da Polícia no Brasil* (Rio de Janeiro: Record, 2003).

Levine, Robert M. *Brazilian Legacies* (London: Sharpe, 1997).

Lovell, Peggy. "Gender, Race and the Struggle for Social Justice in Brazil," *Latin American Perspectives* 27(6)(2000): 85–102.

Mariz, Cecília Loreto. *Coping with Poverty: Pentecostals and Christian Base Communities* (Philadelphia: Temple University Press, 1994).

Mariz, Cecília Loreto and María Das Dores Campos Machado, "Pentecostalism and Women in Brazil," pp. 41–54 in Edward Cleary and Hannah Stewart-Gambino, editors, *Power, Politics, and Pentecostals in Latin America* (Boulder: Westview Press, 1997).

Miller, William and Benjamin Crabtree, "Depth Interviewing," pp. 185–202 in Sharlene Nagy Hess-Biber and Patricia Leavy, editors, *Approaches to Qualitative Research: A Reader on Theory and Practice* (Oxford: Oxford University Press, 2004).

Mingardi, Guaracy and Sandra Goulart, "Drug Trafficking in an Urban Area: The Case of São Paulo," pp. 92–118 in *Globalisation, Drugs and Criminalisation* (MOST/UNESCO, 2002).

Misse, Michel. "Malandros, Marginais e Vagabundos: a Acumulação Social da Violência no Rio de Janeiro," Ph.D. Thesis, IUPERJ, 1999.

Mora, Frank. "Victims of the Balloon Effect: Drug Trafficking and U.S. Policy in Brazil and the Southern Cone of Latin America," *Journal of Social, Political and Economic Studies* 21(2)(1996): 115–40.

Moura, P.L. da Silva. "Um Movimento em Busca de Poder: as Associações de Moradores do Rio de Janeiro e a sua Relação com o Estado—1970–1990." Masters Thesis, UFF, 1993.

NEPAD and CLAVES (UERJ/FIOCRUZ). "Estudo Global Sobre O Mercado Ilegal de Drogas no Rio de Janeiro," October 2000.

Neto, Paulo Mesquita. "Violência policial no Brasil: Abordagens Teóricas e Práticas de Controle," pp. 130–48 in Dulce Pandolfi, José Murilo de Carvalho, Leandro Carneiro and Mario Grynszpan, editors, Cidadania, Justiça e Violência (Rio de Janeiro: Getulio Vargas, 1999).

Nylen, William. "The Making of a Loyal Opposition: The Workers' Party (PT) and the Consolidation of Democracy in Brazil," pp. 126–43 in Peter R. Kingstone and Timothy J. Power, editors, Democratic Brazil: Actors, Institutions, and Processes (Pittsburgh: Pittsburgh University Press, 2000).

O'Donnell, Guillermo. "On the State, Democratization and Some Conceptual Problems: A Latin American View with Glances at Some Postcommunist Countries," World Development 21(8)(1993): 1355–69.

Pandolfi, Dulce. "Percepção dos Direitos e Participação Social," pp. 45–58 in Dulce Pandolfi, José Murilo de Carvalho, Leandro Carneiro and Mario Grynszpan, editors, Cidadania, Justiça e Violência (Rio de Janeiro: Getulio Vargas, 1999).

Parisse, Lucien. Favelas do Rio de Janeiro: Evolução e Sentido (Rio de Janeiro: Centro Nacional de Pesquisas Habitacionais, 1969).

Patai, Daphne. Brazilian Women Speak: Contemporary Life Stories (New Brunswick: Rutgers University Press, 1988).

———. "U.S. Academics and Third World Women: Is Ethical Research Possible?" pp. 137–53 in Sherna Berger Gluck and Daphne Patai, editors, Women's Words: The Feminist Practice of Oral History (London: Routledge, 1991).

Payne, Leigh. Uncivil Movements: The Armed Right Wing and Democracy in Latin America (Baltimore: Johns Hopkins University Press, 2000).

Perlman, Janice. The Myth of Marginality: Urban Poverty and Politics in Rio de Janeiro (Berkeley: University of California Press, 1976).

Pereira, Anthony W. "An Ugly Democracy? State Violence and the Rule of Law in Postauthoritarian Brazil," pp. 217–35 in Peter R. Kingstone and Timothy J. Power, editors, Democratic Brazil: Actors, Institutions, and Processes (Pittsburgh: Pittsburgh University Press, 2000).

Pinheiro, Paulo Sérgio. "Democratic Governance, Violence, and the (Un)Rule of Law," Daedalus 129(2)(2000): 119–44.

Pino, Julio César. Family and Favela: The Reproduction of Poverty in Rio de Janeiro (Westport: Greenwood Press, 1997).

Portes, Alejandro, Manuel Castells, and Lauren Benton, editors, The Informal Economy: Studies in Advanced and Less Developed Countries (Baltimore: Johns Hopkins University Press, 1989).

Portes, Alejandro and Kelly Hoffman, "Latin American Class Structures: Their Composition and Change During the Neoliberal Era," Latin American Research Review 38(1)(2003): 9–40.

Power, Timothy and J. Timmons Roberts, "A New Brazil? The Changing Sociodemographic Context of Brazilian Democracy," pp. 236–62 in Peter R. Kingstone and Timothy J. Powers, editors, *Democratic Brazil: Actors, Institutions, and Processes* (Pittsburgh: University of Pittsburgh Press, 2000).

Ramos, Hosmany. *Pavilhão 9: Paixão e Morte no Carandiru* (São Paulo: Geração, 2001).

Resende, Juliana. *Operação Rio* (Rio de Janeiro: Editora Página Aberta, 1995).

Ribeiro, Rosa and Ana Lúcia Sabóa, "Crianças e Adolecentes na Década de 80: Condições de Vida e Perspectivas para o Terceiro Milênio," pp. 16–39 in I. Rizzini, editor, *A Criança no Brasil Hoje* (Rio de Janeiro: Santa Úrsula, 1993).

Rio de Janeiro, "À Margem, Cresce a Grande Cidade: Favela." *Revista do Tribunal de Contas do Município do Rio de Janeiro* 1(1981): 53–60.

Robben, Antonius. "The Politics of Truth and Emotion Among Victims and Perpetrators of Violence," pp. 81–103 in Antonius Robben and Carolyn Nordstrom, editors, *Fieldwork Under Fire: Contemporary Studies of Violence and Survival* (Berkeley: University of California Press, 1995).

Robben, Antonius and Carolyn Nordstrom, "The Anthropology and Ethnography of Violence and Sociopolitical Conflict," pp. 1–23 in Antonius Robben and Carolyn Nordstrom, editors, *Fieldwork Under Fire: Contemporary Studies of Violence and Survival* (Berkeley: University of California Press, 1995).

Salazar, Claudia. "A Third World Woman's Text: Between the Politics of Criticism and Cultural Politics," pp. 93–106 in Sherna Berger Gluck and Daphne Patai, editors, *Women's Words: The Feminist Practice of Oral History* (London: Routledge, 1991).

Scheper-Hughes, Nancy. *Death Without Weeping: The Violence of Everyday Life in Brazil* (Berkeley: University of California Press, 1992).

Serbin, Kenneth. "The Catholic Church, Religious Pluralism, and Democracy in Brazil," pp. 144–61 in Peter R. Kingstone and Timothy J. Power, editors, *Democratic Brazil: Actors, Institutions, and Processes* (Pittsburgh: Pittsburgh University Press, 2000).

Sheriff, Robin. *Dreaming Inequality: Color, Race, and Racism in Urban Brazil* (New Brunswick: Rutgers University Press, 2001).

Souza, Josinaldo Aleixo de. "Sociabilidades Emergentes—Implicações da Dominação de Matadors na Periferie e Traficantes nas Favelas," Ph.D. Thesis, UFRJ, 2002.

Taussig, Michael. "Terror as Usual: Walter Benjamin's Theory of History as a State of Siege," *Social Text* 23(1989): 3–20.

Tolosa, Hamilton. "Rio de Janeiro: Urban Expansion and Structural Change," pp. 203–23 in Alan Gilbert, editor, *The Megacity in Latin America* (New York: United Nations University Press, 1996).

United Nations Commission on Human Rights. "Report of the Special Rapporteur on Civil and Political Rights, Regarding the Questions of Torture and Detention," Nigel Rodley (August 20–September 12, 2000).

———. "Report of the Special Rapporteur on Extrajudicial, Summary or Arbitrary Executions," Asma Jahangir, (September 16–October 8, 2003).

U.S. Department of State. *International Narcotics Control Strategy Report*, 2002.

Valla, Victor. *Educação e Favela: Política para as Favelas do Rio de Janeiro* (Rio de Janeiro: Zahar, 1986).

Valladares, Lícia. *Passe-Se uma Casa: Análise do Programa de Remoção de Favelas de Rio de Janeiro* (Rio de Janeiro: Zahar, 1978).

Ventura, Zuenir. *Cidade Partida* (São Paulo: Schwartz, 1994).

Vianna, Hermano. *O Mundo Funk Carioca* (Rio de Janeiro: Zahar, 1988).

Zaluar, Alba. *A Máquina e a Revolta: As Organizações Populares e o Significado da Pobreza* (São Paulo: Brasiliense, 1985).

———. "Mulher do Bandido: Crônica de uma Cidade Menos Musical," *Estudos Feministas* 1(1)(1993): 135–42.

———. *Condomínio do Diablo* (Rio de Janeiro: Editora Revan, 1994).

———. "The Drug Trade, Crime and Policies of Repression in Brazil," *Dialectical Anthropology* 20(1995): 95–108.

———. "Crime, Medo e Política," pp. 209–32 in Alba Zaluar and Marcos Alvito, editors, *Um Século de Favela* (Rio de Janeiro: Getulio Vargas, 1998).

———. "Violence Related to Illegal Drugs, Easy Money and Justice in Brazil: 1980–1995," pp. 142–63 in *Globalisation, Drugs and Criminalisation* (MOST/UNESCO, 2002).

Zaverucha, Jorge. "Military Justice in the State of Pernambuco After the Brazilian Military Regime: An Authoritarian Legacy," *Latin American Research Review* 34(2)(1999): 43–74.

Index

Christian Base Communities; declining
participation in, 150; organization
of, 150; and poverty, 151; role in
democratization, 150
Christian Congregation of Brazil,
151
citizenship, second-class, 7
civic groups, 6, 174
civil society; groups in, 83; imagining, 6;
resurrection of, 54; threats to, 5
civil war; between police and drug gangs,
6; for control of favelas, 55
COHAB, 74, 188n. 6
Colombia, 5, 31, 55
Comando Vermelho, 39, 52, 55, 57,
96–97 102, 171, 172; emergence
of, 55–56; and favelas, 55
culto, 3

death squads, 84
democracy; and decline of popular
movement, 150; and favela
movement, 54; and policy towards
favelas, 25, 27; threats to, 5
democratic rights, 6
depth interviewing, 11
discrimination, against *faveladas*,
127–128
divorce, rates of, 196n. 14
dízimo, 140
drug gangs; and addicts, 3, 5, 20, 32, 144,
146; and bailes, 15; and betrayal,
20–21, 52–53, 82, 171; and
childhood, 21; and code of
silence, 7; and the
commandeering of houses, 172;
and their communities. 56, 62, 71,
73, 90, 173, 199n. 16; community
leaders and, 187n. 17; control of
city by, 5; cooperation between,
87; and corruption of authorities,
193n. 18; and death, 30, 131; and
debt, 20, 32, 136, 145–147, 148,
169; and drug sales, 5, 15, 37, 69,

130–131; and drug supply, 69,
147; drug use by, 3, 19–20, 32,
144, 146; emergence of, 6;
executions by, 7, 20–21, 40–41,
46–47, 64; expulsions by, 50–51,
60; and family, 15, 17, 22, 63, 143,
145–146; and guns, 14–15, 32–33,
36–37, 69, 185n. 6, 189n. 16; and
informants, 7, 21; and the law, 64;
and legal representation, 37–38,
145; life of 2, 6, 30, 129, 144, 147;
and local merchants, 87;
manpower commanded by, 187n.
17; and medical attention, 33–34,
43; and money, 16, 30, 32, 35, 68,
71, 130–131, 147, 195n. 5; and
the police, 5, 17, 33–36, 74, 86;
and politicians, 72–73; positions
within, 16, 32–33; and possession
cults, 198n. 12; and prison, 30;
and public works, 56; punishment
by, 18, 56, 64, 78–79, 144, 146;
recruitment of boys and men by,
15–17, 22, 144; and religion, 3,
143; and revenge, 22, 46; and
robbery, 14, 17, 22, 61, 92, 144,
183n. 5; and school, 16, 111, 144;
and social services in favelas, 56;
and street children, 185n. 12;
threat posed by, 27, 55; and
torture, 7, 75; violence between,
5, 13, 38–39, 44–47, 52–53, 55,
57, 60, 91, 145, 171–172; and
women, 6, 14–15, 17–19, 38–43,
47, 49, 60–63, 66–68, 74–80, 92,
126–127, 130, 166
drug free communities, 172
drug trade, attempts to suffocate, 172
drugs; adolescents and, 165;
apprehension of, 173, 186n. 8,
199n. 15; availability of, 5; as a
business, 19, 37; cocaine, 3, 5, 31,
55, 69, 94–95, 100, 131, 173;
consumption of, 5, 11; and

Robert Gay is Chair of the Department of Sociology at Connecticut College. He is the author of *Popular Organization and Democracy in Rio De Janeiro: A Tale of Two Favelas* (Temple).